PRAISE FOR

Pretty Much

"Reading *Pretty Much* is like gaining access to the mind of an unusually talented painter who has now captured family and folk of an entire era, with merely words alone. Be ready for lots of smiles and a few tears as Betty Bell Brown reawakens precious years."

Susan Taylor Block, poet and historian

"*Pretty Much* is a palimpsest of author Betty Brown's mother's diary, Brown's own recollections and research, and her original artwork mixed with family photographs. The result is a richly textured portrait of a South Carolina family over the twentieth century with an unforgettable matriarch at the center. Brown's voice is at once familiar and fresh; she is a detached observer whose vaguely ironic tone permeates the memoir's title and the many narrative strands that verge on tragedy. Her love for her family seeps into even her relatives' least lovable moments. The reader is simply swept along."

Cynthia Lewis, Charles A. Dana Professor of English, Davidson College

"Betty Brown is an esteemed painter who, with an artist's eye for detail and truth-telling, has written a memoir, *Pretty Much*, about her prototypically Southern family. It is an astonishing book. She has skillfully interwoven excerpts of her mother's diary (whose "voice" melds uncannily well with the author's own), as well as exquisite old photos that lend an almost mythological resonance to a story with more than its share of tragedy. Against all odds, with courage and compassion, Betty Brown has gathered all of these pieces, and much more, in one pitch-perfect, heart-rending book to savor."

Michael White, poet and professor of creative writing, UNC-Wilmington

"It takes a skilled memoirist to present her family story both from its heart, as if her readers were cousins with a known place in the story, and from the outside, to present facts and perspectives we need as readers. Betty Bell Brown is just such a skilled writer. In *Pretty Much*, she weaves her readers into the fabric of a complex Southern family in such vivid stories that we are delighted to have been invited there."

Dana Wildsmith, author of *One Light*

"Betty Brown has written my favorite kind of book: an utterly gripping memoir about family. It's the story of ordinary people finding themselves in extraordinary, psychologically challenging situations. This is truly a memorable book."

Judy Goldman, author of *Together: A Memoir of a Marriage and a Medical Mishap*

"Author Betty Bell Brown was exasperated, fearing her mother would be kicked out of another nursing home. 'You've been told not to mess with the other patients, but you do whatever you damn well please… Don't you?' Her mother 'pondered the question only too briefly before she replied, "Yep, pretty much."'

"*Pretty Much* is a meticulously told, engaging story of the toll Brown's mother exacted on her family throughout her life of doing 'whatever she damn well pleased.' In rendering the life of her beautiful, headstrong, self-centered mother, Brown captures fascinating details of the changing world of the twentieth-century South from 1913, when her mother was born, onward.

"The truths and family secrets Brown unravels along the way make for a rewarding read. Brown herself emerges as a hero—her commitment to caring for her difficult mother and her steadfast love for her parents despite their flaws and failures are inspiring."

Maureen Ryan Griffin, poet, essayist, and teacher

To Bonnie
Love, Gretchen

Best wishes!

Pretty Much

a memoir

Betty Bell Brown

Betty Bell Brown

LYSTRA BOOKS
& Literary Services

Pretty Much: A Memoir
Copyright © Betty Bell Brown 2019
All rights reserved

ISBN print 978-0-9996931-7-9
ISBN ebook 978-0-9996931-8-6
Library of Congress Control Number 2019932300

Author's photograph on back cover by Olivia Brown.

Book illustrations by Betty Bell Brown.

LYSTRA BOOKS
& Literary Services

Published by Lystra Books & Literary Services
391 Lystra Estates Dr., Chapel Hill, NC 27517
lystrabooks@gmail.com

Printed in the United States

I dedicate this book to our seven grandchildren.
I write it for you to understand your family history and love
the Geemommy tales from those who knew her.

Author's Notes

Throughout my life, I have been writing my mother's story in my head. I wanted to emulate her, but at the same time, I wanted to be sure that I was nothing like her. When I was about nine years old, Mother began to write her story herself. She placed her treasured Smith Corona on our dining room table, dumped out a box of old diaries, and began to transpose them onto typing paper.

In this memoir, my mother, Clara Scott Bell (1913–1996) speaks in the words from her diaries, random notes found in composition books, and the autobiography she typed. I have quoted her in italics.

I now realize that I didn't know my family until I wrote our story. As a visual artist, I approached writing our lives just as I study a painting in progress. I step back to assess what works, but also to improve the piece, or, in this case, a life—mine.

Dear family, friends, and readers, you may find yourselves within this book. I may have changed your name. Please understand that, as author, I look into one mirror, my own. Our reflections could probably differ.

Betty Bell Brown
Wilmington, North Carolina
January 2019

Prologue

"**Y**ou need to come down here and pick up your mother." It was Mr. Abbot on the other end of my Princess phone, but he didn't sound like the Mr. Abbott I knew, the gentle administrator of Mother's retirement home.

I reached to massage my left side. It contracted into a spasm under stress.

"Come get her right now and don't expect to bring her back."

It was April 17, 1991. My seventy-seven-year-old mother had lived in the Catherine Kennedy Home, a care facility for ladies, since April 22, 1986. She had immediately nicknamed the home "CK." We had moved her from Renno, near Clinton, South Carolina, to be closer to my husband and me in Wilmington, North Carolina. Mother's doctor had diagnosed her with Parkinson's disease at age fifty. She needed more and more help as the years passed and I was the only one around to step in as caretaker. Mother met basic requirements for entry into CK. She dressed herself and attended all meals in the dining room. Impetuous behavior was never mentioned as a deterrence to her admittance.

As she began to feel at home, that impetuous behavior kept her in trouble. The staff frowned on Mother scrounging for her own meds at the nurses' station or trying to "help" workers in the kitchen, a space forbidden to residents. The attic was off limits too, and residents were told they could not go there without a staff member. "Sometimes I need to go check on something where I store my winter clothes," Mother told me.

She turned off all the lights in the stairwells from the attic to the first floor and left the ladies who lived on the upper floors in the dark. They used their wrinkly hands to feel the wall and make their way down the stairs. Mr. Abbott rued the day he told Mother she saved him money when she turned out lights.

She hated to waste a morsel of food from the dining room, and she took a plastic container to save leftovers, or she wrapped her fried chicken in her napkin. Mother had lived through the Depression, which might explain why she hoarded leftover food, along with her obsession to turn out lights. The nurses attributed her behavior to dementia, but, to me, she behaved like the exaggerated colorful personality I'd known forever.

The list of her offenses stretched from the corner of Third and Orange clear to my house in the South Oleander subdivision. The charm Mr. Abbott saw in her when she first arrived tarnished like the gleam on good silver in a dark drawer. Yet, five years in, I wasn't ready for Mr. Abbott's call, certainly not before I had my coffee.

I asked him, myself, and God, "What's she done now?" I listened for a bless-her-heart tone in Mr. Abbott's voice, but he sputtered on the brink of an eruption.

"I'll be right there," I said.

I looked at my cup of coffee and folded the *Wilmington Morning Star.* I'd get a headache if I didn't have my caffeine. The spasm in my side tightened.

I grabbed my keys and rushed out the back door. The empty garage reminded me I'd taken the station wagon to the Dodge place for Freon. I hoisted up my jeans and headed for my neighbor's kitchen door. Like half the women our age, her name was also Betty. Of all my friends, she knew my situation with Mother best, and she had counseled me on dozens of walks around the neighborhood. I didn't know who needed sympathy more, I whose errant mother brought me to my knees, or she with a mother-in-law from you-know-where.

"I just got the dreaded call from CK," I said, "and my car is in the shop. Mr. Abbott wants me to come get her—right this minute."

She handed me the keys to her Buick without a word and I hugged her neck.

Minutes later, I turned into the parking lot behind CK and saw Mother seated in one of the rockers on the back porch. She sat closest to the steps at the end of a row of ladies who looked like tiny birds perched on a power line. Mother appeared no different from the others who lived in the sprawling three-story home, except she rocked three times faster. Her tan cowhide Samsonite weekender sat to her left. To her right, she kept her blue train case packed with necessities, ready to go. I'm sure it contained toiletries, a spare pair of Depends, and prohibited over-the-counter meds.

I parked as close to the steps as I could without blocking the driveway. She popped out of her rocker and picked up plastic bags with more of her stuff. I avoided looking at her while I loaded her belongings into the trunk. I opened the door to the shotgun side and motioned for her to sit there. I'd left the motor on for the air conditioning. She looked cool and comfortable. When I lifted her big suitcase into the trunk, a bead of sweat rolled down my spine. I gritted my teeth.

I had hung drapes in Mother's room and decided to leave them as a donation. It was the least I could do.

I glimpsed a tight smirk on her face. Did she enjoy this? I was her one child close enough to bear the brunt, and I took her misdeeds personally. My younger brother Dick had lived and worked in Atlanta since college days. He had found our mother impossible.

I left her seated in the air-conditioned car and walked to Mr. Abbott's office near the formal parlors. Volunteers from First Presbyterian Church, across Orange Street, delivered their flowers to CK after Sunday services. I passed huge bouquets of cut flowers on tables and chests. They filled the halls with the scent of a funeral—mine?

Though pleasant to all, Mr. Abbott was Baptist-sober when it came to the daily operation of CK—the time-honored sanctuary filled with elderly ladies in downtown Wilmington. He reminded me of the groom on top of a wedding cake—erect, fastidious, and serious.

I saw Mr. Abbott glimpse me through the glass French doors to his office. Before I knocked, I put my left hand on my hip in case the vise of pain grabbed me again. Mr. Abbott glanced at his watch and explained what led to Mother's last day. "It seems Clara tried to force herself into Mrs. Fletcher's room. She reached in and slapped the face of the nurse who blocked her entry."

The movie reel ran through my head as though I had sat in the front row. I grimaced when I pictured the scene.

"We will not tolerate that sort of behavior," Mr. Abbott said, "You know we've put up with a great deal, but no more."

"I am so sorry," I said. Sorry, yes. Surprised? No. She'd slapped before, and then said she was "just playing." She'd finally gone too far.

I wondered if I should stay there and continue to convey my remorse or go back to the car to make sure she still sat there. The motor was running. I decided I'd better cut it short.

Mr. Abbott twiddled a yellow pencil, "You need to come by and get the heavier pieces from her room so that it will be cleared out by 8:30 in the morning."

I gulped. "I'll call Charles to bring his pickup this afternoon." I pictured him rearranging fishing poles and shoving his camouflage mess to one side of his truck bed.

Mr. Abbott answered me with a deep glottal, "Hmph."

Mother sat where I had left her in the car—quiet, for her. I opened my door and heeded advice I had heard from her all my life, "If you can't say anything nice, then don't say anything at all."

The residents seated on the porch watched, leaned in, and whispered about this sensational expulsion. I felt a breeze from their wagging tongues as we left the scene and turned onto Fourth Street. That episode was the end of the Clara saga for them.

I gave her the silent treatment, and she gave it right back. This was as close to humble as I remember her, but it didn't last.

"What did Mr. Abbott tell you?" Then she offered her version—something about "a nurse in my way."

Years later, I discovered Mother's full account in one of her journals:

> *I went to Lula Fletcher's room to see if she was ready to go to breakfast. I was going to help her dress since she hurt her arm the other day. But Linda Simmons (a nurse) was in there and she told me to "Get out." I told Linda I had seen Lula Fletcher naked before because I had been helping her undress at night. Linda came over to the door to push me out, and I patted her on the cheek. For some reason she ran down the hall hollering. I don't know what she told Mr. Abbott, but he came to my room and said, "You start packing. I'm going to call Betty to come after you." He told me he would see to it that I got something to eat, and then he brought a tray full of breakfast to my room. It was more than I could eat so I put some of it in plastic containers to take with me. They are so wasteful with food at CK.*

Part 1

It has been said, "You can't choose your ancestors or parents, but that's fair enough. They probably wouldn't have chosen you either."

Union County
(South Carolina)
Heritage Society

Emily Weaver Scott, Clara Elizabeth Scott,
age 4, & James Carlisle Scott, 1917.

1. Clara's Early Years

My mother was Emily Aileen Weaver of Tryon, North Carolina, the daughter of a well-to-do farmer. She had trained as a nurse but later became a telephone operator where she met my father, Carl Scott, born in Union and raised in Prosperity, South Carolina. He worked as a telegrapher for Southern Bell Telephone & Telegraph Company. Emily Aileen Weaver and James Carlisle Scott married in 1912.

They started in Spartanburg, South Carolina, moved to Darlington, where I was born on 11/12/13, back to Spartanburg, where my sister Aileen was born two and one-half years later. Daddy moved us when I was four after the company transferred him to Charleston, South Carolina.

Our house at 4 Legare Street was near the "Bahtree," as

they say Battery, in Charleston. The house was three stories of gray stucco with two porches that overlooked live oaks and palmettos that lined the street. A tall iron fence surrounded the house.

I first read the story about my mother, Clara, and the iron gate incident in Charleston, written in her typed autobiography. The story was repeated annually at Scott family reunions.

On Tuesdays, Clara's mother, Emily Scott, set up her ironing board next to a second-story window, to catch a cool breeze during the humid Charleston summer. Emily's husband Carl, Clara's dad, had hired Gladys to cook and clean, but Emily insisted on doing the ironing herself.

4 Legare Street, Charleston, South Carolina. *Painting by Betty Bell Brown*

Before she began her task, Emily ushered Clara and her younger sister Aileen outside, "Now you girls play here while I do my ironing at that window upstairs." With the sandbox in her view, Emily kept an eye on her girls while she sprinkled the cotton dresses she draped over the ironing board and steamed the wrinkled batiste flat again.

Aileen took her post in the sandbox that Carl had constructed for the girls. The family had made a special Sunday excursion to the Isle of Palms to bag up white beach sand to fill the box. From one corner of the sandbox, legs crossed and pinky finger out, Aileen served tea to her imaginary friends.

Bored by the tea party, five-year-old Clara climbed onto the iron gate that spanned the driveway, between two seven-foot tabby pillars. The gate, weakened by Charleston's corrosive salt air, creaked and moaned with each back and forth ride. Emily happened to look down just as the gate hinges gave away. The creaking noise stopped, and with a dull thud, the iron gate trapped Clara between bars of iron and the packed dirt of a gritty driveway. Later, Emily didn't remember coming down the stairs, but she was beside Clara in a moment.

Emily had never seen Clara motionless while awake. Emily's slender fingers grabbed the bars. Boosted by a rush of maternal adrenaline, she lifted the gate away from Clara seconds before Clara's father Carl arrived home. Clara picked herself up and scurried out as she backhanded dust from her dress.

Clara & Aileen, circa 1919.

The heavy gate should have crushed Clara, but unscathed and impatient, she ran off to find another adventure. True to the luck that followed her throughout her life, Clara had landed in a deep tire rut—a protective cradle prepared in advance by her guardian angel.

Clara's kin told how Emily trembled at the averted tragedy, and how Carl seated her in a rocker on the front porch and fanned her with *The Evening Post*. Carl and Emily probably looked at each other and wondered what their daughter might get into next.

～

Every day, up with the morning sun, Clara ran to the kitchen as though it might vanish unless she hurried. After breakfast, she grabbed her hair brush and ran to sit at her mother's feet for Emily's daily attempt to train Clara's curls into giving her at least the appearance of perfection.

I loved for anyone to mess with my hair. Mother spent hours training my thick baby doll curls into coils that cascaded down my back to my waist. Every day, Mother pinned a giant-size bow of grosgrain or taffeta on one side to hold back the bulk of my curls.

…Sometimes when I had been in bed asleep I woke up and saw the light from the parlor still on. I often peeped in and saw Mother doing hand work on the dresses she made for us. Aileen loved to get gussied up in the fancy outfits of lace insets, tucks, and other embellishments on fine cotton batiste. I thought it was a waste of Mother's time. My dresses ripped every time I went down the sliding board that Daddy made for us in the backyard. I overheard Mother tell Aileen to try to keep me from tearing my dresses, and Aileen did just that, every chance she had. Who wants a younger sister telling you what to do?

Daddy's brother, my Uncle Pierce, and a friend came to visit us in their World War I uniforms, and Daddy wanted my photograph with them. Then, as an afterthought someone said, "We could put Aileen in the picture too." No bother getting her ready, she stayed spotless and dressed up all the time. Aileen's hair was thinner than mine and straight as a stick. What could they do with that bowl cut and the Buster Brown bangs she peeped through? No fuss needed there.

Uncle Pierce Scott & friend with Clara & Aileen during WWI, 1919.

Clara's mother kept family snapshots in a little black album. Clara got hold of it and wrote names and dates across each photo, a process she continued throughout her life. Aileen hated this and grumbled every time she thought about her sister defacing the family photographs. I had to swear to Mother never to let Aileen have the coveted album. I still have it—names, dates, and defacements intact, easily fixed with Photoshop.

Aileen identified with the Weaver side of the family. The Weavers were British gentry who came from Rhode Island and established one of the early textile mills near Tryon, North Carolina, in 1820. Aileen insisted that the Weaver mill was the first in the South.

Clara took after the Scott clan, a rainbow of colorful characters from Union and Prosperity, South Carolina.

We moved to Greenville when I was six. Daddy had been chief test board man for Southern Bell until American Telephone & Telegraph Company opened an office in Greenville. Daddy transferred to A. T. & T. and became Greenville's first manager. ...

Clara Scott, circa 1919, age 6.

We rented the downstairs of a house on Coxe Street from a twice-widowed lady and her daughter, Miss Ella Mauldin. Miss Ella, an old maid, never had any babies so she took a special interest in me. She taught me to crochet and to read music. She drew musical staffs and the notes on the ground with a stick.

A grateful Emily enjoyed the attention Miss Ella gave to her daughter.

When the family's cook, Tamer, finished her work, she found Clara perched in the fig tree at the back door and called her to the shady porch. She seated Clara and Aileen on a bench while they waited for their father, and Tamer taught them her favorite card game, Rook. It awakened a competitive streak in Clara. They played until Aileen stormed off when she didn't win, or until they heard the crunch of Carl's footsteps on the gravel driveway at the side of the bungalow. Clara ran to greet her daddy and watched his hand to see if there was a piece of candy for her in his pocket.

While Tamer was essential in the household, she sometimes disappeared.

Every now and then, Daddy explained that our cook, Tamer, was put into jail for getting a little too rowdy on Saturday nights. When Tamer was in jail, her daughter Ruth filled in but she was slow. So Daddy bailed Tamer out of jail and let her work out the money over time.

When it was time for Tamer to come to the house to fix supper each evening, Clara made herself a jelly sandwich before crossing a field behind the house to meet Tamer halfway. Tamer teased Clara into giving her a bite of the sandwich. She knew Miss Emily had taught her daughter not to eat in front of others without sharing. But on one occasion, Clara got a bright idea while she spread a glob of apple jelly across a piece of white bread. She went to the back stoop and spooned dirt over one side of the sandwich where the jelly held it in place. She put the top on the sandwich and set off to meet Tamer.

Tamer called out when she saw her young charge walk down the pathway cushioned with chickweed and surrounded by broom straw. "How about a little bite of your jelly sandwich, Miss Clara?"

Beggar's lice clung to Clara's white stockings. Devil horns grew out of her thick brown curls and she smiled, "Sure, Tamer, you can have a bite."

She stuck the dirt side of the sandwich toward Tamer who had closed her eyes before she chomped down. She salivated in anticipation of sweet jelly on fresh white loaf bread.

"Phtttttew!" Tamer spit, sputtered, and gagged over the gritty mouthful. She wiped her mouth with the back of her hand, grabbed Clara by the ear, and marched her back to the house while she spit out grit every few steps. She said, "Your daddy going to give you a whipping when he hears what you did, missy."

There was no whipping, only a ban on future jelly sandwiches when meeting Tamer halfway and Carl's heartfelt apology to Tamer.

But Clara knew she had her daddy wrapped around her little finger.

> *I wasn't the least bit afraid of Daddy. I was his little old gal and that's what he called me. I'd bet a dollar to a doughnut that if you looked hard, you'd have seen a smirk on my Daddy's face the day Tamer and I butted heads.*

———

When Aileen started school the fall of 1919, Daddy asked the telephone company if he could stay put in Greenville and not have to move all over South Carolina. With being in one place, he bought a house on Rutherford Road, about a mile from downtown Greenville. Our brand new house cost $7,500. It had five rooms, with a breakfast room and a sleeping porch. A bath at the end of the hall lined up with the front door. That was the only thing Mama complained about, and she had us keep that door shut every minute, in case someone dropped by. I guess she thought it was a deep and dark secret that the Scott family used a bathroom. At least it was inside the house unlike the bathroom of our Pridmore relatives in Union. When I grow up, I'm going to leave the bathroom door open all the time.

A family of Fletchers bought the house next door. They were rather trashy people, which made for a most uncomfortable situation. They got fiercely drunk, had brawls, and talked real loud. Aileen and I could hear them late at night from the sleeping porch. Except for the noise the Fletchers made, there was no better sleeping than on the sleeping porch. In the summer, it was the coolest room in the house, and in the winter, piles of quilts weighed us down, making us stay put where we were.

Aileen and I had dolls and tea sets and almost everything we wanted, but I'd have given up all my toys for a bicycle. We lived on a highway and Mother was afraid for me to have one. I never got a bike because the traffic grew worse. I hitched rides on the backs of the Fletcher boys' bikes instead.

In order to graduate from Stone School, each student had to give a reading of a poem or short story. I couldn't seem to give this reading to suit my coach, Miss Griffith. I managed to graduate from grammar school but had to repeat the sixth grade.

Mother was known for her flower garden and served on the flower committee for the Susanna Wesley Class at Buncombe Street Methodist Church. Every Sunday morning in the summertime, she carried an enormous blue basket of sweet William, larkspur, zinnias, Dusty Miller, marigolds, and sweet peas to church. Some Sundays Mother wasn't feeling well so I carried the flower basket when she stayed home.

Daddy bought a brand new upright Mathushek piano for Aileen and me. It came in a large wooden crate. He built us a playhouse out of the crate in the backyard and put a window in it that would raise and fasten at the top. He also gave us a tiny lock for the front door. He eventually enlarged the house. It sat near the back steps, under the privet hedge to get shade. I preferred the playhouse over the piano that came in the box.

Almost every weekend, our family went to visit Daddy's step-mother Kate and Grandfather Scott in Union. When we weren't visiting the Scotts, we went to Tryon to see Mother's people. Before Daddy bought us an automobile, we took the train up the mountain from Greenville. Granddaddy Weaver had a horse-drawn buggy and his man Bub met us at the station. If it was snowing, he sent a bigger buggy with a fringe around the top and four to six horses to pull us through the snow. We passed the home of Old Katie, who raised Mother. She clapped her hands and hollered to her brood, "Come on out here and wave to Miss Emily and her children."

Mildred, Lydia, and Harry Reese, my cousins on the Scott side, often came to Granddaddy Weaver's from nearby Hendersonville when we visited.

Mother's cousin Lydia used to say, "The Weavers lived in the mountains, but they were no hillbillies. Fact is they were downright highfalutin."

Cousin Mildred added, "I about died laughing the time Clara stepped out of the rumble seat of Uncle Carl's new car. She had cut out four large pieces of fabric into question mark shapes and sewed them together with long basting stitches using pink thread to hold the sides and inseam. She was determined to ride one of her grand-daddy's horses that day." The relatives smirked at Aunt Em's head-strong daughter who thought she was something in her homemade jodhpurs.

All the kinfolk knew that if Clara didn't make dirt sandwiches, climb trees, or make a pair of jodhpurs, it wouldn't be long before she got into some other form of willful behavior.

Emily Weaver Scott.

2. Emily Leaves

Mama hasn't been staying up nights on her sewing. I think she has worked herself sick. I can tell she doesn't feel well and probably hasn't for some time. But she's trying not to give in. Lots of days I catch her taking long naps in the afternoon. That's just not like her at all.

Dr. R.C. Bruce came out to the house to check on her on January 26, 1928. I heard him telling Daddy to have Mama get plenty of fresh air, lots of bed rest, and nutritious meals. But these things didn't help get her any better. She grew worse, and was diagnosed with tuberculosis.

Clara loved to answer the door when Emily's many friends and neighbors dropped by with food or offers to help. Aileen grew sullen from the lack of her mother's attention. But, she, too, pitched in to try to help Aunt Hannah, Emily's sister, who had come to care for the family. Hannah was Clara's favorite aunt of all her mother's sisters.

Hannah greeted Dr. Bruce when he made a house call in February. By now, Emily was bedridden. After Dr. Bruce examined his patient, he turned to Carl and advised, "You must arrange to have all your wife's teeth pulled right away. If she should get an infection on top of the tuberculosis, it would be tragic and could drain the strength she needs to fight this disease."

Hannah walked Dr. Bruce to the front door and thanked him for coming. The doctor hesitated before he faced Hannah again. "As a matter of fact, Mrs. Scott's hair should be cut short, as well. This, too, will help preserve her strength."

Hannah felt a jolt in her chest and held onto the door as it closed behind the doctor. She mumbled to herself, "First her teeth must go and now this—my poor Emily." The illness was like a crow pecking at an ear of corn, robbing her sister of all that defined her.

Carl nodded at Hannah when she turned and saw him in the hall-way. They exchanged looks and knew what had to be done.

Hannah called out to Clara, "Run, get me two fresh bed sheets." Clara dashed to the linen closet near the back porch and stretched to reach a folded stack near the top. Tamer had ironed that day, and Clara buried her face to catch the smell of hot iron that clung to the cotton.

Hannah spread one sheet onto the center of the bedroom floor. She helped Emily into a chair she had placed in the middle of the sheet. Hannah wrapped a second sheet around her sister's shoulders and followed the doctor's orders. Each metallic snip of the sharp scissors invaded the quiet of the room. Clara had watched the scene from a corner of the bedroom.

Mother looked like an angel wrapped in that crisp white sheet, but her shoulders drooped beneath the folds. Her long locks tumbled down Mother's frail frame. Like Samson, Mother's strength surrounded her feet with waves of red-dish-brown. The ghost-like person who remained was not the mother I knew.

After the last snip, the sheen on what was left of Emily's au-burn waves looked dull against her pallid face. After Aunt Hannah snapped back from a long stare at Emily's appearance, she instructed Clara, "Bundle up this sheet and take it to the garden. Get a hoe and work the hair between the rows of your mother's flower beds. It'll be good for them."

Clara followed the orders after she first saved a lock later held by a red satin ribbon. She put it in the cigar box where she hid secret treasures, stored in her chest of drawers. The hair nestled between a skate key given to her by one of the Fletcher boys, the gold locket she had won in a baby contest, and a dried-out peach pit she planned to plant out back to have her own peach tree.

The fall of 1928 approached. Carl and Emily decided to send fifteen-year-old Clara away to boarding school for a more structured lifestyle. Emily's poor health had left her unable to oversee things at home or to give Clara the attention she demanded. Aunt Hannah didn't need that burden. Fruitland Institute, a Baptist school seven miles from Hendersonville, North Carolina, was a convenient choice.

The headmaster, Mr. Miller, explained to Carl, "We take the children on hikes, picnics, and to basketball games. The students are kept very busy along with their studies." Mr. Miller's words fell on Carl's ears like tonal chords. Carl knew that Clara must be kept busy at all times, and she needed encouragement to get her schoolwork done.

"We try to provide a feeling of family here." The children called Mr. Miller "Daddy," and his wife, the dietitian, "Mother Miller." She was as round as Mr. Miller was lanky—Jack Spratt and his wife.

Athletic and social events, plus plenty of snowball fights, helped expend Clara's bottomless pool of energy. She had a violin lesson each evening at nine o'clock, but by then she was worn out, barely able to play the instrument.

Clara shared a room with Aileen at home and found it hard to abide Aileen or her roommate at Fruitland.

I despise her silly ways, so they are moving me to another room.

Fruitland was nothing to brag about unless maybe you were a Baptist, so Clara shined up the truth and told folks back home that she was at school "up Nawth." About forty-five miles north, that was.

Emily's health continued to decline. The doctor saw a need to upgrade her care. Carl moved his wife to a sanatorium near Asheville, North Carolina.

The family had managed without an automobile for a while. Carl walked to and from the telephone company office, and Buncombe Street Methodist Church was in walking distance. When Emily became so ill, Carl and his younger brother Pierce pooled their resources for a tan Chrysler Coach. The car allowed Carl to combine visits to Clara at Fruitland with trips to the sanatorium. Emily stayed in Asheville for several months before Carl moved her to a sanatorium in Hendersonville, a bit closer to home. She stayed there for nearly two years.

～

Home from Fruitland for the summer, Clara pressured Carl to teach her to drive the Chrysler.

He took me up to West Earle Street and showed me what to do. He'd get so mad sometimes. There were two places in the road going up to see Mother that were perfectly straight for a ways, and Dad let me drive during that part of the trip.

Her driving ability improved, and Carl let Clara and Aileen use the family car on Sunday afternoons, but with a strict limit on how far they could go. Main Street on Sundays was the place to be seen. They parked to "people-watch" or joined the parade of cruisers down the "drag."

Clara couldn't figure out how to turn back that odometer to stay within her twenty-mile limit, but she rolled the car into the driveway as the next increment of twenty rolled into view on the gauge.

～

We had a helper named Eula. She worked for us after Mother went to the sanatorium, but she quit soon after I came home for summer vacation, so Tamer and Ruth took up the slack. Aunt Hannah stayed at home with Aileen for quite a while, but had to leave, so Daddy hired a white lady from Fountain Inn, a nearby mill town. She moved in to keep house for us, but had to leave when I came home the next summer. Dad was at his wit's end by now.

Carl found that the care and supervision of his two teenage girls, trips to visit Emily and Clara, plus the household duties were too much for him while he held down his job with the telephone company. Various members of Emily's family came from Tryon to help but found it impossible to continue indefinitely. The neighbors were helpful, but Carl didn't like dependence on Emily's sisters or the neighbors.

When the last housekeeper left, he placed an ad in the *Greenville News*. As providence would have it, Mrs. Beulah Wilson Parrott, known as Polly, scanned the want ads for employment. She saw the ad for a housekeeper, cook, and caretaker for two girls in their teens. She answered the ad and was invited to 202 Rutherford Road for an interview.

I remember very well the night Polly came. She wore a short green dress with a black flower design at the shoulder. Her hair was black and shiny, worn in a tidy short bob. We all sat in the living room and talked for quite a while. At the time, she worked for a Mr. White with the Goody Headache Powder Company. I think a few days passed before Polly came to live with us as our housekeeper.

I got along with Polly but did not like her at first. I suppose I resented her being there. Looking back, I found out that Polly was one of my best friends. Many times she talked Dad into letting me do things that I wanted to do. And Daddy is relieved to have someone here for us.

After Emily's stays in Asheville and Hendersonville, she told Carl, "I miss my family and I want to see my garden. I want to come home." So Carl set up their bedroom to keep her as comfortable as possible.

They also moved Clara back to Greenville. She was in the ninth grade, but the Greenville School System did not accept the schoolwork she did at Fruitland, so she had to repeat the ninth grade at the high school at the foot of McBee Avenue. Clara was sixteen and Aileen was fourteen years old. Clara had repeated the sixth and ninth grades, which put her in the same class with Aileen. This embarrassed Aileen. Clara explained the situation and blamed history and Latin as "the subjects that caused all the trouble."

Clara and Aileen had not been at school more than an hour on May 5, 1930, when Carl went by to bring them home. "Mother is worse and wants to see you girls," he told them.

Only the birds that sang outside the window broke the quiet while the family gathered around Emily's bed. She lay still and listened to the concert by the birds.

Mama was a little bit of a thing, hardly weighing a hundred pounds, with bobbed hair and no teeth. She barely made an impression lying in the bed.

Emily was no longer the mother who worked in her flower garden, stitched up ripped dresses, and graced their home as hostess to their many relatives and friends. She motioned for Carl to hand her a piece of paper she had tucked inside her Bible. She had listed requests for a simple funeral with galax leaves to adorn her casket. She asked that 1 Corinthians 13, be read at her service and suggested a headstone that resembled a piece of fieldstone. A peaceful countenance masked the usual pain across her face. Emily died at nine o'clock that Friday night.

This is an awful thing to say, but I am not real sorry I lost my Mother. I feel sad, but am a bit glad. Mother was too strict on us in some ways—coming into the room to see what we were doing. I like to be left alone so I can do what I want to do.

I have read this statement in Mother's diary time and time again. I have deciphered it for myself. She lashed out with the persistence of a self-centered girl who had been given a prize that was later taken away. This was her way to say, "I don't care; I didn't want that prize anyway."

After Mother died, Daddy asked Polly to stay on as our housekeeper for the sake of Aileen and me. Polly told Daddy she would stay on the condition she could send for her six-year-old daughter, Sibyl, to come live with her at our house.

3. Polly's Story

Twelve-year-old Beulah Edith Wilson held a fistful of wool sleeve, her older brother John's jacket. Both children lugged tattered, cloth-covered suitcases in their free hands. They followed their aunt and uncle up the front stairs of Connie Maxwell Children's Home in Greenwood, South Carolina.

Beulah and John's mother had died of tuberculosis the previous year. Two months later, their father died. Relatives in Darlington had had to give up farming after another bad crop and were unable to care for Beulah and John.

Beulah took great comfort in books and music and considered her education an escape from a hard-fought existence and the loss of both parents. After high school graduation, Beulah returned to the Darlington area, where she was appointed principal of a two-room country school. She was a natural-born teacher whose gift was to impart academic knowledge along with lessons on how to live a dignified life in spite of hard times.

The new schoolteacher attracted the attention of a local dandy named Reginald Parrott. The attraction went both ways, and Beulah married Reginald in 1921, when she was eighteen years old. Their daughter Sibyl was born a year later, followed by the birth of a son, Gene, in 1927. Beulah accepted the nickname "Polly" along with her new last name. The name stuck with her, but Reginald did not. Reginald abandoned his family and Polly was forced to provide for her children during the Great Depression.

Polly left the school for a better-paying job. She sold Goody's Headache Powder to retailers across that rural area. This single-parent woman became a traveling saleslady. Polly drove her Model T Ford before the sun rose and long after it set—not the safest job, but it allowed her to send money to the relatives who kept Sibyl and Gene back in Darlington.

On the road, Polly received word that two-year-old Gene had contracted pneumonia. Determined to get home to him, she changed her course and watched the setting sun silhouette distant trees on the edge of a cotton field. The car's headlights made the night seem darker along the rugged roads that webbed across rural South Carolina. Gene died minutes before Polly reached his bedside. She vowed to provide for six-year-old Sibyl, and to have her with her at all times.

With Polly as our housekeeper, we continued to take trips up to Tryon to visit Mother's people, the Weavers. Granddaddy owned lots of land where he grew corn as far as you could see, and he kept a stable of fine horses.

When we got ready to go home, some of the more 'air-ish' of Mother's people would pull Aileen aside and say to her, "You go sit in the front seat, so that woman (Polly) can't sit next to your Daddy." Their connivance didn't work though, because Daddy soon planned to marry that woman. Polly was ten years older than me. She was twenty-seven and Daddy was forty-two.

Daddy took me for a ride and told me he and Polly planned to marry. I didn't fancy the idea at the time, but I realized it was the best thing for all concerned. It was especially good for Polly, who had grown up in an orphanage and married Mr. Parrott, who left her high and dry. And, I guess caring for Aileen and me was a better job than the one she had before she met us.

Before Daddy could marry Polly, he had arranged and paid for her divorce from Mr. Parrott. On April 18, 1931, they went to Hartwell, Georgia, for the wedding ceremony since South Carolina didn't recognize divorce. We all went with them—Dad's friends the Millers, Uncle Pierce, Aileen, and I. They had a wedding supper at a famous eating place in Starr, South Carolina.

The following summer our step-sister, Sibyl, came to live with us. I remember the day she arrived. The whole family went to the train depot to meet her. She had traveled alone on the C&W Railway. Even though it was hot, she wore a brown, tweed coat with thread-bare places at the sleeves and collar. Money was pinned between the scratchy tweed and the lining of her coat. I thought that was a great idea so the child wouldn't lose her money, especially when Daddy had to go back onto the Pullman car to retrieve a stuffed dog that Sibyl had left on her seat.

She was a pretty little thing, and I took her under my wing. Aileen pitched a hissy fit when Polly let Sibyl use the silver dresser set that had been Mother's. Aileen didn't want anybody to touch things that had been Mother's. She considered herself her mama's girl and thought of Polly as "that woman who was taking our Mother's place." Again, I was more like Daddy. And Daddy was happy as a puppy with Polly.

Polly and Daddy had some catching up to do after Polly's hard-knock life and Daddy's years spent caring for Mother. Being young, Polly hadn't had a chance for fun until now. They enjoyed their many friends and playing cards into the wee hours. They went out to eat together, went on Lake Murray fishing trips and dances at the Shrine Patrol Clubhouse at the foot of Paris Mountain. Daddy was big into being a Shriner. They had lots of parties and supported a hospital for children with polio. They laughed and told jokes that I didn't quite get. Mother didn't tell me all the things I needed to know. She put it off until I was too bashful to ask questions.

Who knew Clara had a bashful bone in her body?

I could tell that Daddy loved Polly and was convinced of it on a summer day when they came home from fishing. Daddy accidentally mashed Polly's fingers closing the car door. She walked inside, but just as she got into the kitchen, she fainted—dead away, right in the middle of the floor. Daddy ran to the sink, grabbed a pot from the drain rack, filled it with water

*from the tap, and threw the water in Polly's face while she
lay motionless across the black and white checkered linoleum.
Sibyl and I got the giggles over Daddy doing such a thing, but
we stifled ourselves and went back to worrying about Polly,
laid out soaking wet and limp as a dish rag. Daddy got down
by her side, calling her "Honey" and "Darling" and other
names we didn't know he used. She came to, and he took her
to the doctor's office and discovered a bone in one finger was
broken.*

———

*Polly and Daddy had a daughter Edith, born on March
29, 1932, when I was 18. I adored my half-sister, took her for
walks, fed her, and even washed out her diapers. Sometimes
I took her to bed with me. She loved to sleep with me on the
sleeping porch when it was cold. We kept each other warm.
When I didn't have a date myself, I kept Edith for Polly and
Daddy to go out when they couldn't get Ruth.*

Polly adjusted to the sisters' personalities. She let Clara think
she could do whatever she wanted to do, and she stroked Aileen's
ego as needed. Polly never attempted to take Emily's place, and she
didn't change who Clara was.

Aileen & Clara, mid 1930s.

4. Sisters

I wish I could buy you girls for what you are worth,
then sell you for what you think you're worth.

J. CARL SCOTT, FATHER OF CLARA AND AILEEN SCOTT

Clara had her hair cut into a fashionable bob after her mother had died. She replaced the baby-doll curls with stylish finger waves. The young lady grew into her beauty with a movie-star look—Clara Bow had nothing on Clara Scott. One of her hobbies as a teen was to collect movie-star photographs. Aileen pulled her hair to the back and fastened it into a tight chignon. Later, Aileen styled her hair in a pageboy with a middle part and wore it that way for the rest of her life.

Along with their mother's dignity, Aileen had inherited Emily's Dresden-doll-like complexion. Clara's skin was exposed to the elements because she spent her time playing tennis, swimming, hiking, and camping. The activities tanned her with a healthy glow.

Clara's visits with Polly's relatives in Darlington confirmed that she could draw admirers and the young men hovered. Clara had learned as a child that she was special, and she was hell-bent to let the world know it, too. Her steely blue eyes declared her determined nature, and her dresses did not hide the shapely figure beneath. Even tailored clothing and no-frills dresses revealed curves where curves were supposed to be.

⸺

"I said the cutest thing in home ec class today. Everybody just laughed and laughed," Aileen said.

Clara mocked Aileen and told her, "I wish I was as funny as some people think they are."

Aileen was mindful of what others thought of her; Clara only cared that she was noticed, period. Aileen climbed social ladders rung by rung. Clara was not interested in a social climb but loved people's awareness of her presence. Throughout their lives, the sisters raced Narcissus to the pond to admire their own reflections.

When Aileen was a little girl, it was easy to make her mad. I suppose my sister was as good as most, but she'd get real mad at me. I put my hands over my ears when she screamed at me. Aileen's temper got worse in her teens, and the little dickens scratched a mole off my left breast that never grew back.

Another time she got angry and chased me around the dining room table. She picked up a poker when she passed the fireplace and would have hit me had Polly not stopped her.

Aileen resented Aunt Ev loaning me a violin. I took lessons at Fruitland Institute and for two winters from Miss Lennie Lusby at the Greenville Woman's College. I got pretty good and played second violin in the high school orchestra. When Aunt Ev asked for her violin back, Daddy bought one for me.

Polly had Aileen and me take turns washing the dishes after supper every night while she and Daddy went to the parlor to hear "Amos and Andy" on the radio. When it was my turn to wash dishes, Aileen went around the table and licked all the unused flatware to make me have to wash them.

Our cousins Fredree and Lucille visited one night. Aileen and Lucille had set the table, so Polly assigned Fredree and me to clean up. Aileen and Lucille teased us about having to do the dishes. It was getting tiresome, so I told Fredree, "Let's just lick the dessert plates clean. We can put them in the cupboard and no one'll ever know." And they didn't.

Clara and Aileen spent weekends at house parties in the mountains. They found summer cottages at Cedar Mountain, Paris Mountain, or Piedmont Park. Fires roared in huge stone fireplaces while they danced and sang through chilly winter nights.

When we went to the mountains, Aileen would ask her special boyfriend, Dave, to go along, and I picked from my long list of beaus. We'd take a Victrola and get as little as three hours sleep after we danced all night.

When boredom set in, someone might suggest, "Let's hitchhike somewhere."

They walked the dirt road to the highway and took a ride with the first car that stopped. Some of the teens sat in the trunk and dangled their feet out the back if there were too many to crawl inside. They rode from Cedar Mountain to Brevard, swam in the lake at Camp Burgess Glen, and hitched back to Cedar Mountain. They caught rides to the state line several times during the day, got off, and hitched back to the cottage—their idea of an adventure.

One time, a junky heap of a truck pulled over at the state line. An old codger smirked from behind the wheel. "Y'all going my way? Just hop right on."

The weary, hungry kids were ready to get back home, so they piled onto his flatbed. When they approached their destination, the mountaineer flashed his tobacco-stained, toothless grin and chuckled, "I ain't going to let y'all off." Tobacco-tinged saliva crept out of the corners of his mouth.

Clara told her friend Sarah, "I'm getting off of here." She jumped off the back of the truck when it slowed down at the hairpin curve before their stop. She didn't surprise anyone more than the benign hillbilly who played the trick.

I landed in gravel on the shoulder of the road that left me with a burn on the right hip that ran clear down to my knees. I sat out the dancing that night, but everyone was so attentive and worried a lot about me.

Aileen's boyfriend didn't have two nickels to rub together, but he and Aileen had big ideas about someday being business tycoons. Dave had a long way to go because every time he joined the family for a party, or even came by the house, he ran out of gas. It happened so many times, we were never surprised.

Yesterday Aileen and I walked downtown and it snowed pretty hard on the way back. We saw Dave's car in front of our house, and Aileen went all a-flutter. I figured he was out of gas. Smoke came out of the chimney so I knew Daddy had built a fire. We ran inside, and as was my usual practice, I backed up to the open flame and hiked up my skirt to feel the warmth against my exposed back side. You'd think I had thrown ice water into Aileen's sour puss. She about died when she realized Dave ogled me like a pin-up poster. His slack mouth hung off his face like a pair of drawers on a clothesline. He couldn't have seen anything he hadn't seen before. Don't know why Aileen went into such a snit over something like that.

Clara Scott.

5. The Social Life of a Butterfly

You never know if a not so cute boy might have a cute friend to meet. In my opinion, you should take every date you can get, just in case they might have a cuter friend. I couldn't stand Floyd at all, but I did go to the picture show with him several times before I met his friend Richard, and we started dating.

Many times boys called on me, and we visited in the front parlor, making Daddy go to the bedroom to hear his favorite radio shows, "Amos and Andy," "Fibber McGee," or "Jack Benny."

Aileen's old boyfriend Wilbur dropped by one night when Aileen had already gone out with Dave. Aileen didn't want Dad and Polly to realize how serious she was with Dave so she kept our neighborhood friend Wilbur around to fool them. With Aileen gone, Wilbur was satisfied to sit in the parlor with *me. As usual with Wilbur, the conversation lagged, and the silence felt a little awkward.*

Our cat, Velvet, slinked into the room and cozied down on the wool rug between the fireplace and sofa. Simply to break the silence, I blurted out, "I bet that cat can do something you can't do." No sooner than I spoke those words, the cat unfurled, reached his left hind toes toward the ceiling and began to lick his privates, and the cat purred real loud.

Wilbur shifted in his seat and said to me, "Well, I think Mother will look for me pretty soon, so I'd better go now," and he made his way out the front door. I thought I heard him stumble down the steps.

When I told Aileen about it later, she threw another one of her hissy fits even though she didn't care a thing about Wilbur being embarrassed.

Clara boasted of her chair in the violin section of the high school orchestra. The orchestra was recognized with first-place awards at many of the state music contests held in Rock Hill, South Carolina. Clara loved those trips but dreaded the rigorous practice Mr. Rhame demanded. She radiated her enthusiasm each time she climbed the steps on the school bus for another trip. She also held a spot on the GHS girls' basketball squad but admitted she didn't play many important games; she just loved the trips. The GHS senior banquet highlighted the end of the sisters' senior year.

There was not a chance I would miss this event. Boys in the Senior Class outnumbered the girls, so if a girl had a date for the banquet, they kind of rated. Well, I guess I rated since Wayne Ward invited me.

After a graduation ceremony in Textile Hall, Wayne and I went to the banquet at First Presbyterian Church. The decorations were fixed up real cute, and we had baked chicken, green beans, rice and gravy with pecan pie for dessert.

Wayne had borrowed his family car, and he showed off his bubbly date while they cruised all the popular spots. Around midnight,

Wayne went north on Main Street, to take Clara back to Rutherford Road.

"Bam!" The right-front tire made an awful noise, then went flat. Clara felt her side of the car sink, along with her fun. Wayne felt the air deflate out of his ego. Friends drove by and gawked at them. Clara waved as though she enjoyed herself.

Wayne told Clara, "It's too late to get someone to fix the tire." So he called his dad from a pay phone. Clara loved an adventure, but this one got a little tiresome when she saw Mr. Ward clank down Main Street in an old rattle trap—a car made into a truck to haul his chickens. The nasty coops that lined the back bed of the vehicle revealed its main function and far out-smelled her gardenia corsage that Wayne had pinned on the shoulder of Clara's powder-blue georgette gown. Wayne flicked away some unknown substance from the front seat before he helped Clara onto the running board and into the foul-smelling jalopy that reeked of fowl and feathers. It was a long ride out to Rutherford Road.

"Lord, if it be Thy will, don't let the smell of chickens reach Daddy's nostrils." She began all her prayers with "if it be Thy will," so she didn't accidentally pray for undue indulgences.

"What's that smell?" Clara's dad asked as she crept up the stairs.

"I don't know," she answered, but continued toward the sleeping porch, where she hoped the fresh air would dissipate the odors absorbed by the filmy fabric of her frock.

———

Clara and her friends gave small dances at home and invited boys over. They took up the rug in the living room and waxed the floor. Sometimes they borrowed a Victrola in case the radio didn't play anything good. Her favorites were Wayne King, Guy Lombardo, and Sammy Kaye.

Clara also went through a period when she dated boys from Greer, about ten miles from Greenville—Walt, Dillard, Paul, Sidney, John, and two Stewarts. Who knew that many people lived in Greer? Despite her success north of Greenville, nearby Clemson College proved to be the most prolific grounds.

So few girls to so many men, as they are known at Clemson.

Through Polly's cousins at Clemson, Clara found frequent invitations to dances on campus.

On Monday, March 19, 1934, I looked in our closet for something to wear to the dance at Clemson this coming Saturday night. I happened to raise the lid of a trunk that had belonged to Mother. I saw a bunch of pretty silk underwear, night gowns and negligees—things I thought had surely belonged to Mother. I was so excited to find them, and I was fixing to divide these treasures with Aileen when she walked into the room. She was forced to tell me that the finery was actually her trousseau. She had bought these things out of her allowance and no one knew. I thought she was going to chase me around the dining room table again, but instead she married Dave two days later. She loves to hang onto that grudge and broadcast the story as though I tried to steal her trousseau.

Aileen and Dave were married in our living room by a Reverend Piephoff. Daddy gave her away, Polly played "The Wedding March" on the piano, and I lit the candelabra. After the Reverend left, we brought up some growlers of home brew from the basement to toast the bride and groom.

6. Like Magnets

Aileen and Clara had enrolled in a secretarial course at Draughon's Business College in the fall of 1934, but Aileen dropped out after she married Dave. Classes were upstairs over Woolworth's on Main Street. Clara loved to go downtown every day. She hung out with friends for cherry Coke breaks at Armstrong's Drug Store. The school offered bookkeeping, typing, and beginner and advanced shorthand. She mastered them all.

Aileen and Dave moved in with Clara, Carl, Polly, step-sister Sibyl, and half-sister Edith. Aileen was pregnant and Dave didn't have a job. The Depression still took a toll on people and jobs, but Clara thought things were looking up.

> *Herbert Hoover was President, and he let things get in an awful mess. Then Franklin Delano Roosevelt went into office in 1932, and really got things done. Without a moment's notice, he closed banks across the nation and got them straightened out.*

Aileen gave birth to a son in November 1934. Dave got a job in the textile industry, at Southern Bleachery in Taylors. Aileen loved that, since she claimed her Weaver ancestors had the first textile mill in the area. After Christmas, Aileen, Dave, and the baby moved to an apartment on Prentiss Avenue.

Before Christmas, Clara landed a job at Efird's Department Store. They taught her how to do fancy lettering and how to shade block letters for signs used around the store. This led to a compulsion to enhance every block letter she came across — *Life* magazines, letterheads in the mail, and headings in her scrapbooks. She doodled with shaded letters or changed the fonts with a flourish. She was very good at puffy overlapped letters. But her work didn't interrupt her play.

> *I gave a small dance at my house for my cousin Lucille, who spent a week with us. Many boys I knew were out of town so I asked a friend to invite some boys she knew. The party had just started good when the doorbell rang and there were three of the boys my friend had invited. They were Olin Bell, a rather nice looking, tall fellow; Bill Wright, also good look-ing but he thought so too; and John Miller, whom they called "Tokey." He was short but nice. The Bell boy and his gang of friends had gone to the World's Fair in Chicago the previous year, and he grew a mustache. I liked all three but especially Olin who danced so slow and smooth. Also, he reminded me of movie star, Jimmy Stewart, tall, lanky, and handsome. Before the party was over he asked me for a date for the following Tuesday night.*

Clara told her friends, "I like Olin Bell better than any boy I've ever gone out with. He has a car of his own and a good job." Olin worked as a bookkeeper at Ramseur Roofing Company.

The Depression forced Olin's parents to move from Greenville back to their family farm in Renno, South Carolina. Olin stayed in Greenville to keep his job at the roofing company. He lived at the YMCA for a while, before he boarded with Tokey Miller's family.

It seemed to rain every night that Clara dated Olin, but she en-joyed cozy rides in the rain with him. When she dated others, she liked to go to a picture show or some form of amusement, but with Olin she was content to ride around. Sometimes they parked to talk. Clara wrote in her diary that she liked that Olin didn't try to make time on the first date like other boys. Clara invited Olin to several Sunday school picnics or parties. He went for a while, but left early.

They went on group dates with Olin's buddies, Tokey and Gladys, Runt and Melba, Hugh and Kat, or Jimbo and Lois. They packed picnic lunches on Sundays and drove as far as Asheville to see a show.

———

Clara made arrangements with Olin, Tokey, and his girlfriend, Doris, to come for her at the end of a week's visit with a cousin in Chesnee. When they returned to Greenville, they went to Mrs. Miller's for supper before the couples rode out to the Pines, a night club about six miles from town.

Her attraction to Olin didn't stop Clara from dating other boys.

I like to keep my options open by stringing along as many men as I can manage. A girl never knows when she might need an escort for an important event or when something better might come along.

She broke a date with Olin to go with Ross to a dance at Clemson. She often went with Aileen's old beau, Wilbur, to early shows and stayed for the midnight show. Wilbur was like a fixture at the Scott house, always good for a free movie.

It was common to have Wilbur at the front door, but one fall night it was Olin who called on Clara for a movie date. Glued to *The Burns and Allen Show* on the radio, Carl hollered to Olin, "Come on in, Wilbur." But this did not deter Olin. He splurged on a box of Whitman's candy and a Coty compact after Clara reminded him of her birthday being 11/12/13. For Christmas he sprang for a gift box of "Evening in Paris" products. She loved the deep blue box with cobalt bottles nestled in a satin package.

Olin and Clara planned a house party near Cedar Mountain with Runt, Hugh, and their dates. Jimbo and Lois were not much older than the others, but were married, which qualified them as chaperones. Olin, Clara, and Dot went early to set up. After a fried chicken supper with potato salad, they sat around and listened to the radio in Olin's car. He found Sammy Kaye and the notes wafted out of the partially opened window along with the smoke from Olin's Lucky Strike. Earlier, he had taken the small light bulb out of his radio, since there was no moon. Now, a few fireflies and the occasional glow from a drag on his cigarette punctuated the darkness.

Back in Greenville, Olin and Clara went over to the Pines and sat in the car while Olin drank a couple of Ram's Head beers. Clara noticed that Olin drove around town the same way every time—down the "Main Street drag" and over to the Pickwick, where he drank a couple of bottles of beer. Then out Augusta Road, around by Conestee Mill, and back to Laurens Road. The nights ended with a trip out to the Pines for a few more beers for Olin.

Olin often had a beer or two with the boys before a date with Clara, and after a few, he liked to take off his shoes. He called ahead to make sure Clara was ready to go. He told her, "Be on the front porch because I have taken off my shoes."

It amused Clara to see how he avoided Carl or Polly this way, so they wouldn't smell the beer on his breath. He asked Clara to get behind the wheel since he didn't like to drive after he had a few.

Kat invited Clara, Olin, and her boyfriend, Hugh, for supper one night. Then they took Hugh's new car out for a test ride. For once, Olin and Clara were passengers in the back seat.

> *It was the first time Olin ever tried to make any time with me. I had dated him for eleven months to be exact. I remember it so well. We had been across Paris Mountain and the moon was so pretty. He had nothing to drink either. Our romance was so different from other boys I went out with. Olin moved gradually. He made other dates seem superficial.*

One July night, Olin showed up at Clara's house driving a brand-new black Chevrolet sedan with a radio. He told Clara, "The boys and I plan a trip to Pawleys Island in August. I'd like for you to go with me if you can." They rode around a lot, to break in the car. He and Clara took slow rides to Boscobel Lake for swims, over to Greer and back, then on their usual circuit around town.

Clara's cousin Louise invited her to come to Tryon for a visit. Olin told Clara, "I'd like to drive you up there and I'll pick you up next Sunday."

The day after he had delivered her, Clara received a letter from Olin. His handwriting was like no other she'd seen—oversized capital letters between almost horizontal lines of lower-case that were jagged and stretched out, long and lanky just like him. He wrote, "I forgot to ask you if you want to ride with Runt and me to pick up Melba in Charlotte for the house party at Pawleys? I forgot to tell you on the way up there because I can't think of anything when I'm around you anyway." He signed the letter with, "In a hurry, but with slow love."

They stopped to hear Art Kassel's band in Hendersonville but didn't stay long since Olin didn't care for crowds. They stopped at a self-service photo booth—four pictures for a dime.

The night before the Pawleys Island trip, they ate dinner at Mrs. Miller's before they took Clara home to pack, but Clara hated to wait for things to happen, and she had packed her bags the day Olin first invited her to Pawleys.

Runt and Melba rode with them in the new Chevrolet. They left about five o'clock in the morning and stopped in Columbia for breakfast. Runt bought what Clara thought was a beautiful blue bottle of a cordial liqueur, but she found out it looked more enticing than it tasted.

They unpacked their bags in the Pawleys Island cottage. It nestled under a canopy of myrtle and live oak trees a short walk to the creek on the western side of the island. They bought a can of pork and beans and Vienna sausage for their dinner, then rode over to Myrtle Beach and back before the others arrived.

They fished the inlet on the south end and went past the breakers in a rented, thirty-two-foot boat. They had a cook named Myrtle and a creek boy named Bubba, who taught the ladies to crab. They crabbed with chicken necks or bony backs all day. Melba said, "We'd better quit now. We've run out of places to put this big mess o' crabs."

For supper that night, Myrtle cleaned the catch and fixed a sumptuous crab dish flavored with a touch of sherry. She served rice, sliced tomatoes, corn on the cob, field peas, and hot biscuits that oozed butter. "Mighty fine low-country meal, Myrtle," said Runt as he rubbed his belly and reached for the pretty bottle of liqueur. They hadn't eaten so much that they couldn't dance at the Pavilion that night and every night they were there.

It was not compulsory to wear evening clothes since Pawley's is a family-oriented beach community. We took off our shoes the minute we hit the beach and didn't put them back on until we started home.

———

September 20, 1935, Fredree and I churned some ice cream and invited her beau, Dr. Northrop, and Olin to come over. Later Fredree went with her friend to check on a patient so Olin and I drove around our usual route. We parked awhile and talked about getting married.

On Thanksgiving Day, 1935, after a hard rain that morning, the sun came out for the Furman-Clemson football game. Olin, Clara, and Melba went to Clemson with Runt in his flashy new yellow convertible. As usual, the game drew a huge crowd. They hit a traffic jam in Clemson, so they parked and the men ran into a liquor store. They had a few nips while they waited for the traffic to clear.

Someone suggested they go to the Pines for chasers. Polly had invited them to supper along with Dave, Aileen, Fredree, and Dr. Northrop. Dave ran out of gas again, so Clara and Olin went for Dave and Aileen. Fredree spent the night and slept with Clara, who was up and down all night—sick as a dog from all the little sips she had had that day. Clara and too many drinks didn't go so well. It was hard for Clara to keep up with Olin and his gang of friends.

———

Just after Thanksgiving my Aunt Bess called long distance to tell us that her brother, my Uncle Coxe Weaver, had died. Bess had to go to Gainesville, Florida, where Uncle Coxe worked as an electrician for the university. Aunt Bess had to attend to his affairs, and wanted me to go with her to help drive his car back home. Uncle Coxe's wife had divorced him since he was so hard to get along with. He had an awful temper.

It seems he had gotten into an argument with his assistant. While Uncle Coxe worked in the basement under the

auditorium, his assistant walked in and shot Coxe dead. Coxe's
temper probably got him into that trouble.

Clara Scott.

Clara was convinced that red-head-
ed people had worse tempers than most,
based on stories she had heard about
her mother's people, the Weavers.

Once Uncle Coxe's affairs were in
order, Clara and Aunt Bess had about
two more weeks to toodle around
Florida. They rode over to Gainesville
to hear the Red Nichols Orchestra play
for the Military Ball at the University
of Florida. They stopped by the Ravine
Gardens at Palatka, went down to
Tampa, and to Silver Springs to ride the
glass-bottom boats. They went to a carillon concert at Bok Tower and waited
around to have the carillon player auto-
graph their programs. They also went
to Ocala and had their fortunes told.

Clara could make a party out of any situation. That included Uncle
Coxe's murder. Her absence from Olin made hearts grow fonder.

On December 7, 1935, I worked late at Raylass Department
Store and Olin picked me up from work. We saw Runt at the
Pickwick and he offered us a drink, but Olin told him, "Not
tonight." Later we had a talk that ended with the decision to
get married the following Monday. Olin told me that he had
turned down Runt's offer for a drink since he planned to pro-
pose and wanted to be sure he remembered it the next morn-
ing. I thought that was very responsible of him.

When I came home that night I told Polly about the propos-
al. Daddy was in Atlanta for some telephone company train-
ing. Polly couldn't wait until the next day so she called long
distance about 12:30 that night. The next day Olin went to
Renno to tell his mother and daddy about our plans.

Olin Bell.

7. Olin's Story

So, out of Rupert, Ross, Walt, Wilbur, John, Dillard, Paul, Sidney, and all the Stewarts, Clara decided to marry Olin—the serious one who had a job and a car, the one slow to make a move, the one who drove the same way every time, the one who kicked off his shoes after a few beers, and the one with a mustache grown in Chicago at the world's fair. When friends teased Clara that the mustache might get in her way, Olin replied, "She doesn't mind going through a little brush to get to a picnic."

In the South, from whom and from where you come is of significant interest. The Bell ancestry traces back to Scotland. They migrated south from Virginia in 1762 and settled in Laurens County, South Carolina, where they obtained a land trust in the community of Renno.

After a day of chores, Mattie East Bell, Olin's paternal grand-mother, wrote poetry by lamplight in precise penmanship. She shaped into verse the beauty of nature or recounted acts of heroic officers and soldiers who fought in gray uniforms.

Olin's mother's people were Quakers from Great Britain; my cousins and I thought Janie Bell was quite regal. Her parents died young. Janie and her brother be-came dependent on relatives in the community. They grew up in a small house, literally on the other side of the railroad tracks from cousin Johnny Bell's store and the post office at Renno. Janie was soft-spo-ken and sensitive, even when she wrung a chicken's neck for Sunday dinner.

Janie Maria Hollingsworth & William East Bell on their wedding day.

She endured a double mastectomy after her eldest child was born. Who knew of breast cancer in the early 1900s? Everyone accepted Janie's bo-som as a roll of cotton padding that rested above the belted waist of cotton dresses she made from the same pattern.

My grandparents, Willie and Janie, raised their family of four in Greenville. The eldest was William, then Mary B. The B. didn't stand for anything; B. was her middle name. Then came my father, Olin, and finally Martha.

Olin was passionate about automobiles and aircraft. He skipped school if an air show was in town. He was an honest hooky player though. He let his mother Janie know his plans. When the school checked on his absence, Janie covered for him, since Olin educated himself with an independent study that day.

Olin's father had lost his wholesale grocery business along with valuable real estate during the Depression. His parents moved back to Renno to eke out a living in the early 1930s. They raised hogs and chickens and grew cotton.

Willie Bell's friend, Mr. Vardry Ramseur, who owned Ramseur Roofing Company, hired Olin, so he stayed in Greenville to work. As a boy, Olin had hung around Ramseur's place of business and learned to drive at age eleven when some of the truck drivers allowed him behind the wheel. Later, Mr. Vard hired Olin as a bookkeeper and trained him personally. Olin was loyal and respectful of his boss.

Clara, the independent extrovert, sought fun, and Olin sought a quiet existence as a conscientious introvert. Where would they find enough middle ground on which to build a solid foundation for their marriage? Would Olin's mustachioed kisses and wry humor be enough to "keep her in," as in Peter, Peter and his pumpkin-shell?

8. The Wedding

Polly and Clara went downtown for a trousseau and a manicure and to have Clara's hair done. They bumped into Olin when they walked through the back door of Myers-Arnold Department Store. "My car is just down the street. Can you come with me for a minute?" he asked Clara. Polly hung back and window shopped while the couple scurried off. They reached Olin's car, and he opened the passenger door for Clara to slip in. When seated in the driver's seat, he whipped out a ring he had just purchased at Smithwick Jewelers. Right then and there he gave her the tiny diamond flanked by even tinier diamonds set in yellow gold. She wanted to throw her arms around him, but they were in sight of all the passersby, so she saved her affection for later.

An elaborate wedding didn't cross their minds. The Depression had squelched everyone's extravagance, so they settled for a ceremony at the Methodist parsonage in Clinton. Olin picked up Clara before he stopped for Runt and Fredree, their witnesses. They stopped in Laurens for the marriage license. They arrived at the parsonage a little late. A group of ladies filled the living room, ready to start their missionary circle meeting at 4:00 p.m. sharp.

The couple apologized to the minister, who hushed the chatter. "Ladies, I know you all lead very busy lives, but I want to ask your permission to delay our meeting long enough to perform a wedding ceremony for this delightful young couple. You are all invited to share the joy as God joins these two in matrimony." The circle members giggled and nudged each other during the brief ceremony. The ladies sat through the benediction and resumed efforts to save the world through their Methodist missions.

Clara and Olin took Runt and Fredree back to Greenville, and the newlyweds went by Clara's house for her suitcase. Edith and Sibyl had filled the luggage with rice and stitched up openings in her slinky new lingerie. The couple planned to go on a honeymoon to Atlanta, about two hours away.

Though Clara was heady from the excitement of her wedding day, Olin allowed her to get behind the wheel. She played with the spotlight attached to Olin's car and flashed the light at a train going parallel to the road. The engineer thrilled Clara when he blew his shrill whistle long and loud. She had never heard an engineer respond with such enthusiasm. Olin noticed a sign that showed the track would veer right in the path of their speeding car. Preoccupied with the spot light, Clara had not seen the railroad crossing signs. Olin told Clara, "Put both hands on the wheel, your foot on the brake, and pull onto that wide shoulder ahead."

She pulled the car to the side of the highway. They sat dazed as the train rattled past them. Distance muted the rhythm of the wheels against the tracks, and the caboose lights grew tiny before they disappeared into the night. Then Olin drove the rest of the way—it was the beginning of a marriage full of surprises and unexpected sharp curves in the road.

They spent the night at the Henry Grady Hotel in Room 1114 and returned to Greenville the next day because Olin didn't want to miss any more work.

On December 10, 1935, on page two of the society section, *The (Greenville) Piedmont* announced:

Scott-Bell Marriage of Interest Here

Popular Young Couple to Make Home in Greenville Following Brief Wedding Trip. Wedding Quiet Affair

A marriage of the most cordial interest to scores of friends in Greenville took place on Monday afternoon, December 9, at 4 o'clock at the home of the officiating minister, Dr. J. C. Roper, in Clinton when Miss Clara Elizabeth Scott, daughter of Mr. and Mrs.

Olin & Clara, 1935.

James Carlisle Scott, became the bride of Olin Bates Bell. After a brief wedding trip the young couple is returning to Greenville to make their home.

The wedding was a very quiet affair taking place at the home of Dr. Roper with only a few friends in attendance. The ring ceremony was used. The bride was lovely in her wedding costume of aquamarine crepe with trimmings of silver braid, made in the popular tunic pattern. The frock was not only smart but most becoming. With it she wore accessories of black, including a modish hat of velvet, and a corsage of Talisman roses.

Immediately after the ceremony the young couple left on a wedding trip after which they will be at home for a time at 202 Rutherford Road until their apartment is ready.

The bride has scores of friends in this city where she was educated at Greenville High School and at Draughon's. The bridegroom, the son of Mr. and Mrs. William East Bell of Clinton, was also educated in this city, and is now connected with the Ramseur Roofing Company.

The wedding is one of the interesting events of the mid-winter season in this city.

Friends honored Clara with many showers. On December 22, Olin took her to Renno to meet his parents. Clara and Olin lived with Carl and Polly while they looked for an apartment. A place at 403 McDonald Street Extension seemed to work—one bedroom, a kitchen, and a semi-private bath for $4 a week. They bought a maple bedroom suite, an oil stove, and later a Frigidaire refrigerator. They moved in on Christmas Day and Olin's older sister, Mary B., and her husband, Harry, brought Olin's parents by.

Harry gave his sister-in-law the nickname "Bullet," based on her driving and how she ran in and out of their house. A few weeks into the marriage, Clara "forgot" to stop at a stop sign while she drove their new car. She didn't cause an accident but was charged for the violation. Somehow it didn't prevent her from forgetting many more stop signs in years to come.

Another young couple, Madge and John, moved into the apartment below Clara and Olin. Madge and Clara spent all their spare time walking and shopping. The ladies were both pregnant, or "PG," as they called it. Clara had not felt well in the third month of her pregnancy, so Dr. Daniel confined her to bed for four days.

Olin's sisters, Mary B. and Martha, gave a stork shower for Clara at Mary B.'s house. They set up three tables of bridge and one for Monopoly. Later, Dr. Daniel put Clara to bed again and told her not to stay up more than four hours a day. Mary B. had given birth to a daughter a year earlier, so she knew what Clara was in for.

I felt better but the doctor wouldn't let me drive the car, so whenever I wanted to go anywhere, Madge drove for me. We went everywhere together anyway.

The summer drug by. Olin took me out to pass the time, either to a show or down to Williamston where they had some real good steak sandwiches.

The telephone company transferred my Dad to Gaffney, thirty miles from Greenville. He and Polly went house-hunting then came by our house on August 4. The baby was due in September. When they left, Olin and I went to bed and got a bit too romantic for this late stage of my pregnancy.

I had some bleeding so I called Dr. Daniel. He told me to go to the hospital. We called Daddy and Polly just before they went to bed and asked Polly to go with us.

The moon shone so pretty and full that night. I told Olin I didn't feel a bit bad and would much rather ride around in the moonlight.

At 2:00 a.m. Clara was admitted to Room 314. Polly stayed with her the whole time. Her labor stopped and started, so Dr. Daniel administered drugs to keep it going. After thirty-eight hours of labor, Clara delivered a baby girl at 3:00 PM on Thursday, August 6, 1936. The baby was born posterior. Dr. Daniel said, "Some call it sunny-side up, or face up, or some say the baby is born looking at you."

That night Polly came back to the hospital with Aileen, Dave, Mary B., Harry, and Olin. Carl stayed home to keep the children.

> *They had been celebrating and were feeling fine. The baby and I had lots of company at the hospital—Weavers from Tryon, Madge and John, and the Ramseurs. Olin's sister Martha came with Mom and Dad Bell, who brought a stack of baby clothes that Janie had made.*

Mother had hired a girl named Fannie to help her. She paid Fannie in advance so that she would come to work after they brought the baby home, but Mother had seen the last of Fannie. Daddy brought his younger sister, Martha, to help Mother with the baby. Martha, Mother, and I came home in an ambulance.

Mother leaned toward the name Susan, but switched to Elizabeth Maria, her middle name and Grandmother Janie Bell's middle name. But Mary B. convinced them to use Mother's middle name and Daddy's middle name. Mother thought it was funny that Mary B. was such an expert on middle names since she only had a "B." for hers.

They named me Elizabeth Bates Bell and nicknamed me "Betty."

"Born looking at her," was indeed a prescient first glance I paid my mother, Clara.

Part 2

"I'm a pretty little girl.
Oh, what a figure.
Stand back boys,
'Til I get a little bigger."

Clara's song

Olin Bell in 1936, age 25.   Olin Bell in 1936, age 23.

9. New House, Nursemaid, Washer-Woman, and Baby Boy

My parents bought a two-bedroom house at 4 Glenn Street in the Eastover section of town.

Olin sent two men with me to the house to get it cleaned up before moving in the next day. I bought living room curtains, a living room suite, kitchen cabinets, and an electric stove. A lady from Duke Power Company came out and demonstrated the new stove for me.

On moving day, Mother spotted a group of school children walking to their homes a few blocks past our house. Mother stopped a girl named Pauline. "Do you know a washerwoman in the neighborhood?"

"Yes ma'am, I'll get my mama."

Betty Bell, 12 months old,
& Pauline Hall in 1937.

That afternoon, Pauline's mother, Daisy, walked up to our house and Mother hired her to do our laundry. She also hired Pauline to help around the house and to be my nursemaid. Mother bought Pauline a gray uniform for work, and by Thanksgiving, she got her a white one with a matching cap for when company came. When there was heavy housework like waxing the hardwood floors, cutting kindling, or working in the yard, Daddy sent Tom and some of the other men from the shop to help Mother.

Pauline, only sixteen years old, was there for me while Mother gallivanted around town, held a hand of bridge, or shopped. I didn't love anyone in my family more than Pauline and her mother Daisy. I thought they loved me, too, even though it was their job to take care of me and do our laundry.

Daddy built trellises for climbing rose bushes he planted at each end of the porch. He placed cement stepping stones from the street to the front door, had the side yard filled in, and built a rock wall. He made a metal lamp for the end of the walkway since there were no street lights. Mother took photos of me by the lamp to show how I grew.

Since Mother and Daddy were the first of their gang of friends to have a child, our house became headquarters for Saturday night dancing, drinking, cooking steaks, or ordering from Charlie's Steak House. Daddy, Runt, Hugh, Tokey, and Jimbo

Betty at 9 months old.

preceded their meal by knocking back a few. Another Christmas was nearly here and along with the birth of Jesus came lots of late-night partying.

Daddy may have celebrated a bit too much. This could explain why he came home for lunch. He took short naps on the bed with a cold washrag draped across his forehead. Pauline took me outside to play on the opposite side of the house so he could have about fifteen minutes of quiet.

Mother and the wives and girlfriends of the gang organized a bridge club and had a Wearever Aluminum Company party. Mother bought a Bungalow set of pots and pans for fifty dollars. While Mother pursued her fun, Pauline kept me during the day. She walked three blocks to our house. She cleaned, fixed enough dinner to re-heat for supper, took me for outings, fed me, bathed me, and put my pajamas on before she walked back home.

My daddy gave up trips to the world's fairs, but his passion for air shows and new cars remained, even with the burden of a family that cut into his freewheeling times. Many nights Daddy worked late on the books for Mr. Ramseur. When he came home on time, Pauline stayed with me and he took Mother bowling. If they couldn't get Pauline, he left Mother at home and went out with Uncle Harry or Mr. Vard. Mother admitted in her journals:

> I despise being alone when Olin works or goes somewhere without me, so I pack up Betty, and we drive over to Gaffney to visit Daddy, Polly, Edith and Sibyl. Since Betty's birth, we call my Daddy, "Pop."

Daddy didn't drive damaged cars, but someone dented our new Chevrolet while it was parked in front of his office. He traded for a Plymouth coupe. Soon he lost interest in the coupe since the back was too small to take friends along. Mother put a ding in the next car when she backed into a taxi while she shopped downtown. He traded for an Oldsmobile sedan. An old man ran a stop sign and crashed into this new car when Mother drove my cousin Jane and me downtown to see Santa Claus. Daddy's cars were an extension of his ego—clean, in perfect condition, and sleek to look at. Not many things upset Daddy more than when our cars got dinged. Mother tried his patience when she supplied dings. I'm sure these pressures got to him, but he appeared cool on the outside. He seemed determined to hide his stress from Mother, but she was pretty good at reading him. She rode his moods like Barney Oldfield drove his Ford, with speed and masterful manipulation.

Daddy was what they called "jimmy-jawed" because his top front teeth fit behind the lower ones when he closed his mouth. The veins on his temple swelled and moved in time when he ground his teeth. Most of the time, Mother knew to stay within limits before he lost his temper.

Betty, 17 months old, & Clara, in Miami, Florida, 1937.

We took day trips to the mountains or weekends at the beach; Pauline came along to help with me. Mother and Daddy decided to take the most extended trip yet in December 1937. We went to Miami, Florida, down the east coast and up the west coast.

Everyone was very accommodating about our having Pauline with us. Restaurants fixed her plates and fed her in their kitchens. We stayed in tourist homes overnight. The owners prepared a cot for Pauline to sleep on a porch or some out of the way spot.

I didn't understand; Pauline was not in my way at all. She could have slept with me, but Mother said, "There's not enough room." There was plenty of room when we napped together in the back seat of the car.

We stopped at Silver Springs and rode on the glass bottom boats. This was my second time there after my trip with Aunt Bess when Uncle Coxe was murdered.

━━

The next New Year's Eve, Mother and Daddy went to a party and left me with Pauline. The whole gang and more were at that party. Pauline came to work the next day, but Mother nursed a hangover and stayed in bed all day. She still hadn't learned to keep up with Daddy and the gang when it came to alcohol.

━━

On the afternoon of February 10, 1938, Olin drove Betty and me over to Gaffney when he got off work. Polly was in the hospital giving birth to their second child. I had taken Edith and Betty for a walk when Pop pulled to the curb. "The nurse called and told me, 'It's a boy,' but I just can't believe it," he hollered. We all piled into his car and went to the hospital to welcome the baby boy, my half-brother.

Pop was so tickled after six girls, a daughter who died as an infant in Charleston and another one in Greenville who lived a few hours, my whole sister Aileen, my step-sister Sibyl, my half-sister Edith, and me. We called the baby boy Jimmy.

Daddy was supposed to pick us up in Gaffney the following Saturday. He didn't come; we waited, and he still didn't come. As usual, Mother was antsy to get wherever she was going. She had packed our clothes that morning. The suitcases sat by the front door all day.

In those days people didn't just pick up the phone and call. "It's long distance!" Mother loved the fact that Pop had free long distance as manager of the telephone company, but Pop knew Clara's excesses, so he was very stingy with this privilege. Mother flitted around the house and finally blurted out to Pop, "Olin was due to pick us up hours ago. Could you please call to see what's held him up?"

Pop reached Daddy at the house with Runt where they were "taking on a few"—I learned early all the euphemisms for alcohol intake. Daddy made the sixty-minute trip by 7:30 p.m. He had forgotten to eat any dinner and felt sick to his stomach. So we spent another night and came home the next day.

Edith came down with whooping cough and Mother brought her to our house so the new baby wasn't exposed. Mother took me to see Dr. Grimball, my pediatrician, and told him I had been exposed to whooping cough. The doctor gave me a couple of shots. After work Daddy took Mother, Edith, and me back to Gaffney where the Scotts' doctor gave me two more shots. Was this more of Mother's excessiveness? If one dose is good, two must be better?

Back home, Betty woke up with swollen feet. Dr. Grimball put her on a diet but she got worse. He told me she had a severe case of bronchitis and was on the verge of pneumonia. At the age of eighteen months, she contracted whooping cough on top of all that.

That night Betty was a lot worse, probably because things seem worse at night. I thought I'd better take her back to the doctor the next day. About that time, Mrs. Bryant came to see if she could help me with Betty. Even though it had been dark outside for a long while, Mrs. Bryant went for Daisy.

Olin had a fire going in the fireplace, but he went to bed. He had a headache and needed to be able to get to work in the morning.

I felt better when I saw Daisy follow Mrs. Bryant through the front door. Daisy took Betty from my arms and told me to get a bunch of quilts to make a pallet in front of the fire. She passed the baby to Mrs. Bryant and began to concoct onion poultices. I kept the fire stoked, and the ladies took turns, putting Daisy's warm muslin-wrapped remedy onto Betty's feet and chest. They were back and forth from the kitchen to the living room where Betty lay on the quilt pallet that cushioned the warm tile hearth. Mrs. Bryant and I did whatever Daisy told us to do.

I never heard a worse cough in my life. Then it suddenly stopped, and her little body went limp as a dishrag. A hush fell over the living room. I wondered if Olin would wake up. The silence seemed much worse than the terrible coughing.

She was turning blue. Daisy felt for a pulse but there was none. Before I could think what happened, Daisy whisked the

*baby up by her heels and gave her a whack on her backside
that brought a harsh gut-wrenching sound. The next coughing
sounds comforted us, unlike the rasps that led up to the silence.
The women stayed into the night until things got better. Mrs.
Bryant went on home, but Daisy stayed. I fell asleep on the
sofa while Daisy rocked and cooed to Betty until the sun came
up.*

Somehow, Dad's sister, my Aunt Mary B., got wind of the drama
that had taken place the night before and called Daddy at work to
check on things. Daddy played it down. He knew his sister had little
confidence in Clara's ability as a mother. Mary B. didn't want to
come by the house since she was PG with her second child, so she
called Mother's cousin Fredree, "You might want to run by Clara's.
Please don't tell Clara and them I called, but I think someone needs
to check on Betty."

Mother was truly glad to see Fredree at our door. "Betty is really
sick," she told her.

It thrilled Mother when people sent me things and asked about
me. Dr. Grimball came to the house to see me every day, and six days
later I was able to go to his office, where he told Mother, "She needs
to get plenty of sunshine," which was pretty much what he told her
every time we went.

We were hardly over the whooping cough scare, when a frantic
knock on our door woke us in the middle of the night. "If you're
in there you'd better get out, the house between us is on fire," our
neighbor Mr. Mathis shouted.

Daddy called the Greenville City Fire Department, even though
4 Glenn Street was just outside the city limits. With foresight, Daddy
had paid an extra dollar on his insurance premium to cover a run to
our neighborhood.

The sound of the sirens cut through the silence of the city asleep.
The scream of the alarm became louder as it approached Glenn Street.
Neighbors lined the street to watch. Some late-night cruisers had
followed the blaring trucks and circled by to get in on the act, much
like Mother did when we were on errands and she heard a siren.

Things that made a noise or promised excitement got her attention.

I felt Daisy lift me from my crib and bundle me in a blanket. She shook all over, but I knew I was in good hands. She found a safe place for us in Mr. Thompson's car across the street, where we felt the heat of the fire and watched the firemen at work from a distance. But Mother got as close as she could; her face reflected the orange flames.

The men went to several hydrants before they found one with water. Finally, water shot through the flat canvas, and the hoses went to work on the blisters of paint that bubbled on the side of our bungalow. The

Daisy Hall holding Betty, 13 months, in 1937.

wind whirled embers through the night air like giant sparklers. The sparks landed on our roof. The neighbors' house was too far gone and it burned to the ground. Thank goodness the Dickerson family was away and no one was hurt.

Mother was pleased that the insurance company paid for a new paint job and roof for our house. The remains lay around next door for the longest time. We relived the event every time the ashy smell drifted our way. When it rained, the odor of burnt ruins filled the air.

~

Mother, Daddy, Pauline, and I went to Myrtle Beach for a weekend, but we ran into rain so we headed for Washington, D.C., and sites along the way. Mother felt yucky. On August 27, 1938, she realized she must be PG again.

She stuck close to home during the early, nauseous months, but the gang didn't hesitate to drop by. The doorbell rang about nine o'clock on New Year's Eve; they played Chinese checkers until 2:00 a.m.

Dr. Daniel told Mother, "I don't want you to drive the car during this pregnancy." She didn't like to miss anything, so she got Mrs. Bryant to drive her wherever she wanted to go. They went for groceries on Saturday afternoons. Mother recruited Pauline's boyfriend, James, to drive her places, too.

Olin in 1937 at age 26.

Daddy itched for a new car before the baby came, so he went to Lansing, Michigan, and bought a new 1939 Oldsmobile sedan straight from the factory. It was the color of a clay flower pot. He loved it along with every other car he had owned. He saw only two automotive philosophies—either trade cars every year or drive it until it wouldn't go. He chose the first option and often traded before the first year was over.

Mother watched the calendar for her due date. She complained to Dr. Daniel, "This pregnancy is slowing me down. What can I do to bring on labor? My nine months are up this weekend."

"I don't suppose it would hurt for you to take a dose of castor oil."

She called James, and we hurried off to Campbell's Pharmacy to pick up a bottle of the nasty liquid.

I took castor oil at 8:50 PM. and forty-five minutes later the pains started. They continued all night and Olin went for Pauline at 5:30 AM. He was driving along kind of slow, and I told him he'd better hurry. Olin left before I delivered—for

*some reason I didn't want him around. His smell took me back
to those morning sickness days.*

*I went to the delivery room at 12:40 PM and had a nine
pound, seven and one-quarter ounce baby boy at 3:16 PM on
April 25, 1939. After the baby came, the hospital called Olin
and told him he had a boy, and he came over after I woke up
good. Pop and Polly came about 6:30 PM and stayed overnight at our house so Pauline could get some sleep. We named
the baby James, after the James in Pop's name and Dixon, Mr.
Vard's middle name. We called him "Dicky."*

The social buzz around Mother came back to life after the delivery. She knew lots of nurses at Greenville General through her cousin Fredree. They hung around her room and gave her the attention
she loved. She had so much company with neighbors and the gang
that Dr. Daniel put up a "No Visitors" sign for a while.

Pauline stayed at our house while Mother was in the hospital. She
took me by the hospital on the city bus every day, sometimes twice a
day. Mother and the baby took a Jones's Ambulance home, and they
entertained the gang that night. I think Pauline was more worn out
than Mother.

Dr. Daniel didn't let Mother drive for about a month, so James
drove. He took Pauline and me to Buncombe Street Methodist
Sunday school while Mother recuperated. Until, that is, an epidemic
of infantile paralysis came along and they kept me home.

By June, Mother was ready for outings—picnics to Table Rock
State Park or over to Gaffney for a few days at a time. Pauline came
along after frying a couple of chickens for our picnics and James
drove us wherever Mother wanted to go.

∽

Mother didn't take seriously the fall I took, riding piggy-back on
the girl next-door. But when I continued to complain, she relented
and took me for an X-ray. I had broken my collarbone. She kept
me busy while I stayed strapped up for twenty-three days. To keep
me entertained, she took me at the age of three to my first movie

show—*Babes in Toyland*, with Judy Garland and Mickey Rooney. I also remember how she scared the pudding out of me when she took me to *The Wizard of Oz* with about a million other children piled into the Roxy Theatre.

———

The tea party table and two chairs Pop Scott made for me sat near the kitchen in the central hallway where the floor register for the furnace was—the register that I walked around because I knew the things that dropped through the grate were never to be seen again. I imagined they burned in the hell below. But I felt safe when my favorite playmate Pauline sipped tea with me, like the ladies we were.

My days with Pauline's undivided attention were numbered. My best friend, Pauline, married James. They moved into a little white house down the road from Daisy. I remember Mrs. Thompson from across the street asked Mother, "Is that James good enough for our Pauline? She could pass for white and that boy is blacker than midnight."

I knew Pauline would be a wonderful mother, but I was a little jealous to lose her attention. I wondered if Pauline's babies would be black or white or if it really mattered at all.

10. 113 Aberdeen Drive

When Daddy came home from work on Dicky's first birthday in 1940, he told Mother, "I traded our house for the one we saw off Augusta Road."

You couldn't hold her down. Mother started to pack that night and even wrote in her diary, *I got the pip from the excitement of moving to a new house.*

The front rooms were painted dusty rose, straight out of *Better Homes and Gardens*. The living room opened onto a porch where they put our Adirondack chairs and the glider with green and red-striped canvas cushions. A bathroom separated my pale peach room and Dicky's mint green room. He had a crib, a chest of drawers, and a toy chest that Pop Scott had made. Mother and Daddy bought a mahogany four-poster bed with a matching chest-on-chest and a sit-down vanity with an oval mirror attached. Their blue bedroom had a bath with our first shower. The kitchen was across the front so Mother could wash the dishes and watch the world go by on Aberdeen Drive. A special commode room for Pauline was off the kitchen. Mother told us not to use that one, even in a hurry.

We still took our dirty laundry and linens to Daisy on Mondays. Even though it was farther, I begged Mother to take us the way we called the "funny road," off Laurens Road to Daisy's house. Mother, a master at going over the rolling mounds in this road, drove at just the right speed to make our stomachs bounce into our throats.

Before we came to Daisy's house, the asphalt in front of the white peoples' homes stopped and a dirt road continued in front of the other homes. Daisy and her husband, Clarence, lived in a two-story white frame house at the end of that road—larger than our new house on Aberdeen Drive and way larger than our old house on Glenn Street. Chickens and strange guineas roamed the backyard and wandered into the front. The smell of Rinso laundry powder was everywhere. Daisy's house brimmed with fancy doo-dads for me to investigate. She had porcelain figurines of old-fashioned women and men dressed in elaborate clothing and a stand of porcelain fruit in the middle of her dining room table.

Clara in her Victory Garden in 1943.

Pauline gave birth to a daughter one week before Dicky was a year old. The baby girl was born a lovely shade of brown, like milk chocolate. Pauline's cousin, Mary Lee, helped Mother since Pauline had her hands full with her new baby. Mary Lee was nice enough, but she was no Pauline. We went through several other helpers for Mother—Ruth, Christine, and Helen. Mother became more available to Dicky and me. The bridge table must have bored her; she found things she enjoyed at home.

A war went on overseas. People helped out on the home front and grew their own food. Mother loved outdoor activities, so she became a busy gardener for Uncle Sam. The backyard was a grassy playground large enough for a swing set and Mother's Victory Garden.

Mother claimed the groceries at Kash & Karry were the least expensive in town. We went every Thursday and she flirted with Elmer, the manager, as though he could reduce the prices or give her more sugar than had been rationed to her.

Housewives wore cotton hose and used coupons to save on sugar. I think most women wanted the war to end so they could get nylon hosiery and sugar again and stop the need for star flags in their windows. But it was gas-rationing that gave Mother the excuse to fulfill her lifelong dream to own a bicycle.

Her new dark blue bike had a basket on the front and a luggage rack
over the back fender. A speedometer
measured how far and how fast she
went, and a jingly bell on the handle
bar let people know they had better
get out of her way. She put Dicky in
the basket as a little thing, and I rode
like luggage on the rack behind her.

Clara, age 29, on her bicycle.

Mother bought me a pair of brown
jodhpurs that I wore with a yellow
pullover sweater and red cropped
jacket. She told me, "I made a pair of
jodhpurs when I was your age. They
looked darling."

A jodhpurs outfit on the back of a
bicycle instead of a horse seemed a little odd, and I felt more secure
staying at home with Pauline or Mary Lee rather than taking a wild
ride on the back of Mother's Schwinn in a darling outfit.

Dicky didn't worry about anything dangerous, so as he outgrew
the basket, he took my place on the luggage carrier over the back
fender. Mother looped two of Daddy's leather belts to the seat for
him to put his feet in—like Roy Rogers's stirrups. She probably recalled the time she caught her foot in spokes on the back of one of
the Fletcher boys' bikes on Rutherford Road. She used the mistakes
she had made as warnings to us. But even if we had made six dozen
mistakes a day, we couldn't catch up with her.

Mother and Dicky liked the hill on the way to Aunt Mary's house,
where she got up some speed before she kicked her legs straight
out to allow the pedals to spin as fast as possible. Dicky so enjoyed
the roller coaster lifestyle that Mother created for him. They were
Batman and Robin. I preferred a coloring book, paper dolls, or visits
to my cousins Jane and Annelle's house.

But Santa brought me a light blue bicycle, smaller than Mother's,
with a basket up front and a jingly bell. I named my bike Blue Streak
and had the notion I would go faster if I pointed my forefingers

toward the wind while I gripped the handlebar. My aerodynamic fascination probably came from Daddy.

Santa brought Dicky a big green wagon with removable wooden slats for sides. Mother fixed it up with a pallet, blanket, and pillow, and let Dicky take his naps there. She also hitched his wagon like a trailer to the back of her Schwinn and pulled him around the neighborhood.

Mother taught me to spit watermelon seeds into a paper cup with the skill of a tiddlywinks champion. She saved the seeds to plant in her Victory Garden. Dicky learned to climb trees, as she had done in her white batiste dresses. Before long, he shinnied up a pine tree like a Hawaiian after a coconut.

I had a strategy to maneuver out from under her supervision. I gave her a minute of quiet, until her attention moved to something else, then I continued whatever I had wanted to do.

Dicky and I loved to jump on beds, but Mother warned, "We can't afford to buy new springs."

While Mother ran the vacuum one day, I decided to teach Dicky how to do somersaults on my parents' bed, which they had placed against the wall in their blue bedroom. He caught on fast, but his next tumble took him toward an open window near the foot of the bed. I watched the scene unfold in slow motion; the window screen bulged from his uncontrolled weight before the hinge gave way, and it cartwheeled through the air. Dicky somersaulted through the opening and fell out of sight, swallowed by the window. I knew he had to be dead, so I ran to break the news to Mother.

We found that Dicky had landed in the cinder pile on the tall side of the house. He was left with no more than a scar the color of the cinders, shaped like the letter C etched into his fat cheek. How appropriate—the scar could stand for courageous since he didn't even cry, other than a little snigger. That boy wasn't afraid of the devil himself. I was convinced that we should watch him more closely. I feared his stupidity might cause him to try it again just for the thrill. But Mother told us we were not allowed to use the word "stupid."

"If you can't say anything nice, just don't say anything at all," she added.

I couldn't think of anything nice about Dicky having fallen out of the window, so I muttered "fool" under my breath.

"And," Mother interjected, "If you call someone a fool, you will go to hell—it's in the Bible."

I cried and wailed at the thought of going to hell until she told me, "You can ask forgiveness and not go to hell, if you feel bad enough."

| Olin on Main Street in Greenville. | Clara & her sister-in-law Mary B. Bell Powell. | Betty, age 4, & Clara. |

11. Places to Go and Things to Do

If you saw Mother walk down Main Street in the early 1940s, you might confuse her with Judy Garland or Jane Wyman. Her gait was quick, and I was attached to her by the hand, a full step behind. Even though we were always in a hurry for some reason, she kind of slowed down for the photographers who hung out on Main Street to take pictures of passersby. She loved it and bought the photos.

I can see her seated at her new mahogany dresser where she kept a black and white photograph of Daddy. A cobalt blue gift box of Evening in Paris toiletries sat in the center of her dresser. It had satin niches for a fifty-cent-size compact of rouge and a tasseled bottle of eau de toilette. She made it clear to me that was a French name—not actual water from a French toilet. Daddy never let her run out of this luxury in the blue box.

Mother let her wavy burnt-umber bob grow longer. Her new hair-do mimicked Betty Grable's. She pulled the back into a bun that made a bow of hair at the nape of her neck. Or, she added fullness with what she called a "rat" held in a snood. Hairpins held her hair on either side, swept straight up then folded under. A wavy pompadour stood between the upswept sides.

~~~~

She loved to hang her head off the side of the bed for me to brush her waterfall of hair. I smelled the warmth that arose from her scalp. My hand followed the brush through each coarse lock that kicked up at the end. The scent of her Evening in Paris cologne mixed with the scent of freshly brushed hair

~~~~

To live in Greenville, a textile center, was to have access to monster rolls of cotton string wrapped around cone-shaped bases and sold at the outlet store. The string gave Mother a lot of creative ideas. Her crocheted doilies served as mats on end tables, the coffee table, and the dining room table. String doilies adorned the headrests and arms of every stuffed chair. She cut billions of bunches of string in uniform lengths, and with her largest crochet hook, she knotted the strands of string through a loose-weave fabric base, also available from the mill outlet. These became white shaggy rugs that decorated our floors. I pretended they were hides off exotic animals found only in the woods around mill towns.

It was my job on Saturdays to fluff the rugs. I shook them outside since the Hoover choked on the long strings. I had to do this when Daddy wasn't around because flying dust gave him a headache. Many things we did gave Daddy headaches.

~~~~

One day, we heard sirens up the street. Mother and I hustled up there to see what was going on. The two-story frame house across from the Blandford family had caught fire. We stood with the neighbors who watched from across the street, then Mother broke away and ran inside the burning house to see if she could help save something or someone. So I thought that I should help, too. I went to the front door and dragged a small rug from the entrance into the

Clara, age 32, in 1946. Olin, age 24, in 1937.

front yard so it wouldn't burn. My noble Wonder Woman imitation ended when two firemen on either side of Mother ushered her out through the front door and into the yard with stern looks on their faces. We stood on the sidelines with the other neighbors until Mother got bored and took me home.

The Blandford family, across the street from the fire, had three boys. The middle one, Joe, was my age. Joe's mother Ludie and Mother were pretty close friends. Every Christmas Eve, the Blandfords had a party for the whole neighborhood, even the children. They served eggnog to the parents and punch to the children and all sorts of goodies were on the dining room table. I was impressed by the grandeur.

But Mother was not to be outdone at Christmas time. A Pickwick-pine-paneled wall in the living room was her bare canvas during the holidays and Scotch tape was her medium of choice. She either taped red velvet bows all over the wall or displayed Christmas cards taped to the panels. Sometimes she strung the cards around the door jambs with her cone of string.

The fireplace became a wintertime village scene. The black-soot background made a perfect night sky. She splattered it with Ivory soap suds to look like snowflakes. The floor of the fireplace, built up with crumpled newspapers and covered with cotton batting, was a perfect setting for tiny fake trees on a hillside with miniature porcelain houses and stores. Single bulbs from a string of Christmas lights were inserted into the floor of each building for the nighttime scene. Miniature ice skaters did their thing on a mirror lake. Reindeer pulled Santa in a sleigh strung over the scene with fishing line. Every year, the end of the living room was a bit different except for the snow scene—that was a staple.

———

When Mother went to bed at night, she took a flashlight with her in case there was something she wanted to see in the dark or to light the way when she thought of a reason to get up. She often came into my room and either turned on the overhead light or shined the flashlight inches from my face to see if I had gone to sleep. By then, I was pretty much awake.

As I grew, I watched Mother dream up ways to make the world turn faster and to have more fun. She dragged friends and family—even strangers—along on her joy rides.

12. Cousins and Them

My cousins Jane and Annelle Powell were my pretend-sisters under another roof. We could walk to their house about four blocks away on Tomassee Avenue, but I didn't like to walk because unleashed dogs along the way frightened me. Mother warned me, "They can tell you are frightened by the scent you give off." I knew I had no control over how I smelled. I was afraid of as many things as Dicky and Mother were unafraid.

Jane, Annelle, and I sat on their front steps and heard their help, Eva, crunch up the gravel driveway from the back door. At the sidewalk, she turned left, headed toward Augusta Road to catch her bus.

Annelle often fussed that Eva was too strict, or Jane complained that Eva wouldn't talk to her when "One Man's Family" was on the radio.

"I don't think that bright green sweater goes with Eva's dark blue uniform," I said.

"That is not a very nice thing to say, Betty. It might be the only sweater she has," Jane scolded me.

Then Annelle chimed in. "I like those colors together, and I don't see anything wrong with how she's dressed."

Even though blood is thicker than water, I learned you don't talk ugly about someone else's help.

My cousins' house smelled like Lifebuoy soap. I asked Mother to buy Lifebuoy, but she said, "It has a medicinal odor and I don't want our house to smell like Aunt Mary's."

Mother put Yardley's Lavender Soap in her drawers to make

her underclothes smell good. We bathed and washed hands with a cheaper brand, Ivory Soap.

It didn't take much for my cousins and me to get the giggles at the table. Grownups didn't seem to see the humorous side of eating. Aunt Mary's jaw popped every time she chewed, so Annelle and I exchanged looks and stifled our giggles. Jane told me not to laugh because her mother couldn't help it. But Annelle and I thought it was hilarious.

When I dawdled over my cereal until it was mushy, Jane fussed at me. I turned to her and asked, "How you eat that soggy stuff?" The milk from Annelle's cereal actually came out of her nose she laughed so hard. This became our running joke whenever something struck us as repulsive.

I left about a half inch of milk in my glass since I didn't know what might lurk at the bottom—gravity and all. The idea probably came from Mother, who told Dicky and me not to eat the bottom tip of an ice cream cone. "Some drug stores have bugs, and a dead one could be trapped in the point." Warnings like that have remained with me.

The Powells' neighbor, Mr. Anderson, had a plant nursery next door. A tree on the edge of the property was easy for us to climb and we adopted our own personal limbs. Jane's tree limb was "Pie" from the movie *National Velvet*, and she rode that limb as well as Elizabeth Taylor rode her horse. Sometimes Jane also pretended to be Margaret O'Brien, who had a fake smile and was way overly dramatic for my taste. Annelle was Natalie Wood and I was Peggy Ann Garner.

When I spent the night with them, we put ourselves to sleep by telling movie plots. If one of us had seen a movie that the others hadn't seen, we gave a detailed account. Jane said, "If you tell it right, the narration will last as long as the movie itself." Annelle fell asleep before we finished.

Among Uncle Harry's numerous business ventures was a watermelon garden where customers bought beer and slices of watermelon. They stood at outdoor picnic tables he provided. When that enterprise lost its luster, Uncle Harry stored the tables in a shed in their backyard. It made a good hide-out for Annelle and me to smoke the Viceroy cigarette butts stolen from Aunt Mary's ashtray.

We were good at hopscotch and I could skin the cat on the monkey bars at Augusta Circle School. Jane, Annelle, and I practiced after school and weekends since they lived a few houses from the playground. Jane said, "When we get older, we can get jobs as acrobats in the circus if we practice." But I was pretty sure Mother would not allow me to join the circus.

Betty in ballet pose, age 5.

In spite of my skills on the bars, my pediatrician, Dr. Grimball, noticed a murmur in my heart and suggested that Mother enroll me in the Sherill School of Dance classes for some proper exercise. The school was run by two sisters. Miss Kathryn Sherrill taught acrobatics. She placed me face-up on a gray mat to see how far my legs would go over my shoulders. I heard Mother's voice over Kathryn's shoulder. "Push harder," like a German soldier calling for her to torture me harder. I wondered if the Sherrill sisters had ever permanently injured any little girls this way.

We wore two-piece blue uniforms with white Peter Pan collars and an "SSD" monogram. It was one of the most fun things Mother ever allowed me to do. I won a silver loving cup as the most improved and heard Mother tell Mrs. Blandford, "I guess if you start at the bottom there is nowhere else to go but up."

The Sherrills put on a slew of recitals. Only Shirley Temple outdressed us in our costumes. For my ballet number, I wore a powder blue tutu with a sparkly silver bodice that went over one shoulder and pink toe shoes with satin ribbon straps laced around my ankles. For my tap solo, "I've Got Rhythm," I wore an alluring purple satin costume, trimmed with pink fluff. A group of dancers performed a military-themed routine to "When Johnny Comes Marching Home Again," to honor the soldiers who defended America. Two other girls and I portrayed the Russians. You would have thought Red Skelton was on stage the way those families and friends laughed each time my hat fell over my eyes during our Cossack dance. But we were told, "The show must go on!" Jane, Annelle, and I had seen enough musicals on screen with Mitzi Gaynor, Ginger Rogers, and Cyd Charisse to know that this was the truth.

Jane knew a lot about shows, and we put on a zillion of them for our parents under her direction. The arched doorway from their living room to the dining room was our stage. "If you can't remember what comes next, just make up something," she told Annelle and me.

We charged a penny a piece for the adults to watch us. Daddy forked over a penny for Dicky to watch, but it was a penny wasted. He never stayed until the end of the show. Even Mother got a little antsy when she sat still that long. Sometimes she told me, "We can go over to the Powells' if you promise not to put on a show."

Daddy complained that the pounding of hammers gave him a headache when new neighbors built a house behind us in the field where may-pops grew. The people in the new house were not Americans—the father was very serious, wore rimless glasses, and looked intelligent. I think his name was Hans or Fritz or something out of "Katzenjammer Kids." His wife was much shorter, a little dumpy, but pleasant. They had a son named Bernard Caesar, but we called him "Heide." He was about twelve years old. His adopted sister Evelyn was a couple of years younger than Dicky.

The father had a fancy camera that he put on a tripod. He set the camera to take our picture, after which he ran to be in the photo too. I was impressed.

After the house was built, we watched Hans/Fritz dig in the red clay until he had a wide but shallow hole near a water faucet on the side of the house. He mixed up a batch of cement and lined the hole.

Once the cement set, he filled the hole with water, and it became a wading pool, like a bird bath for children. I could not believe my eyes when they let Evelyn play in the wading pool without a bathing suit. Thank the good Lord they didn't have Heide doing that. I asked Mother, "Why in the world do those neighbors let Evelyn go in her wading pool naked as a jaybird?"

Mother answered, "I think it's something Europeans do." But Mother, an American, allowed Dicky to go over there and get naked and play in the pool. Mother didn't have a modest bone in her body—I suppose I became overly modest to counter her immodesty, and I wore my bathing suit every time I went to that wading pool.

That family turned out to be famous—at least Hans/Fritz's father was. Daddy said he was the father of modern physics, Albert Einstein. Daddy also told me that Dr. Einstein probably encouraged his son to come to America because of the war. When Dr. Einstein visited them, we got all dressed up to go over and meet him. I couldn't look at his face, because I was lost in his fuzzy hair. He spoke to me like he spoke to an adult.

～

Daddy had the same men who put up swings out by the Victory Garden lay boards across sawhorses, to make tables to stand around and eat ice cream and cake at the grand birthday parties Mother gave for us. Daisy's freshly ironed sheets served as tablecloths. Mother made individual hats from crepe paper, even though I told her, "I kind of like the ones from Woolworth's."

When Daddy came home from work each day, he brought pieces of candy for Dicky and me. Dicky popped his in his mouth, but my miserly strain prompted me to store these treasures in a cast-off Whitman's candy box. I hid it in the bottom of my chest of drawers. At my sixth birthday party, I noticed Dicky and his friend with their mouths stuffed full of candy. I realized that they had helped themselves to my stash. At that point I was convinced that little brothers were not all they were cracked up to be, and I learned to hold a grudge.

Then there was Easter—store-bought baskets were unnecessary

because Mother adapted her large-brimmed straw hat that she wore in the garden. She turned the hat upside down and attached a ribbon for handles. "This will work perfectly well for your Easter basket without buying one," she told me.

Dicky and I were given two baby ducklings for Easter. His was blue and mine was pink. When the ducklings grew into adult ducks, they lived in our backyard. Their quacks about drove Daddy crazy, until one day the noise stopped. Mother told us, "They must have flown away."

Betty, age 7, & friend Jordan Jones with Easter baskets, April 1943.

Later Joe Blandford told me, "Your mama gave the ducks to my mama and we ate them for supper one night." I had a hard time with that visual.

That fall, Joe Blandford and I entered Mrs. McCuen's first grade at Augusta Circle School with the children of Mother's friends and bridge partners.

⁓

Daddy's boss at Ramseur Roofing Company paid for Daddy to take a correspondence course in accounting. The house on Aberdeen was full of mammoth red leather-bound books that Daddy studied in the evenings before he mailed in assignments. When Daddy studied, we were required to be silent—no sound louder than breath in and out was acceptable.

Dicky and I were not allowed to touch the red books, but when Daddy wasn't around, Mother used one to weigh down something she might have glued or to act as a door stop when the breeze through the house was too strong. But she always put the books back in their place before Daddy came home from work.

⁓

It was past time for Daddy to trade his 1939 Oldsmobile. He chose a 1941 greenish-gray hydrodynamic-drive Oldsmobile with white sidewall tires.

We rode everywhere, down to Columbia, up the mountains as far as Gatlinburg, Tennessee. But we didn't keep this car long before Olin traded it to a man for his 1938 Nash. We kept this car for a week or so and then traded it for a new Ford, the cheapest model they make. I think Olin was afraid Mr. Vard didn't like for us to have a car that was nicer than his.

After naps, we often went for rides with Mother's friend Kat and her three children. We went for "co-colas" at the Pure Oil place that Kat's husband, Hugh, owned. These were the only times Mother allowed us to have a Coke, but Kat's kids drank them all the time since they got them free at their daddy's business. Those children had olive complexions and tanned easily. I thought their coloring might have come from drinking too many Cokes.

Our four-door car was loaded with five children in the back seat. I stood on the floor behind Kat with my back against the door. When Mother pulled into the backyard turnaround, my door flew open, and I fell onto the gravel driveway. Mother didn't hear the door open above the noisy children. She continued to turn the car around. I looked to my right and watched the tire bump over my shoulder before Mother realized that she had backed over her only daughter. Kat dusted me off and we headed out for our Coke.

"I can't wait to tell Daddy I fell out of the car and you ran over me," I said, still in the drama of the moment.

"Oh, Daddy won't be interested in hearing about it," Mother told me. With that, the incident became another one of those "no need to bother Daddy" things.

13. The Pathé News

Dicky and I were in the yard, playing. Mother called us to come in the house. We hadn't seen that look on her face before—a serious look. When we got inside, Daddy shushed us and pointed to the radio. The Japanese had attacked Pearl Harbor, wherever that was. After the announcement, everyone in the neighborhood drifted out to the sidewalks to talk about it— December 7, 1941.

I saw it on the Pathé News at the Carolina Theatre. The world participated in a full-fledged war when the United States became involved after the Pearl Harbor attack. The news people called it World War II. The bad guys were Hitler, Hirohito, and Mussolini, very scary men. Daddy explained to me that they were power hungry. He told us, "Hitler stirred people into a psychological frenzy and caused them to do all sorts of crazy and mean things." Daddy warned me not to get caught up in things without first questioning other people's motives. "Just because someone is in authority, it doesn't mean they know best—that includes teachers, politicians, and others in authority," he said.

"And Mother," I muttered.

I couldn't understand why we had to be at war with people who lived that far away. Why couldn't Hitler, Mussolini, and Hirohito just have lunch, play a game of bridge, and talk it out? They could sit around a table with Roosevelt, Churchill, and maybe Stalin. Some bourbon and water might get them loud and happy like Daddy's gang. It should have been evident that no one was content with the way things were, so why not end this foolishness? I wondered, where was the love my Sunday school teachers preached.

Daddy often had important letters, probably job applications, that he wanted to go out immediately, so I rode with him to the post office. A poster of Uncle Sam sat outside the main post office. Uncle Sam pointed right at people and said, "Uncle Sam wants YOU." I presumed that meant me, but I wasn't clear what I could do. I did save my money to buy bonds and stamps to support the war effort.

Donaldson Air Force Base, out Augusta Road, brought crowds of families to Greenville. A plea went out for patriotic people to make room for boarders in their homes. My patriotic parents moved me into Dicky's mint green room and rented my pale peach room and bathroom to an officer and his German-born wife.

Dicky and I went down the hall to use our parent's bathroom. Mother still forbade us to use Pauline's bathroom off the kitchen, even though it seemed perfectly good to me. Mother also kept an enamelware potty in Dicky's room for emergencies. I sat on that potty one morning while Daddy occupied the blue bathroom. I looked around Dicky's room and noticed toys all over the floor. He was too young to know how to take care of his things, and with the war on, our toys would not be replaced; I could hear Mother's warning in my head, "These toys have got to last until the end of the war."

Mother was not very fond of the German wife who boarded at our house with her air force officer husband. I thought Mother disliked her because she was German. She sat at my dresser and fixed her hair and make-up every morning. She had a piping hot glass of water there and drank from it as though she savored a cocktail.

"I think that's what Germans do to keep their bowels regular," explained Mother.

"Wonder why they don't find something that would taste better?"

"Germans are very tough and they don't mind if some things don't taste good as long as it is healthy for them," she told me. Mother knew a lot of stuff about people.

I watched the German lady and I had lived with Mother for six years. It made me wonder what it was like to be an adult. Curiosity led me to dress up in Mother's blue taffeta slip with the fluted ruffle. She kept it in the bottom drawer of her chest-on-chest. I accessorized with jewelry and silk scarves draped around my neck. My curiosity also led me to sneak a touch of Mother's Evening in Paris eau de toilette, a dab behind each ear.

I stood on a stool to see what things looked like from a grown-up perspective, but the best way to find out about being tall was to find Daddy's friend Jimbo, who got to be fun after he hung out in the kitchen with Daddy's gang. If I caught him before I was shooed away, he squatted down and spread out his big, stubby hand for me to sit on. When I sat on his hand, his strong arm rose up like an elevator that lifted me until I could touch the ceiling.

Betty, age 6, in dress-up clothes.

Everyone in Greenville became very patriotic after they saw the awful things on the Pathé News. Men either volunteered or the government drafted them. The army wanted the fittest of men. Daddy's friend Jimbo was called into service with the Army. He was so big and strong. Jimbo was not the most handsome of men—his hairline receded until he was almost bald and after a few drinks one eye wandered around without the other one. But Jimbo had attracted the prettiest wife. Lois had flawless, transparent skin and dark naturally curly hair that she wore short with deep waves cut into a stylish bob. She worked in lingerie at Ivey-Keith Department Store, and I imagined she wore silk and lace at night. She probably looked like Rita Hayworth at bedtime.

The Miller brothers, Runt and Tokey, were too short to be drafted. The recruiters deferred Uncle Harry. When his deferment ran out, he was too old. I overheard Daddy tell Mother about his trip to Columbia where he had to get naked and stand in a line to see if he was fit enough to be called into service. He was not inducted because of his flat feet. What a shame he had to get naked when he could have just taken off his shoes. The army graded him as 4-F.

I guess the draft board in Columbia never noticed how Jimbo's eye wandered when he was drunk. While Jimbo fought the war in Italy, we wrote letters to him on a regular basis. Mother asked Daddy to bring home a roll of adding-machine tape from work, and she started a letter on that roll. She carried it with her for weeks and asked everyone she ran into, whether they knew Jimbo or not, to write a note to him on the roll of paper. When she got to the end, she re-rolled it so the messages from hundreds of Greenvillians would be in the proper order.

Daddy's boss, Mr. Vard, had a son, Jack, who started work at the roofing company. Jack had a Piper Cub airplane. He took Daddy up in the plane with him for company and to help balance the weight in the plane. Jack gave Daddy flying lessons, and they flew most every afternoon here and there.

Dicky, 3, Olin, & Betty Bell, 6, in May 1942.

Daddy and Uncle Harry became members of the Civil Air Patrol since Jack had taught them to fly. Daddy had to go to meetings and record the hours he flew. I imagined they did all sorts of clandestine things at the airport. They met on Sunday afternoons and we went to the airport and watched. Dicky loved that. Daddy loved it, too. He wore a khaki-colored uniform and hat like a soldier. Mother bought Dicky a miniature uniform and a sailor dress and hat for me.

Daddy also served as an air raid warden. He grabbed his billy club from the secret place in his closet and put on a flat metal hat with an insignia on the front. He walked through the neighborhood to check on things, whatever that meant. Mother told us that when sirens blasted at night, it was called a black-out that warned us of possible air raids. She said, "They practice in case the air force base is ever attacked."

All the lights in the houses were supposed to be out and the shades pulled so enemy airplanes couldn't tell Greenville was down there. Daddy told us, "My job is to knock on doors if someone hasn't turned out their lights." We curled up with Mother in Daddy's scratchy red twill easy chair in the dark living room and waited for him to come back home from his mission.

Aunt Mary and her friends were known to put blankets over their windows and continue to play bridge by candlelight. Jane remembers walks through the neighborhood with her air raid warden daddy. Jane was braver than Annelle or me.

Mr. Vard groomed his son Jack to take over the business. Daddy thought it was time to spread his own wings rather than fly with Jack. Even though Mr. Vard had treated Daddy like a son, Mother reminded us, "Blood is thicker than water." Daddy wanted to make a career change and found a job at Ecusta Paper Corporation, near Brevard, North Carolina. He moved there in August of 1943, to start his job and find a house for us. Mother sold her bike before the move. Daddy had told her that there were no sidewalks out in the country. I felt apprehensive to leave Pauline, Daisy, my cousins, and Greenville.

14. Almost Tacky

Daddy lived in Brevard for six weeks before he found a house for us to rent. Mother drove us in Daddy's black Forty Ford and followed the moving van from Greenville to Brevard. I saw a double garage to the left of the house when we turned into the driveway. "That's probably a big reason Daddy picked this house for us," I told Mother.

The house was jointly owned by the Osborne and Hawkins families who lived on either side of our red brick rental. A little creek and a field separated us from the Hawkins and another field before the Osborne house. Water was piped down to the house from a spring.

Daddy wrestled an extra key off his gold chain and handed it to Mother after we entered the kitchen door. It was a big room. Mother didn't need that much kitchen. It didn't take a lot of space to open a can of Le Sueur English peas, a can of peach halves, or salmon for croquettes. I did, however, enjoy her Sunday fried chicken and her pimento cheese on a slice of Claussen's white bread.

The door from the kitchen to the dining room had louvered swinging half-doors. If my parents' gang visited, I thought, they could pretend it was a saloon in a cowboy movie. I wondered if Dad's buddies would come all the way from Greenville, or would this be the end to Saturday-night dinners? With gas rationed, they might stay at home. Mother couldn't get enough sugar for Daddy's coffee, so I couldn't see Hugh, Runt, and Tokey with enough gas to drive the fifty or so miles from Greenville just to knock back a few drinks and share a pot of spaghetti. But the war didn't keep the gang away. They came to Brevard several times, just not every Saturday, like before.

A dark brick exterior and ecru paint on every interior wall replaced the white siding and pastel walls on Aberdeen Drive. I felt sure that the people in Brevard didn't read *Better Homes and Gardens* like people in Greenville. I think they read *Progressive Farmer* instead.

The RCA radio was placed next to the empty bookcases built in on either side of the fireplace in the living room. Daddy's maroon chair and the hassock were within easy reach of the radio. The hassock seemed more threadbare than it did in Greenville. Everything about this house seemed worn and dark.

Mother and Daddy's mahogany four-poster was in the bedroom behind the living room. Dicky and I were relegated to two smaller rooms on the right side of the house.

"Don't be jumping on that bed, Dicky," Mother yelled from the hallway when Dicky bounced into his new room.

I slinked like a hermit crab into the ecru shell that was to be my room. I wondered how I might get some color in there. I looked out the window and saw a bank of shrubbery that separated the front

Dicky & Betty on homemade parade float.

yard from the back. Giant, round, white flowers blanketed the huge shrubs. Mother called them snowballs. They were the prettiest things about this house. Mother showed us how to cover the wagon in snowball flowers to make a float like in the Santa Claus or Rose Bowl parade. I wondered if Brevard had Santa Claus parades.

Mother took me downtown to the elementary school and enrolled me in Miss Billie Aiken's second-grade class. I adjusted to the new school except for feeling alone when I walked onto the playground surrounded by strangers. A girl named Joan came over and talked to me. She became my best friend.

Her mother plaited Joan's hair each morning. Her pigtails were long enough to cross over the top of her head. Pretty soon Mother went through a period when she plaited my hair. It must have been easy for her because I knew the hairdo didn't become me. She wrapped the last rubber band and stood back to admire her work. Mother laughed while I sat at the mahogany dresser.

"What's so funny?"

"You look like a skint rabbit." But the skinless bunny look didn't stop her from plaiting my hair every day.

Before Christmas I sat at the dresser for the plaiting ritual before school. I told Mother, "Some of the children at school say that our mothers and fathers are Santa Claus instead of the one at the North Pole."

Her hands continued to weave sections of my hair together and without a bat of her eye she said, "Well, yes. They're right. It is the parents who play Santa."

"What?" I couldn't help but bawl even though it meant I went to school with red eyes. "Even if it is true, you didn't have to tell me. How can you be so cruel?" I was a livid seven-year-old.

She snapped the last rubber band in place and turned to leave the room. With a second thought, she added, "Just don't let Dicky know."

———

The trick I used on Mother—I got her mind on something else before I proceeded to do what she told me not to—didn't work on Daddy. Like a lot of eldest children, I had to toe the line and there was no way to escape his scrutiny. But the same rigid rules weren't focused on little Dicky, who was disgustingly cheerful all the time. If we had been really bad, Mother uttered the dreaded words, "Jus' wait 'til your father gets home."

We knew that meant the wooden brush left by that pushy Fuller Brush salesman. Daddy called Dicky in first. Daddy sat on the commode with the lid down and we draped ourselves over his knees to get spanked. Dicky hollered real loud while he was spanked, but he left the bathroom with a laugh and a grin, toward me, through very few tears. That child could endure anything and then laugh about it. When my turn came, Daddy fumed over Dicky's laugh and took it out on me.

———

I only played with Joan on Saturdays because her mother had a job downtown. She seemed very tough, as a woman who worked in an office might have to be. Joan's father was tall with black hair, like Daddy without a mustache. Joan's father looked like Ray Milland and Daddy looked like Jimmy Stewart.

The whole family came to pick me up after a day at Joan's house. I got into the car and Dad and Mother continued to sit in the driveway to chat with Joan's parents before Dad drove off rather abruptly. Out of sight of Joan's family, Daddy pulled the car to the curb. For once, Daddy's scrutiny targeted Dicky. He laid a fuss on Dicky and accused him of a poot in those people's presence. I didn't hear it or smell it, but Daddy sure must have because that was the angriest I ever saw him get toward Dicky. It could've been that Daddy was afraid they thought it was him, but anyone who knew Daddy also knew he would never poot in public. I wondered if it could have been Mother.

———

Mother was early wherever she went. I think she wanted everyone else to be early like her so she could get on with whatever came next. She woke me up for school earlier than she needed to, and I walked to the Osbornes' house to catch the school bus at 7:20 every morning. Once I got to their house, I still had time to eat a bowl of Rice Krispies in heavy cream from their cows rather than store-bought Biltmore milk that Mother used. When Mrs. Osborne offered me cereal, I always ate it since I obeyed people in authority, except for Hitler and Mother when she wasn't attentive.

In the spring I walked across a field straight out of William Wordsworth's poem—through "a host of golden daffodils." Louis Osborne had planted the bulbs to sell the flowers downtown.

"...For oft, when on my couch I lay in vacant or in pensive mood, they flashed upon my inward eye..." My teacher Miss Aiken loved this daffodil poem and so did I. Even if I had gone blind, the scent of the flowers would have guided me through a shortcut to the Osborne house to catch the school bus. Past the daffodils I took another short cut, a path to the house through a field of peas, beans, or whatever crop it was.

I had to wear my galoshes to school when it was wet. I put up a fuss but I couldn't win that battle. The galoshes and shoes were too big since Mother bought our clothes so that Dicky and I could "grow into them." About halfway up the flat wet path, the mud held onto my left galosh, with the shoe inside. Before I realized what happened, I put my white sock into the mud for balance. My library book took flight and landed in the mud. Then both hands sank into the mire. I tried to pull my galosh up, but the sand had a hold on it. I imagined the quick sand could suck me under like the bad guys in Tarzan movies. At first, I was afraid to scream since I knew that quicksand swallowed the movie villains faster when they screamed and flailed around. I soon gave in to my fear and screamed so loudly that Mrs. Osborne heard me. Her daughter called Mother, and they both ran to my rescue. The experience was the opposite of a heavenly walk through daffodils.

Daddy didn't like for me to go out of the house with red eyes, but I knew my eyes were red by the time I walked into my classroom, tardy by thirty-five minutes. Miss Aiken was sweet enough to ignore my eyes and the tardiness. She smiled and motioned for me to take my seat.

The Hawkins girls and the Osborne girls were older than me, so I didn't have any friends near our house. Bonnie Hawkins told me, "A family with a whole bunch of children lives in a shack in the woods, up the dirt road behind our house. But we're not allowed to play with them."

"Why not?" I asked.

"Because some of the children have six toes on one foot," Bonnie said.

I looked for those children at school and counted the toes on every bare foot I saw. Soon I decided the deformed children were also uneducated because they weren't at my school. I didn't ever see them come down the mountain, but Bonnie swore they were up there with their extra toes.

No one to play with meant I played with Dicky. At a gully hidden in the woods behind our house, Mother showed Dicky and me how we could make a village. We dug roadways into the red clay and ran some of Dicky's toy cars along these ridges. We made it look like the cyclorama in Atlanta with tiny cars and trucks rather than dead Confederate soldiers. When I was tired of the village, Mother taught me to dig a hole in the ground the size of a shoebox and bury the box up to the top edge at ground level. I made scenes with special things I had found like moss, stones, feathers, and snowball flowers. We covered the scene with a piece of glass with duct tape around the edges and placed it on top of the box. Mother cut a rectangle into the lid and made a window. I charged Daddy a penny to see my peep show. Mother told me, "You probably shouldn't call it a peep show since some people think that means a naked woman is in there."

"Why would anyone pay a penny to see a naked woman?"

—

We had a big grassy front yard, so Mother bought a croquet set. She encouraged us to play a lot, and she always won the game. Dicky and I had a playroom, too, upstairs under the Dutch hip roof. She found some cardboard playhouses in the Sears Roebuck catalog and bought one for Dicky and one for me. She told us how she enjoyed the playhouse Pop Scott had built for her and Aunt Aileen when they were little. Like villages, peep shows, and croquet, Mother enjoyed the playroom as much as Dicky and I.

Mother had me cover one wall of the playroom with movie star pictures. *Life* magazine had a good supply of star photos and I could cut up the copies once Daddy had read them. Mother bought me movie magazines like *Photoplay* and *Modern Screen*, for the pictures. She typed letters to some of the stars and they sent autographed copies of their photographs.

I told my cousin Jane that these were very valuable, but Jane laughed. "They hire signers who write pretty so the real movie stars won't be bothered." I didn't want to believe that, but Jane knew the truth about pretty much everything.

Soon, one whole wall was covered with photos and I knew the names of all the stars. Betty Grable was my favorite because she had my name, and because she made soldiers happy with her poster—the one in her bathing suit where she smiled over her shoulder at the servicemen.

People told me I had pretty legs like hers. Jane said, "If you can hold a 50-cent piece at the ankle, knee, calf, and thigh, your legs are considered perfectly developed." I could hold the coin at my knees that sort of faced each other. Mother could hold dimes at all four places.

Betty, age 7, cousins Jane Powell, age 9,
& Annelle Powell, age 5, in 1943.

When we moved to Brevard, I had to stop dance lessons from the Sherrill sisters. I guess my heart murmur had improved enough that Daddy's new job was more important than dance lessons. But I kept the old costumes in the playroom. When Jane and Annelle visited Brevard, we dressed up and gave recitals to Dicky when we could get him to sit still. Since Jane was the oldest, she pretty much decided which dancers we were. She was Jane Powell because she already had the name. I liked to be Cyd Charisse because she was trained, like me. We told Annelle to be Ann Miller who was a good dancer, but Jane and I didn't want to look like her in the face. She was funny though, and Annelle was real funny.

My August birthday rolled around. Bonnie Hawkins had a birthday just three days after mine. Mrs. Hawkins knew Bonnie and I loved fried chicken. She told us, "I'm going to cook fried chicken for you girls so you can eat as many pieces as you want until you can't eat another piece."

We sat at a card table covered with a bright white cloth with strawberry plant borders and matched napkins and ate nine pieces of chicken between us. We didn't have to eat vegetables with it, either. After the feast, I thought about the pink and blue Easter chicks

Dicky and I were given by the Easter bunny. I realized I hadn't seen the chicks lately and worried they may have been Mother's contribution to the meal.

———

I didn't have a snooty bone in my body even though I was a native of Greenville where they say there is a tendency to be snooty. But I do think Mother let us get a little tacky when we moved to Brevard. Of all people, she should have known tacky, the way she looked down her nose at her own Pridmore kin and the drunken Fletchers who lived next door to her on Rutherford Road. She allowed Dicky to go barefoot all the time, which was pretty tacky to me.

She said, "It's because his shoes cause warts." Brevard was not citified like Greenville in the 1940s. When you went downtown in Greenville, children wore shoes and dressed like they should, but in Brevard it was all right to wear your play clothes and go barefoot anywhere—except church, of course. We didn't go to church much that year because Dicky couldn't get into his shoes with all the warts on his feet.

———

After our year in Brevard, Daddy decided to leave his job at Ecusta Mill and go back to Greenville. Maybe because we might get too tacky or maybe he missed the old gang and the weekend parties at our house. For whatever reason, he started to watch the want ads in the *Greenville News,* and he took the Greyhound bus into Greenville for several interviews. He found a job in the accounting department of Judson Mill and started to work there on August 14, 1944. Rather than tell people that Daddy's flat feet kept him out of the service, Mother bragged that his work at Judson Mills, where they made nylon for parachutes, was considered "essential service."

He stayed at Aunt Mary and Uncle Harry's house for a while and later got a room in a boarding house on Pendleton Street. He took the bus to work and left the car in Brevard for us. I'm sure he missed his car.

Mother grew impatient to join Daddy and for him to find a house for us in Greenville. Gas was still rationed but she took off for Greenville on several occasions to find us a place to live rather than wait for Daddy.

Mother took us to Sunday school one day and bought us a milk shake for our lunch at McFie's Drug Store. Next thing we knew, we headed down the mountain to push Daddy to buy the most recent house he told her about.

15. Back to Greenville

The house that Daddy found, and Mother pushed for, looked and smelled like an antique. It was twenty years old, a 1920s-style bungalow. I wondered how it could be that old and still stand. The brown shingle exterior and corbels under the eaves seemed straight out of Hansel and Gretel.

Mother had been packing ever since Daddy first left Brevard for his new job, and she greeted the workers from the moving company like old friends.

In October, 1944, the same men from Smith's Dray Line moved us back to Greenville for $54. The men put the furniture in place as well as possible, and I did the rest. With all that had to be done, of all things, I woke up the next morning with the pip.

She placed a lot of significance on her menstrual cycle.

Mother brought us to the house at 11 Vannoy Street. My feet stepped across the porch's broken-tile floor before we entered a paneled front door onto the hardwood in the living room. A brand-new room-size cocoa-colored wool rug made by Olsen, with a lifetime guarantee, welcomed us. That meant I would spend the remainder of my days seated Indian-style on a scratchy rug to play Monopoly and Parcheesi.

Daddy's chair and the green easy chair with matching sofa graced the living room, as always. I ran my fingers over the intricate wood-carved trim and memorized how it looked in case I should ever go blind.

We were not allowed to sit in his chair when Daddy was at home, but I didn't like the prickly doses of scratchiness anyway. If we sat there while he was at work, we were obliged to re-fluff the down cushion that molded his lanky frame. He swept into the chair with the grace of Roy Rogers mounting Trigger. He deftly flicked his ashes into the amber glass ash tray atop a manly bronze smoking stand.

We were not allowed to read the funnies until Daddy had seen the paper. The undisturbed *Greenville News* waited for him on the footstool; he propped his wing-tips where straw-like contents peeped through the seams. His bony legs created a lectern for the newspaper. He folded each page onto itself with precision.

Dicky and I were not allowed to play on the stool so it would hold its shape. The stool conformed to the pressure of Daddy's feet, like those of us who bowed down to his rules. He held court from this easy chair. His throne smelled of Lucky Strikes and Schlitz.

My parents had the front bedroom. My strongest memory was the time Daddy suffered with one of his headaches and tried to sleep it off with a cold washrag on his forehead, his usual remedy before he resorted to a BC Headache Powder. He must have heard me in the living room, as I sang along with Dinah Shore on the radio. He got up and guided me to his room and sat me on the dresser stool next to Mother's Singer sewing machine cabinet. "Sit there without a peep until I get up."

He resumed his mummy-like position, the cold washrag placed just right. I stared out the window with nothing to look at. I heard the sound of a distant lawn mower. I craned to see if it was Mr. Eliazar, the Syrian man from across the street, but saw no sign of anyone mowing a lawn. After a while, I figured out that the lawn mower noise was the way Daddy breathed and his muffled snore. I 'bout got tickled but knew better.

Dicky's room resembled a sunroom. It was on the back corner of the house, next to mine, and had windows around two sides. Mother and Daddy bought an army surplus bunk bed for him. On the inner wall they hung the huge blackboard we had received for Christmas.

I'm sure it was her lack of modesty that caused Dicky to draw a picture of Mother in one corner of that blackboard. He drew her naked as a jaybird and showed all her privates. When I saw it, I about died of embarrassment, and I ran to tell Mother. She just erased it and didn't say *pee turkey* to little Dicky. But a few days later, she got between us on my bed and started to read aloud books from the library about birds and bees which were not about birds and bees at all.

I told her, "I don't want to participate in this activity with Dicky here." But he wouldn't budge. I preferred to educate myself about such matters. I found two little rubber balls that had broken off our paddleballs. I put them in my panties and sat down to teach myself how it felt to sit, if I were a boy.

Dicky's room led through a tiny hallway toward the kitchen. To the left was a screened-in porch where we ate in the summer. To the right was the door to the basement and the furnace. Mother fixed us a playroom down there in a floored room across the back of the house. That's where we kept our comics and my dress-up clothes. She painted a rug on the floor to make it look like a real room.

Our dining room was large enough to hold the Duncan Phyfe suite. A fireplace was on the end wall. The floor was bare except for a large register where air returned to the coal-burning furnace below.

Mother came across a stash of leather books with fancy brass locks and miniature keys. "I'm tired of moving these diaries from place to place." So she removed her Smith-Corona manual typewriter from its case and placed it on our dining room table. The diaries surrounded the typewriter most days, and she transcribed events during her life from the diaries to the white pages. The only time she put the typewriter back in the carrier was when the gang came over for spaghetti. She wrote her first entry on January 30, 1945.

> *My parents named me Clara Elizabeth Scott after my father's youngest sister. I was born November 12, 1913....*

Mother didn't always use her beloved typewriter. Her script, bold and curvy, slanted to the right. She recorded, in cursive, the date and the name of who married whom, plus their marriage or death dates across the pictures of classmates in her Greenville High

School yearbook, the *1926 Nautilus*. She kept countless lists that recorded marriages, births, deaths, and other information that pertained to friends, relatives, or famous people—useless data to anyone but her or maybe the South Carolina Department of Archives and History. Mother also made lists on legal pads so she wouldn't forget what happened during the day. She often slipped into Gregg shorthand as though more fluent in a second language. She checked off each item after she shared the news with the family, usually at the supper table.

Mother stuffed the typed pages about her life into a manila envelope along with other loose pages handwritten with no. 2 pencils on notebook paper or yellow legal pads that she got free from the telephone company where her father worked. She liked free things. I knew where she kept the autobiography and I often curled up in the scratchy green chair to read those pages.

Sometimes Dicky took a nap before Daddy came home from work. While he slept, Mother took the opportunity to rest too. I crawled up next to her on our scratchy green sofa and studied her round features up close. Peach-curved cheeks merged into smile lines like parentheses down to her round chin. Curvy nostrils flanked a small ball at the end of her nose that pugged up just enough to be cute. Naturally curly hair, in a rich brown, flounced at her forehead and encircled her cushion-like ear lobes. I reached to touch a lobe with one finger and felt the softness. She often wore pearls or beads with earbobs to repeat the round shapes in her face. I had angular features and straight dirty-blonde hair. Her curvy, full buttocks pooched out below a tiny waist. Before she sat, she lifted her skirt, just a little, so it didn't become "rump-sprung." There was no chance of a rump-sprung look to my skirt. My backside was wide and flat like those of Daddy's sisters, Mary and Martha, on the Bell side. From behind, my butt had the shape of a double ice cream cone. My bird-like legs might have held up a robin, but Mother had muscular calves from biking, hiking, camping, and tennis. My lips seemed narrow next to her full, plump ones. Mine quivered when I cried, became frightened, or felt embarrassed or uncertain. She consoled me with, "Beauty comes from within." But I pretty much wanted some beauty on the outside, like hers. My mother's looks made her a shining star, and I felt dimmed by her glow.

When we left Brevard, the Osbornes gave Dicky and me a six-week-old black rabbit. Mother and Dicky fixed up a pen for the rabbit in a tiny room under the garage. We named him Thumper. And he did.

We discovered that Thumper was a she after Mother allowed a neighbor to board her rabbit in Thumper's pen. Our rabbit disappeared about the time Mother realized Thumper was PG. I never found out who of her acquaintances had rabbit stew for supper.

Our neighborhood had lots of squirrels, maybe because of the proximity to McPherson Park. Mother tried her best to run over the squirrels that crossed her path. She may have known someone who could make Brunswick stew from squirrel road-kill, but I hoped not.

Next to the squirrels that she called "bushy-tailed rats," Mother despised the coo sounds made by pigeons. Pigeons roosted under the eaves of our house and she did everything to discourage them. She threw rocks up there, banged on the walls, and shot at them with Dicky's Red Ryder BB gun. I wondered if Ludie Blanton liked squab.

It made Daddy uneasy to pull the car into the rickety single garage over the rabbit pen at the foot of a steep, narrow driveway, but he did it during awful weather. I had a nightmare that I had pulled the car into the garage and an anvil crashed through the roof. It fell on top of Daddy's car like the anvil dropped by the Road Runner onto Wile E. Coyote. The weight caused Daddy's car to crash into the rabbit pen. I woke up before he discovered the damage.

Many memories began in the kitchen at our enamel-topped table. I picked at my food while Mother told Daddy she wanted to start a Girl Scout Troop for me, so I could hike, camp, and work on badges, even though I had no interest in those activities. An explosion interrupted their conversation and shook the twenty-year-old house. Daddy thought the furnace had blown up; I just knew the car had fallen through the garage floor into Thumper's pen. Mother hollered when she saw soot fall through cracks in the ceiling and onto our supper. Dicky pushed the soot aside and continued to eat.

A radio announcer said that the main plant of Ideal Laundry and Cleaners had exploded. Along with the rest of Greenville's curious population, Mother, Dicky, and I drove out there to see what had happened. Daddy was content to stay home. We found a parking place blocks away from the Ideal plant and started to walk in that direction. We knew which way to go because the night sky was like an orange sunset over the exploded plant. The police had roped off the area. By then Mother had edged us as close to the disaster as possible. Unable to get to the action, she said, "Let's go—those police won't let us get any closer," and we headed home.

———

The day after we moved back to Greenville, Mother enrolled me at Billy Cleveland Elementary School a couple of blocks away. She wore a rose-colored dress with swishy gray flowers and huge sunglasses. I wore the pastel striped dress I had worn the previous Easter. Mother said, "First impressions are lasting impressions."

Mother stopped by my school often. She wore the sunglasses that all but covered her face. Tad Hudson teased me, "How long has your mama been a highway patrolman?"

Billy Cleveland School had one classroom per grade and Miss Georgia Fant was my third-grade teacher. Daddy said, "Thank goodness her parents didn't name her Ella."

The children in Greenville had learned to write cursive in second grade, so I had some catching up to do. When the other children had free time or worked on other things, I had to practice my letters alone at the blackboard. Nothing but perfection was good enough for Miss Fant, but I wound up with pretty good penmanship. After the class elected me secretary, Mother told me it was because my handwriting was pretty.

Mother also learned her way around the neighborhood and soon knew everyone on our street. However, she told us, "I want y'all to stay away from those Pridmores three doors up."

"How come?" we asked.

"Because, with a name like Pridmore, they are bound to be tacky. You can hear that country music they play clear out to the street."

I remembered that her grandmother Scott had been a Pridmore from Union County. Mother always looked down on them as countrified.

I didn't understand why Mother didn't call the Graysons next door "tacky" because they raised chickens in their backyard. Our garages were attached and they kept chickens in a coop next to Thumper's room.

Mrs. Grayson was big in the Presbyterian Church, and she trained her children to be ladies and gentlemen. I don't think I ever touched Mrs. Grayson, but I'm sure she was soft because she smelled of Jergen's lotion.

Dicky played in the yard one day with our Uncle Jimmy. They overheard Mother tell Mrs. Grayson something cute that Dicky had said. When we went inside, Dicky said to Mother, "You know what you told Mrs. Grayson that I said?"

"Uh-huh," answered Mother.

"Well, I didn't say that."

"Yeah, but it would've been real cute, if you had."

Snow came to Greenville, and Mother, Dicky, and I ran toward the park. Snowsuits swaddled our bodies and we walked like little Frankenstein's monsters. Mother placed plastic bags over our shoes and held them in place with rubber bands from the rubber band bank over the pencil holder. She plopped our stuffed bodies onto the sled that belonged to her when she was little. As she shoved us down the bank, I began to pray with my eyes open, "Thank you, God, for that flat place before we get to the creek."

Our day ended at the fireplace in the dining room where Mother draped our wet clothes over a rack. The air smelled like steam. Then, as always, Mother sidled up to the fireplace, lifted her skirt, and backed up toward the fire. I asked her, "Why do you always lift your skirt and back up to fires?"

She answered, "I don't want the fire to scorch my clothes, but mainly because it feels good."

That dining room floor had to be waxed after all the wet we tracked in. When she got the Johnson's paste wax out, we knew we were in for some fun. Dicky and I were human buffers who donned white socks and skated around the room to bring out the sheen. Sometimes she made pads of rags and tied them around our bottoms for us to slide around. The chore usually ended with a splinter in somebody's butt.

By spring, we smelled dookie and feathers from the chickens the Graysons kept in their backyard. Along with chicken odors, Dicky's warts returned to his bare feet. The warts started out small, then become bug-ugly nickel-size protrusions that grew out of his wide five-year-old flat feet.

Mother tried everything to get rid of them. Doctor Daniel told her to leave them alone, but Mother didn't leave anything alone, especially when someone told her to. She had some castor oil from when she was PG with Dicky, and every time he came into her sight she rubbed that stuff onto his nasty warts. It didn't take them away, but the warts looked a lot softer. I guessed, because I wouldn't touch one for the life of me. They say you can catch a wart yourself when you touch someone else's.

One day Mother had picked up the laundry from Daisy. She threw the sweet-smelling sheets onto the Duncan Phyfe table and grabbed little Dicky by the arm; his wart-infested feet cleared the floor. He waved behind her like an unfurled flag. She was Donald Duck and he was Huey, Dewey, or Louie. She had a small brown paper bag of corn kernels. They high-tailed it next door to Mrs. Grayson's house.

Daisy had told Mama, "You can get shed of warts with a prick of a needle, till it bleeds. Then you put a drop of the blood onto a kernel of yellow corn, feed it to the chickens, and the warts will go away."

Mrs. Grayson was too polite to look sideways at Mother and her weird remedy. In her non-judgmental way, Mrs. Grayson went along with Mother's medical procedure as they hurried toward the chicken yard for Mother to begin her magic. I thought I saw Mrs. Grayson smile a little for the first time. Mother said, "That Daisy knows her stuff."

I don't remember warts on Dicky's wide, flat feet again. Such a blessing that was, especially after our move back to Greenville, where bare feet were not that acceptable.

Mother and I went to the mill outlet store one Saturday to pick out slipcover material for the scratchy twill in the living room. As a devout reader of *Better Homes and Gardens,* I planned to have a sophisticated interior design shop when I was older. I drew floor plans and cut out pictures from magazines. I glued them onto a piece of cardboard to give my imaginary customers some good ideas. I convinced Mother to get the jungle print with a life-size banana-leaf motif. The covers hid the monotonous upholstery on the living room furniture during the summer season. It was like the middle of a hot, steamy jungle—very appropriate for Greenville summers before the days of air-conditioning.

We had to live in a house for a long time before Daddy allowed Mother to hang pictures on the walls. He didn't want holes in the plaster in case Mother changed her mind where she would hang them. Dicky had a "Blue Boy" in his room, an etching of a European street scene hung over the telephone table, and a pair of botanical prints hung over the buffet. I didn't get a picture since they let me choose some blue wallpaper with white eyelet stripes threaded with pink ribbon for my bedroom walls. Daddy hung the paper and lined it up perfectly.

With my own money, I bought a blue taffeta pillow for my bed. The touch of that taffeta was a welcome relief to the feel of the dry, chenille tufts, which made my skin crawl, on my counterpane. Dicky was not allowed to touch the pillow since his hands were grimy most of the time.

Even though I detested Dicky's griminess, I didn't mind the grimy stable at Cleveland Park where Uncle Harry took Jane, Annelle, and me horseback riding on Saturdays. But I wasn't keen on the horse left over for me.

I told Jane, "My horse twitches and shudders—I don't think he likes me."

Jane said, "It's how he scares flies away."

None of the other horses twitched their tales or stomped their feet. I took his stomps personally. I didn't truly love to ride horseback, but I followed Jane's adage to get back on every time I fell off.

Georgia, a friend from Sunday school who was very cool, loved horses and had one of her own. Maybe if I liked horses too, I would seem just that cool. Like Georgia, I bought bronze horse sculptures with baby-sitting money. The metal horses adorned every vacant space atop my dresser and chest of drawers. I had a horse poster on my bedroom door. He was tan with a white face, and I named him Bill after the handsome school bus driver in Brevard. I pretended he was real and that we kept him in a stable. Mother told me, "It's against the law to have a horse in the city limits, and we don't want to move to the country where we would waste a lot of gas to and from." That satisfied me since the real me didn't want an actual horse anyway. I just wanted to be like Georgia.

Horses didn't frighten me as much as things that crawled. If the family vacationed in the mountains, I had nightmares about snakes and spiders. If we went to the beach, the nightmares were about crabs that walked sideways along the strand. If we were at home, the nightmares were triggered by things that might have happened during the day, like the time Daddy found a nest of baby copperhead snakes in the weeds near the creek. The first time I witnessed a neighborhood dog in heat and saw that pink thing on the male dog sealed my fear of dogs and triggered nightmares too. I had nightmares about lions that chased me up the hill on Poinsett Avenue. In the dream, I was unable to run, even though I worked my legs as hard as I could.

I had a recurring dream about the end of the world. The setting was at the intersection of Bennett Street and Park Avenue, in front of Billy Cleveland School. A group of monks presided over a ceremony that proclaimed the end of the world. They instructed people to hang onto massive posts scattered around the intersection. Those who could not hold on were consumed by a dreadful unknown world to be revealed when the asphalt broke away from beneath our feet. I searched in desperation for my parents, so they could help me hold onto the post. The nightmare ended just as I lost my grip. I also screamed like bloody murder at the end of each dream when the crabs started to crawl up my legs, or a snake headed right for me. The screams woke everyone but little Dicky who could sleep through a bomb explosion—or a need to pee, and his room smelled like it. I did, however, slip into his bottom bunk to be a little closer to another human being after my bad dreams.

Mother taught me Psalm 23 to help me cope. I memorized the psalm and woke up from nightmares to repeat it the way a Catholic hailed Mary.

Mother told me she went to the Bible for answers to life's problems. One of her shortcuts was to let the Bible fall open. Some people called it "cracking the Bible." "Just let it fall open, and the solution to whatever bothers you will be revealed on those pages," she told me.

I likened this to the magic of Jane's Ouija board. I tried it many times, but often felt the Bible kept secrets from me. Mother said, "Ouija boards are like black magic." She wondered why Aunt Mary would buy one for Jane.

I asked Jane's Ouija board if my parents would buy me a piano like the Graysons had. The board answered, "Maybe." Lots of people had noticed my long, bony fingers and told me I would make a good piano player. Daddy agreed to buy a piano on one condition: "The first weekday you miss practice, the lessons are over, and the piano will be sold."

No one enjoyed that piano more than Daddy. He got a little bourbon on his breath and taught me "Chopsticks" and "Heart and Soul." I practiced every day and walked up Vannoy Street to Mrs. Lucien Earle's for lessons. Mrs. Earle's fingers were not very long but they were bony. And I'm certain that it was her breath that turned the ivory keys yellow.

On the days I had piano lessons, Mother took the opportunity to run around town for another hour or two. She left the door unlocked for me to pick up my music books and practice before I walked to my lesson. I gave up good intentions to practice when I heard inexplicable sounds in the house. Maybe ghosts. I grabbed an apple from the bowl in the kitchen, gathered my music books, and sat on the curb to wait until time to go to Mrs. Earle's house.

Mrs. Earle gave recitals in her dining room, where her piano sat catty-cornered next to a window. She put up folding bridge chairs where the parents sat. She scattered candles throughout the room for a Liberace ambiance. I wore a dress handed down from my cousin Vance on the Weaver side. Vance was about four years older than me, and I became heiress to her hand-me-down clothes since she was an only child. She had given me a baby blue chiffon dress, fit for royalty. Narrow pleats hung from the yoke to the hem. Satin ribbons streamed from the shoulders to my waist. When I twirled in the dress the pleats rippled into a circle that stood out from my body and the ribbons took flight.

Carolyn Grayson played "The Spinning Song" from the red John Thompson book. I was next. I took a big inhale of the burning candle wax scent and made my way to the piano bench. By then, it was darker out the window. I stumbled over the notes at the beginning of my piece and started over several times. The correct notes had stayed at home. I sensed someone from the folded chair section get out of their seat. I heard a bridge chair creak and someone shuffle across the floor. It was—Mother. She went to the window where one of the candles glowed, picked up the candlestick, and held it over the keyboard where I struggled to remember my piece, as if my problem was poor lighting rather than nerves. She saved her reputation and mortified me. I stopped my performance and dodged hot wax about to drip onto the yellow keyboard. Great fortune also kept candle wax off my gorgeous frock. This all happened just before I confessed a loss of interest in the piano, and Daddy sold the piano out from under me in less than a week.

～

Daddy sat on his maroon throne during my impressionable years. He became a king whom I wanted to please, a king I needed to obey, and a king who demanded perfection of himself and of me.

On his birthday, Mother agreed to help me make a fresh coconut cake with Grandmother Bell's recipe. I put candles on top and Mother lit them. I was to carry the cake from the kitchen to his easy chair as a surprise. I felt important, mesmerized by the candles as I stepped through the dining room. Before I rounded the corner where he sat, my shoe caught on the edge of the monstrous floor register in my path. The cake lifted vertically like a helicopter. My arms and legs flailed like those of a cat who landed on all fours. The register imprinted a grid pattern across the remainder of the cake—the part that didn't go to hell in the furnace below. I ran to my bedroom and cried, careful not to tear-stain the taffeta pillow I had bought with my own money.

16. Fires and Fireplaces

Aunt Mary, like my Daddy, had a hot temper. "Damn it," she hollered as she slammed our front door on Vannoy Street. Mother or Daddy had probably made her mad. The dramatic exit took her right into the game of jacks my cousins and I played. We sat on the cool broken-tile floor of the front porch.

We quizzed each other with looks until Jane took her turn and bounced the ball again without comment. I think Jane had heard her mother say that word before, but it scared me to death. Aunt Mary settled into the squeaky glider on the other end of the porch and lit one of her Viceroys. I really didn't think Aunt Mary could get any angrier than that "damn it day" until the dreadful Sunday afternoon when Mother embarrassed Aunt Mary at her neighbor's house.

Sunday afternoons were designated to visit kinfolk and friends or ride around neighborhoods and look at things we had seen a million times before. One cold winter Sunday, Mother told Dicky and me, "Get your coats on. We'll go over and visit Aunt Mary and them and give Daddy a little quiet time." That meant he planned to read the want ads in the *Atlanta Journal*. It hadn't taken long for him to complain about his new boss at Judson Mill.

We got to Aunt Mary's and Mother took a notion she wanted to run next door to the Andersons' house and tell Mrs. Anderson something. When Mother got a notion, she acted on it. I tagged along, either to satisfy my own curiosity about whatever adults talked about or to try to keep things as sane as possible.

The fire in the fireplace spread warmth through the Andersons' living room. Flames licked the logs that rested over a bed of red coals.

The Andersons' daughter Liz and her date were curled up on the sofa like a scene out of a romantic movie. The Priscilla curtains hung behind them swayed from cold air that crept through cracks around the window panes.

I had heard Aunt Mary say that Liz had her eye on this Furman College senior, Class of 1947. He was the latest in a long history of boyfriends. I had also overheard Aunt Mary say, "I think this might be the one."

Mother saw the fire and made a bee line for the hearth. She backed up to it, planted both feet, grabbed her hem, hoisted the back side of her plaid wool skirt to her waist, and exposed her rayon-pantied buttocks toward the flames.

"Ummm, that feels good."

Liz's date's mouth flew open and he gaped at the crazy woman until he remembered that gentlemen don't look, and he turned his crimson face toward the Priscilla curtains.

Aunt Mary was a few seconds behind Mother and me. Like most folk from Greenville, where daughters routinely married native sons and pushed Chippendale chairs under their dining room tables, Aunt Mary knew decorum.

Mother was "raised right," as well. "Don't cut but one bite of meat at a time; don't eat bacon with your fingers; don't talk with your mouth full; never walk across a ballroom floor without an escort; write thank-you notes immediately after you receive a gift; cross your legs at the ankles or at the knee and keep your legs parallel to each other; don't wear white after Labor Day, and never kiss a boy on the first date…" Mother knew all the rules and instilled them into me, but discarded them like a bad hand in bridge for herself.

Aunt Mary gushed apologies to Liz Anderson, and ushered Mother back to her house next door. She had ahold of Mother's elbow like a guard who led a bad prisoner to see the warden. She knew Mother's ears grew deaf to reason, so Aunt Mary gave Mother the silent treatment. Then hell-bent to tattle, she waited until we left before she called my daddy.

I could imagine what she would report to him. "Clara mortified me in front of the Andersons, and I don't appreciate that."

Daddy's ears probably still ached from the lecture by the time Mother returned me, Dicky, and her warmed butt back home. I figured Aunt Mary had him on the phone for the entire time it took us to drive across town. Daddy didn't say much around me and seemed to have chalked it up to another of Aunt Mary's tirades. He knew by now Mother would not change, so when Aunt Mary fussed, he just fussed back. But the quiet of his afternoon was over.

For a long time, everyone tiptoed around the hiked-up skirt incident and avoided the mention of the sore subject, especially in Aunt Mary's presence.

———

All her life, mother struggled against constraints, whether they pertained to marriage, motherhood, or manners. From her role as a genteel lady to her competitive streak in games of Rook or rummy, she made up her own rules. I pretty much knew that winter Sunday at the Andersons' would not be the last time Mother pulled up her skirt.

17. Nurse Clara

I had a brave notion to ride the bike that belonged to Rudy Anderson, who lived next door to Jane and Annelle. I started with my left foot on the left peddle and swung my right leg over the back wheel to avoid the bar down the middle. Sad ending—to avoid Aunt Mary's boxwoods, I swerved and stopped. I slipped off the seat and my privates crashed onto the bar across the middle. I about died from the pain. Really, I about died. Mother called Dr. Daniel to see if she needed to bring me in, but he thought I'd be fine. I wondered if he knew how badly I hurt. He was a male, after all. Mother's explained, "You could have broken your hymen."

"Huh, what's that?"

"It's a covering of skin over your privates, and if it is broken, your husband might think you lost your virginity before your honeymoon. You'll have to remember this day and explain it to him."

That seemed like a long time to remember something. "Why would that be so important?"

"It's like someone else having opened his birthday present before he had a chance."

I felt a birds and bees talk looming, and I didn't want to hear it. I asked myself if there was anything about the human body she didn't know. I hushed her as fast as I could and went back to playing.

———

The walk to Billy Cleveland School felt like miles, even though it was two long blocks. But I didn't complain about that walk up Park Avenue since Camilla, who was a polio victim, walked three blocks on crutches. Camilla missed lots of school days to go to the Shriners Hospital for treatment during the year. When she did go to school, we children took turns and carried her books for her, because she was as sweet as a piece of pie. I decided polio attacked sweet people like Camilla, President Roosevelt, and my crush Marion.

I had a weakness for blond-haired boys ever since I fell in love with Bill, my school bus driver when I was in the second grade. A boy named Marion Lesesne had blond hair, piercing blue eyes, and was the best baseball player at Billy Cleveland before polio left him with a slight limp. Doctors thought that his twin sister and younger brother probably had mild cases of polio as well. Mother told Dicky and me, "The children probably ate some Christmas candy that had been left out for mice to get into." That put a real damper on Christmas candy for a while.

Children across the country contracted polio—many died or were left crippled. The Pathé News showed children in iron lungs to help them breathe. That summer of 1944, polio was so bad that the city closed swimming pools so people wouldn't get the disease from swimming together. We sweated through an extra-hot summer because parents heard that playing in cold water from garden hoses could also cause polio.

Other less malicious diseases also threatened the children in our school and neighborhood —measles, mumps, and chicken pox. Mother felt it was inevitable that we would get them all, so she moved things along by sending Dicky and me to the homes of newly infected children. She was in a race with the health department man sent to nail a "Quarantined" sign on the front doors.

All the childhood diseases struck Dicky and me, except for polio.

During our bouts with measles, mumps, and chicken pox, Mother put us to bed and furnished one of the bells from her collection on the what-not shelf, so we could call Nurse Clara, like sick people buzzed for a nurse in the hospital. She also provided a big, thick coloring book to entertain me and plastic soldiers for Dicky. She brought meals on a tray or a glass of water when we rang the bell.

She pulled out the bottom drawer of my maple desk next to my bed. The drawer was the right size to nestle an enamelware potty there—a makeshift commode to save steps. I endured a feverish bout with measles, and I got up in the night to pee into the potty invention. In my sleepy state, I didn't realize she had not put the potty back into the drawer after she emptied it. That was one wasted pack of Blue Horse notebook paper. For the rest of the desk's life, the rippled wood veneer in the bottom drawer was a reminder that pee-pee paid a visit in the wee hours during a feverish stupor.

Mother could diagnose and had a cure for anything that ailed anyone; if she didn't have an answer, she knew Daisy could whip up a cure. She used a flashlight on Dicky's butt in the middle of the night to check for pinworms. Another reason for Nurse Clara to sleep with a flashlight next to her bed.

Many of her remedies were bought over the counter, but their use was often embellished far beyond the claims of the manufacturer. As if she knew better than any physician or pharmacist, she administered her own dosages.

Mother kept her medicines in the bathroom closet. The old bottles and jars were pushed to the back of the closet like last week's leftovers in the recesses of her Frigidaire. She used iodine for the most serious healing, but the red liquids, mercurochrome and methylate, were standards for every infinitesimal scratch. Cotton balls and Band-Aids in every shape and size were there and we had enough rolls of gauze and adhesive tape to wrap a few mummies. Eye drops, ear drops, nose drops, drops for most openings in the human body were in the closet. She couldn't leave a doctor's office without asking for a few complimentary tongue depressors for her collection.

She slathered her favorite remedy for cold or cough relief, Vicks VapoRub, onto the soles of our feet before bedtime. She covered our feet with white socks and we were expected to be well by morning. She also used it for the added side effect of smoothing dry heels and calluses. She put a dab of Vicks up both her nostrils when she felt a cold or cough coming on—it didn't matter how unattractive it was for a booger of Vicks to protrude from her nostrils. She also used the miraculous remedy on bee stings, mosquito bites, minor abrasions, chicken-pox sores, measles, moles, blisters, splinters, chapped lips, and yellow toenails.

She trapped Vick's fumes from a vaporizer under a sheet tent suspended over Dicky's bed. If one of us had a cold, she put both of us under the tent as a preventative measure and to save on Vicks. She gave us lots of comic books to keep us content. That worked fine until our little eyes began to burn. Soon gummy buildup of the cure coated the windows, walls, woodwork, furniture, and our eyelashes. When we whined about the treatment, she threatened us with the stuff that smelled like asphalt.

Vicks became available in cough-drop form. I have seen her remove a drop from her mouth in order to sing a hymn in church. She wrapped the partially used drop in a Kleenex and popped it back into her mouth at the Amen. I cringed at the thought of the fuzzy drop on my own tongue. But it didn't bother her since she never wasted a perfectly good, partially used cough drop.

A new invention called "penicillin throat troches" came along. We were told to suck on one anytime our throat got scratchy.

In cases of irregularity, we were given a large glass of milk of magnesia. Mother preferred Phillip's because the empty cobalt glass containers decorated the kitchen windows with a flair. She tried to fool us by mixing it with a glass of milk. A maraschino cherry drifted to the bottom of the viscous concoction, our reward for drinking the whole thing. I no longer consider maraschino cherries tasty.

She took aspirin whenever she had nothing better to do. Nurse Clara claimed they cured headaches, fever, inflammation, or insomnia. Soon the wonder drug Benadryl came along to be used for the onset of colds, influenza, allergic reactions, and insomnia. Mother carried bottles in her purse and swigged at will. She was never without it whenever she expected to be in the company of boring people or on lengthy car trips with family.

Family and friends were cautioned against the onset of constipation. She told them, "Eat a bowl of Bran Flakes before you go to bed. Or even better, eat a mellow apple, or one as close to being rotten as you can tolerate." But she warned, "Never drink a Coca-Cola with a mellow apple. It causes a gaseous reaction that can kill you. And never take an aspirin with a Coca-Cola," for the same reason.

She told me, "Never sit on a cold stone, brick, or concrete wall. It can give you the piles," known by its medical term as hemorrhoids.

I made myself scarce about the time Mother rattled those pots and pans to heat up supper, the witching hour when Mother whipped out her silver-plated teaspoon from the top of the fridge. She grabbed the economy-size bottle of cod liver oil and whistled her commanding "Whew-whew" for Dicky and me to come get our daily dose.

That didn't bother old Dick. I was the finicky one, suspicious of things Mother tried to put in our mouths. Dicky gulped his cod liver oil and ran back outside to play. I cringed when I looked into the spoon and noticed the ever-present green patina that grew where the silver plate was worn off.

"I rinse it off under the faucet," she assured me.

My doses were topped with an additional elixir called S.S.S. Tonic with iron to improve my appetite. In the sixth grade, I weighed six-ty-four pounds. Dr. Daniel diagnosed me as anemic. Nurse Clara's tonic did work though. Soon I noticed that roast beef gravy on rice tasted really good.

18. Keeping Up Appearances

It was no surprise when on the way to the drug store, Kash & Karry for groceries, or Daisy's house, Mother might take a notion to drive over to Gaffney to get Edith, her half-sister who was four years older than me. It was even easier after they built the super highway.

We rode around town on one of Edith's visits and went through Cleveland Park. Mother pulled the car into a parking place by the skating rink and asked Edith, "You want to drive?"

"Sure," Edith said. She was about fourteen years old. She drove all around the park with Dicky and me in the back seat.

After Mother got behind the wheel again, she gave a little speech to Edith. "Now when you get older there will be times when you don't tell your husband everything you do."

I translated that to mean, "Don't let Olin know I let you drive." Edith was so cool that she kept her mouth shut about driving Daddy's car.

As far as grown-ups go, I also thought my Aunt Mary B. was pretty cool. I liked it when friends and family said I looked more like Aunt Mary's daughter than her own daughters. I didn't mind this, except for the flat buttocks and jutting Bell chin. Granddaddy Bell gifted all us Bells with a jutting chin. I often studied my profile through a hand mirror, and hid my chin with two fingers, to imagine how cute I would be without it.

I was afraid of the flat-butt curse. Nobody's butt looked as flat as Aunt Martha's. I spent the night with Aunt Martha, Uncle Chick, and my cousin Anne and got a jarring preview of what an adult Bell rump looked like. I happened to open my eyes in the middle of the night and watched Aunt Martha go down the brightly lit hallway from the bathroom back to her own bedroom. She was dressed in a tee shirt and panties that bagged over her skeletal frame. The butt part hung several unnecessary inches below the edge of her undies. I closed my eyes and prayed that age wouldn't pull this trick on me.

Aside from Aunt Mary B.'s physical flaws, she cared about things that I thought were important—looking good to go to a party, keeping a pretty house with fancy furniture, and encourag-ing Jane, Annelle, and me to put on shows for the grownups. Her fa-vorite show-stopper was our trio of "Whispering Hope" in three-part harmony while Jane accompanied us on the piano.

She also knew how we should fit into Greenville's social whirlwind of pre-teen girls. When the children of Aunt Mary's and Mother's friends gave what folks in Greenville called "prom parties," Aunt Mary made sure I looked presentable and found formal dresses from friends and neighbors for me to wear. In return, Aunt Mary required Mother and me to go by her house before each prom party so she could see if I looked all

Betty, age 9, & Jane, age 11, going to a prom party.

right. She always found reason to reinforce at least one or two of my curls with her curling iron, still piping hot from doing Jane's hair.

When we arrived at the party, the host's or hostess's mother hand-ed us a bridge tally and stubby pencil. The boys huddled togeth-er until the hostess mother encouraged them to ask us for a prom, which meant they walked with us around the block at designated times. The boys were to write their names on the girl's card next to a number, and we wrote our names next to their corresponding number. The hostess mother rang a cow bell for the start and end of each prom around the block with the boy who signed up for that allotted time. Aunt Mary's curling iron must not have worked on me, because I didn't have many boys' names written on my card. One host's mother, Mrs. Spann, noticed that I was a wallflower and she told her son Don and even his little brother Henry to walk around the block with me. One time her husband Mr. Spann walked me around the block. It was hard to stand out next to a cousin who looked like Elizabeth Taylor.

19. Christmas Time

It was a Friday night in December 1944, and I still had a fishy taste in my mouth from the salmon croquette Mother had fixed for supper. Dicky and I were fed early, and Daddy unwound with his friend Jim Beam. He had been cooped up all week in his windowless office as office manager, a job he daily dreaded. Daddy seemed mellow, at least for now, but I knew that Jim Beam would soon kick in, and we would see the other side of his personality.

A knock on the door made us look up, and Mother greeted the other Betty Bell from across the street. How strange for me to be named Betty Bell and have a grown lady with the exact same name across the street. But there were few similarities other than the name. I had turned eight, but she was very old, probably in her twenties. Like lots of ladies during wartime, she was an "old maid." Mother had told me, "There are not enough men to go around anymore since so many boys have been killed in the war, and the rest of them are still overseas."

I'd seen enough Pathé News at the Carolina Theatre to know how bad things were in the world. Even after the soldiers and sailors would come home from overseas, I was afraid Miss Bell would never find a man. She was no Veronica Lake. She didn't get a tan in the summer and her cheeks looked like biscuit dough, with dents where she had pimples as a teenager. Miss Bell and I were both blondes, but Mother said my hair was "dirty blonde," and she called the old maid's hair "bottle blonde." I'm pretty sure that meant she combed peroxide or Marchand's through her hair, then sat in a window for the sun to give her that "bottle blonde" look.

This year, Mother had Scotch-taped Christmas cards around the double door frame between the living and dining rooms for decoration. Daddy told Mother, "You can use the tape if you wash the stickiness off the door frame before New Year's." Daddy didn't like a mess and Mother knew how to make one.

We had gotten some mistletoe when we cut our cedar tree from Granddaddy Bell's woods the previous Sunday. We draped the tree with strings of colored lights, glass ornaments with fake snow on top, and silver icicles from a box saved year after year. The green scent went all through the house.

Even though Daddy didn't like holes in the walls or in the woodwork, he let Mother hammer a tack in the center of the double door frame where she hung a mistletoe ball wrapped in red ribbon around her embroidery hoops. Miss Bell planted her feet between the living room and dining room under the mistletoe ball while she talked to Mother. I liked to hear grown-ups' conversations and Miss Bell and Mother acted right giddy. I guess they were excited about the holidays, too.

Bing Crosby crooned "White Christmas" over our RCA Victor radio. I looked up just as my own daddy laid his Lucky Strike onto the ash tray. Like movie cowboy Sunset Carson, Daddy sauntered toward the other Betty Bell, swept her into his arms, leaned her back, and flat-planted a kiss right on the lips of the old maid. My jaw jerked like a hooked fish, and I felt right faint from what I saw.

When she got her balance, Miss Betty Bell left, through the front door, her doughy skin as pink as a rosebud. I ignored the smirk on Daddy's face and turned to Mother and asked, "Why did Daddy do that?"

Mother explained, "She was standing under the mistletoe."

Daddy added, "She asked for it."

I wondered if that was the only kiss the other Betty Bell had ever had, or would ever have, even after the boys returned home from The War.

20. Planes and Trains

For Christmas, Santa brought Dicky a toy that had a map, a periscope, and bombs. You looked through the periscope and dropped bombs onto a map placed on the floor. Every child in the neighborhood came by to try this toy. When the gang came over that night, even the grownups got into it. Daddy pulled out the kitchen stool for people to stand on so the bombs had farther to drop.

Dicky ate a lot of cereal and each box contained a miniature army-green airplane as a prize. Dicky had all of them— flying boxcars, B-29s, B-25s. He knew the names and what they were used for. He and the Creech boys had camouflage suits and helmets. They played army about every day. It made me cringe every time they shot at each other.

The Creech boys with Dicky Bell, age 5, in 1945.

Mother didn't like the guns either, but she did nothing to stop the boys. I vowed that my children would not have guns to play with, and that they wouldn't be allowed to point even a finger or a stick at an enemy. Sometimes the boys let Carol Grayson and me be the nurses who saved their lives. Or Carol and I pretended we worked in factories where we built airplanes to replace those that were shot down by kamikaze pilots who committed *hari kari* and took out American planes. We heard about some bad people who pretended to be good, like Tokyo Rose who spread propaganda, and Russians who were supposed to be our friends, but we were not so sure.

Like Daddy, Dicky loved airplanes and airports so much that Mother took us to the airport and parked our black Ford at a spot she knew about, where a road ended below the edge of a runway. The airplanes lifted off the ground just feet over our heads. We sat there for hours. In those days, things like airplanes excited people, especially little boys and our mother. We also killed a lot of time at the train depot, not to meet or pick up anyone, but just to watch the trains come and go, or watch freight trains unloaded then reloaded.

The idea of a parachute intrigued me, and I decided to make one. But with nylon in such high demand, I had to use Mother's table cloth with a green border, adorned with daisies and bumblebees. I found the middle of the table cloth and tied string to each corner. I tied a big knot around an old jump-rope handle. When I was ready, I told Dicky, "Go gather up the neighborhood kids who want to watch me float to earth. I'm headed to the brick wall at the corner of Poinsett and Vannoy. I might even let y'all take turns and try it." I imagined a new means of entertainment that would keep all the neighborhood kids happy for hours.

The crowd gathered but consisted only of John, the youngest of the Creech brothers, and Dicky. I must have competed with some very important appointments scheduled for the other children. I slipped up the eight or so steps that took me into the corner neighbor's yard. I tip-toed so they wouldn't notice me or hear my heart beat—they didn't have any children and I didn't know them well enough to ask permission to launch my parachute from the corner of their yard. Also, I think they were the people who complained when we played kick the can in the street in front of their house.

I stood at the corner of the wall and strained to hear Mother call me to come home. She didn't shout our names—she said that was tacky. When we heard her whew-whew whistle, we responded like puppies headed to a kennel. I sort of thought the whistle might save me from the jump, but I heard nothing.

I took the plunge off the wall, but it wasn't high enough to give my chute time to fill with air before I hit the sidewalk. The chute crumpled around my turned ankle. Neither Dicky nor John Creech wanted to try it after my awkward splat. Dicky took little John by the hand, turned, and walked him back home. I realized there were no pinnacles high enough for my parachute in this neighborhood.

I imagined how Jimbo might feel if he had to hobble back to camp in Italy with a failed chute. My crumpled tablecloth and tangled string dragged behind me. The injury didn't hurt that bad, so I didn't tell Mother. Besides, Mother thought it was tacky to cry or express pain when we got hurt, even at the doctor or dentist offices. "Don't let on that it hurts. Be like a soldier. You don't see them holler when they get hurt." Brother Dicky, the smiley, easy-going one, relaxed so much that he once fell asleep in the dentist's chair.

I needed that ankle because we had to save gas during the war. We walked to school, the library, and the cowboy shows at the Rivoli Theatre, the only kind of movie Dicky would go see with me, and he complained to Mother, "I don't like to go with her. She squeals and grabs my arm when she thinks it's scary."

I preferred a musical with Jane and Annelle but settled for Dicky and the cowboys when my cousins weren't available. I liked Roy Rogers and Dale Evans best — maybe Gene Autry, but Sunset Carson was a little sleazy for my taste.

No matter what the movie was, we all got quiet when the Pathé newsreel came on. War news was a duty, like going to church.

Mother's restless nature kept her eager for distractions. When Barnum & Bailey Circus came to town, she woke Dicky and me in what I thought was the middle of the night to go to the tracks and watch the circus unload, then set up for their show. We watched them raise the big top and herd animals past us. Those were some hard-looking people. Mother said, "They look like that because they are on the road all the time, kind of like gypsies, but more honest." Mother had opinions about everyone, and I knew she was wary of gypsies.

I was stunned when I heard that President Roosevelt had died. Mother told us about it after she heard it on the radio. She wrote about it in her diary.

I came home from my weekly grocery shopping on April 12, 1945, and turned on the radio as I started supper. I heard the shocking news bulletin that President Franklin Delano Roosevelt had died with a cerebral hemorrhage at 4:35 PM. It was 5:20 PM when they interrupted with the news. All regular broadcasts were discontinued and there was nothing on the radio from that time until Monday morning except for things about FDR, slow music, hymns, and things about the events in his life. It got boring toward the end, though. The country was officially in mourning for thirty days. He died at the little White House in Warm Springs, Georgia, and Mrs. Roosevelt flew down that night. The next day, his body was taken by train to Washington for the funeral. The train went real slow and every stop it made was broadcast over the radio. It hit Greenville at 6:50 PM and Mayor McCoullough made a short talk. We didn't go down to the station but listened on the radio. Harry S. Truman was vice president, and he became president.

21. Peace

When President Harry S. Truman took over, he killed and injured thousands of people when he had an atomic bomb dropped onto Hiroshima. This is how he celebrated my ninth birthday, August 6, 1945. Three days later, he bombed Nagasaki on Bonnie Hawkins's birthday with the same result. I wished he had picked someone else's birthday, but it seemed to end the war. I hated to think what survivors lived to tell. I went to the concession stand for Milk Duds or Boston Baked Beans when the movie news showed the survivors.

It had just gotten a little dark outside when Mother burst out the door and hollered, "It's over! It's OVER, the war is over!" Other neighbors ran out of their houses too. Mother piled us into our Ford, along with whoever else stood around. The Ford was soon stuffed with neighborhood children. She sent me back into the house to see if Daddy wanted to go, but he had already begun his evening intake and wanted to stay home.

Mother headed downtown to Main Street. She blew the horn the whole time. I don't know why the battery didn't go dead. We crept down our lane of traffic with everyone else who sat on their horns. Several times she yanked up the emergency brake and ran to the sidewalk to hug and kiss friends and strangers too. Maybe Hitler, Mussolini, Hirohito, Churchill, and Franklin Roosevelt should have hugged and kissed, then we wouldn't have found ourselves in this hateful mess.

My Sunday school teacher, Tommy Thomason, said, "Like Jesus, we learn from our suffering and are made stronger," so I guess something good must have come from all this. God knows, Jimbo and the other men surely suffered.

We cruised down Main Street, bumper to bumper, with the rest of Greenville, minus Daddy. We circled back down McBee Avenue, took right turns on Richardson, then College, and back to Main Street again and again. The traffic grew thicker as more people joined the party.

At the next movie show we went to, the Pathé News showed sailors kissing women on the street and families being reunited at the ports. I don't think people realized how anxious and unhappy everyone had been during the war, until we saw how happy we were to have it over.

Jimbo came home for good and brought back a bazooka and a German helmet as souvenirs for our family. Mother, Daddy, and Dicky were in awe of the special gifts, but they told Dicky and me we couldn't tell anyone about them because Jimbo was not supposed to bring things home. I wondered why we wanted a bazooka and helmet if we were not allowed to tell anyone.

Jimbo went back to work at the Chevrolet place. It was not easy to buy cars after the war, but later Jimbo fixed up Daddy with a two-tone green Fleetwood Chevrolet. Daddy loved to surprise us when he bought a new car. We squealed and danced when we saw the surprise. He had strict rules, though. We couldn't eat or rough-house in the car, and we could never touch his driver's seat from behind.

Daddy loved to travel, but Mother told us he didn't make the kind of money needed to take extended trips. The summer I was eleven and Dickie was eight, he took us on a trip across the country for us to see the sights. His goal was to drive to California and back over his two-week summer vacation from work. Mother told us he borrowed against his life insurance policy to be able to take the trip.

All in the span of Daddy's vacation, we saw the Hoover Dam, skipped Las Vegas, which was not a good place for children, saw the Grand Canyon, the Redwood Forest, Yosemite, Yellowstone, and

Mt. Rushmore. The back seat of the Fleetwood Chevrolet provided fleeting glances across country and back to Vannoy Street.

I knew from past experience that it was easy for me to forget home when on a trip, so I picked up a piece of mica from the front yard to help me remember what home was like. I stored it in the ash tray in the back seat. When we arrived at the Sequoia National Forest, I put a cutting from a redwood tree with the mica to help me remember California.

Mother had filled up the back seat with comic books but fussed at Dicky and me because we read the comics rather than looked at the scenes that whirred past our windows. We did, however, look up to read the Burma Shave signs.

Mother's fascination with the postal system should have led her to a stamp collecting hobby, but it was less expensive to collect free postmarks. She started a collection of them for Dicky. She bought a scrapbook at Woolworth's, and in her fancy lettering, she printed the name of each state at the top of the pages in the scrapbook. She helped him cut out the round shapes and paste them onto the appropriate pages. She liked LePage glue with the beveled rubber tip.

Before we left on the trip, she self-addressed a stack of postcards and mailed one home at every opportunity. She made sure she got at least one from each state we entered. As hurried as we were, we had to take time to find a post office in offbeat towns so Mother could mail a postcard to beef up Dicky's collection. Dicky continued to read his comic books throughout these efforts, but it kept Mother busy, which was a good thing.

Aside from the opportunity for Dicky and me to become well-traveled, we visited Dad's long-lost brother, our Uncle William, and his wife, Adelaide, in Yuba City, California. Uncle William worked for a newspaper there. We had to wait for him to come home from work before we went to supper. While we waited, Aunt Adelaide let me look through my cousin Billy's sketch books. I found them to be stunning.

When Uncle William came home, we went downtown to eat. Supper meals started with a snort or two, so Dicky and I whiled away an eternity on the sidewalk outside the bar, while the adults fulfilled their ritual.

When we got back home to Greenville, Mother cornered Dicky and me. "I want you to kiss Daddy on the cheek and tell him good-night when you go to bed each night. He sacrificed a lot by spending so much money on this trip for you."

I preferred acts of affection to be more spontaneous than to pay him back for the trip with hugs and kisses as Mother encouraged us to do, but I did as I was told, at least for a day or two.

⁓

I didn't like how Mother manipulated Daddy. Her encouragement for Dicky and me to gush over him with scripted hugs and kisses instead of unprompted acts of affection was just one example. Perhaps this accounted for my feelings of despondency and my desire to live through the lives of my friends rather than the reality I lived.

22. Crafty Clara

Cars and airplanes were Daddy's passion, but Mother's passion was to make things. She found a new hobby that she did to death. The workers at the dry cleaners, seamstresses, mothers of scouts in her troop, other den mothers, anyone she knew, or anyone she didn't know heard her one-liner, "Save me your wool scraps!" I couldn't count the times we pulled to the curb of Ideal Laundry & Dry Cleaners, honked her horn, and the attendant either waved her on or brought out a pile of unclaimed wool clothing for Mother to recycle into crocheted, braided, or hooked rugs.

After she filled our home with these products, she was on a mission to fill the houses of family and friends, whether or not they wanted or needed handcrafted rugs. Be careful what you teach a rambunctious child. Little did old Miss Ella Mauldin know that her protégé would someday enshroud the world in woven pot holders, crocheted doilies, hooked and crocheted rugs.

I'm not sure what became of the lifetime guarantee on the scratchy brown Olsen rug on our living room floor, but Mother replaced it with her own crocheted wool rug. She started the process while seated in a chair until the handicraft became too large. Then she took to the floor, folded one leg under her, and bent the other leg at the knee, so she could scoot about to crochet her way around a living-room-size oval rug, and later a round one for the dining room.

The leftover scraps were not wasted but were made into smaller rugs. She plopped a large frame across her lap in her scratchy green chair and bought a steel cutter to cut uniform series of strips. As soon as the whole world had a hooked rug, she started to hook placemats for everyone's dinette tables.

Even though quilting has been a skill handed down through generations of Americans, Mother found easier ways to make a quilt. Annelle told her, "Aunt Clara, I want to show you this Cathedral design I have learned to do." Mother tried it but got no farther than making enough folded squares and triangles to make one throw pillow. "It's too slow," she told Annelle.

No tedious, prideful stitches for Mother when she could use her Singer. She slapped a worn-out cotton blanket as batting between a piece of flannel and the squares, then stitched those suckers up. Everybody got one, then two, maybe more. She made crib size, double and twin-bed size, and odd sizes she called throws. The size was determined only by the amount of materials she had on hand at the time.

We drank lots of Dole pineapple juice, Blue Bird orange juice, or Hi-C bought in large tin cans. She arranged the empty cans in a circle and duct-taped them together. She padded the top with cotton batting. She had a pattern to use as a cover for the bundle that resulted in a scallop-shaped footstool.

Mother was introduced to textile painting by a lady who taught classes in a meeting room of the Ottaray Hotel on Main Street. Students equipped themselves with stubby bristle brushes with short wooden handles and jars of paint in various hues. The instructor brought stencils the students could buy. Mother called them "just darling designs." The ladies held the brushes perpendicular to the stencil and stippled the colors onto the fabric of choice or a piece of clothing.

Soon, not a surface in our house went untouched by the technique. She embellished the edges of our pillow cases with bouquets of flowers. Plump pieces of fruit decorated every tea towel. Christmas motifs adorned cocktail napkins and centerpiece doilies for the dining room table. She had a design with a crowd of teenagers who spilled out of a hot rod car, and she stenciled that design onto the back of my windbreaker. She made me a pink flared skirt from a Simplicity pattern. She decorated it around the hem with cowboys and cowgirls. "It's a little much for me to wear the windbreaker on the same day I wear the cowboy skirt," I told her.

"I don't think so at all. They look cute together," she insisted. Mother loved the combination that was as busy as she stayed.

Grandmother & Granddaddy Bell's house
in Renno, South Carolina.

23. Renno

For as long as I can recall, on more Sunday afternoons than not, my cousins Jane and Annelle, Aunt Mary and Uncle Harry, and our family visited our Bell grandparents in Renno. Our cousin Anne and her parents, Aunt Martha and Uncle Chick, lived in nearby Clinton, so they were usually there too. Dicky and Anne played together since they were younger.

One of the Bell ancestors had built a frame house around a two-story log house. I remember that all the paint had peeled off Grandmother and Granddaddy Bell's home place, leaving raw wood rather than paint. Later, they screened in the front porch, painted the house white, and added an indoor bathroom. We were happy they had an indoor bathroom, but in cold weather we dreaded to go in that icy unheated room. Even though they had a new bathroom, our grandparents kept an enamelware pot under their bed. Aunt Mary called it a chamber pot but Mother called it a slop jar.

We sometimes ventured into our grandparents' bedroom to get a peek at a shadow box frame that hung over the mantle. It contained a crown woven of human hair. Mother said, "It was a fad in the olden days to save a woman's hair as a memento of the deceased."

We never saw Grandmother Bell's hair down, but we knew it must be very long. We wanted so badly for her to let us brush it and fix it, but we were not so privileged. Aunt Mary told us, "Ladies only let their hair down in their boudoir."

Cousin Jane said, "I bet Grandmother's hair might someday become a crown in a shadow box."

Annelle and I assumed she was right; she always was. But I questioned whether or not the crown weavers might be as dead as the ancestors. I didn't know a living person who knew how to weave hair into a crown.

Aunt Mary liked for us to wear our Sunday dresses to Renno, to impress her folks. Mother liked for us to change into "play clothes," but we went along with whatever Aunt Mary wanted us to do. The Sunday attire didn't slow down our play. We wore those dresses to the chicken yard where we peeped through fingers splayed over our eyes while Grandmother located the chicken du jour. Thank goodness she was fast—just a crank or two on the chicken's neck like a cowboy swings a lariat.

We played Dorothy from *The Wizard of Oz* and walked around the rail fence of the pig sty in our black suede heels and Sunday dresses. It was an added thrill when Granddaddy came out to feed the hogs. We knew what he was up to when we heard him holler, "Slop, Su-eeeey, Pig, Pig, Pig." The hogs knew too. We saw them flock toward the troughs to see what good stuff had been prepared to fatten them into bacon, pork chops, and country hams.

I remember a space heater that replaced a trash burner in the main room where we entered from the front door. Folks sat in a semi-circle of rockers around the heater to warm their toes. When it was real cold, Granddaddy built a fire in the parlor fireplace, too. This is where Aunt Mary and Aunt Martha hung out. They pulled chairs close to the fire and smoked cigarettes. They blew their exhales up the chimney. Granddaddy must've never known he had two grown daughters addicted to nicotine. I suppose it was all right for his sons to smoke. Daddy didn't have to hide in the parlor.

Mother didn't stay still like the other adults. She was in the main room for a while, out in the yard for a while, and then she might burst into the parlor. She bounded toward the fireplace to lift her skirt and warm her butt in front of the open fire between Mary and Martha. As though she was afraid to miss something, she was hardly there before she left again. A few minutes later she barged into the parlor and ran toward the fire again. Mary and Martha had pitched their newly lit Viceroys into the flames when they heard Mother turn the door knob. They waved the air with the *Progressive Farmer* to disperse their smoke. "Clara, for God's sake! That's the second cigarette you've made me throw into the fire in the last ten minutes. Would you please decide to come or go?" Aunt Mary said. Mother got on Aunt Mary's nerves, but there was nothing I could do about it.

Jane, Annelle, and I played the piano in the parlor and sang from the *Golden Songbook* and *Cokesbury Hymnal*. We also spent countless hours on the second floor of the log house where we rummaged through steamer trunks. Country hams hung like stalactites overhead. We descended the stairs to ask the names of unfamiliar faces on daguerreotypes.

We also ventured up a second set of stairs in the newer section of the house. We slipped the funnies from the fat stack of Sunday's *Greenville News* and settled on feather beds covered in satin-soft white cotton. Grandmother and Granddaddy didn't have overnight guests, so the beds were not used very often. The linens had that unused bed-scent—sort of musty, but sort of crisp and clean, too. The massive oak posts of the bedstead were old and dry from their places upstairs where it was too hot in the summer and too cold in the winter.

Grandmother made all their feather mattresses and down coverlets. They caressed us like a nursemaid who wrapped her arms around us. The warmth of our slight bodies softened the fabric. The fluff whispered "swoosh," as we plopped onto the clouds of feathers.

Cousin Jane pointed out to us a truth that we had never faced before. "You know, don't you, that the feathers in all these mattresses, coverlets, and pillows came from the chickens pinned up out back? Grandmother wrung the necks of all the fried chickens she ever served on Sundays and saved their feathers to stuff inside these linens." Jane had ways to force a dose of reality on Annelle and me in any given situation.

A young woman named Jo was Grandmother's help in the kitchen, but our mothers pitched in, too. Meals were served at a dining room table in one corner of the main room. If there were too many people, the children were fed in the more casual dining room off the kitchen. They placed leftovers on a large table in the middle of that room. A white damask cloth covered the food. Jane, Annelle, and I snitched Grandmother's 50-cent-size biscuits from under the linen cloth all afternoon. They were sweet and light as a cookie with crunchy outer crusts. She was the best cook in the world—even to picky me. I loved her macaroni and cheese, ambrosia, and fried chicken, in spite of the wrung-neck visual. Her fresh coconut cake was a favorite for Daddy and me. She was also known for her canned peach pickles, which she served as a staple. I didn't understand the appetite that everyone held for country ham. To me, it was as though someone spilled the salt shaker onto the meat.

In pretty weather, we tested the rusty chains that held up the porch swing. Granddaddy sat in a rocker with a spittoon next to it. If he looked as though he was about to use the spittoon, Jane said, "Let's go." We didn't like to see him spit into the spittoon.

Granddaddy knew everyone who walked or drove past his house on Sunday afternoons. He knew the white folks that drove by in their cars, but he also knew all the men who walked toward Tip Top, the country store on the highway. If it was close to Christmas, he called out, "Christmas gift!" and they hollered it back to him.

Mother explained, "That is an old custom. The person that first shouts the greeting gets a Christmas present from the one shouted to." I don't think he collected many of those gifts.

About mid-afternoon, Granddaddy took us to Tip Top for ice cream. The country store sat where Bell Road ran into the Whitmire Highway. Our trips to Tip Top ceased once we became teenagers. We wore shorts in the summertime, and Mother explained,

"Granddaddy doesn't want y'all to go down there in shorts where the men hang out."

Mother explained that white people had some fears when it came to their domestic workers, in those days always black people. One of those fears had to do with them as sexual beings—as if the white people were any different. She tried to describe the notion that whites also feared getting diseases from them, so they had them drink from different water fountains, have their own toilets, and such. These attitudes seemed strange to me since the people she described worked for the white people, cooked for them, cared for them when they were sick, and saved their lives when they had whooping cough and pneumonia. I didn't get it.

Granddaddy took us for long walks in the woods because he was the only one who wouldn't get lost. And Granddaddy knew where the good cedar trees grew when we looked for Christmas trees. Sometimes he shouted real loud, and I asked Daddy, "Why is he hollering like that?"

"He thinks he hears some hunters in the distance and wants to let them know we are here so they won't mistake us for deer or other wild animals."

Good idea, I thought. I trusted it to work and hoped there were no deaf hunters around.

Sometimes we took Dicky's Red Ryder BB gun to shoot tin can targets off fence posts in the woods. The older we got, the more often Daddy and Aunt Martha's husband, Uncle Chick, carried a .22 rifle and a shotgun. My shoulder is still sore from when I shot the shotgun without a snug hold against my shoulder.

Our parents told us some of Grandmother Bell's dislikes. "She can't abide laziness or selfishness." So we stifled any such traits in her presence. "But more than laziness and selfishness, she becomes very angry if anyone shoots a songbird in the woods. Nothing upsets her more." We didn't want that either. If someone accidently shot a bird, we were instructed to keep that to ourselves.

24. Gaffney

Mother and Daddy sent me to my Scott grandparents' in Gaffney for visits in the summer. It never occurred to me to wonder why. I spent weeks at a time with my grandparents Pop and Polly and my aunt Edith, four years older than me, and my uncle Jim, two years younger than me. I think they kept Dicky at home because he wet the bed for so long.

The Scotts had a piano in their living room on Petty Street. Polly encouraged me to play for her. Polly told me I was "smart and pretty." She made people feel good about themselves. I never heard her say anything ugly about anyone, even Aunt Aileen, Mother's sister. Everybody loved Polly, except Aileen.

It suited me fine to spend time in Gaffney. I loved to go through Edith's clothes. It was like a walk through the ladies' department at Belk-Simpson. I loved her red plaid taffeta formal.

The Scotts belonged to a golf club with a swimming pool. Edith was as glamorous as Dorothy Lamour without the lei, and she swam like Esther Williams. Her black hair made her look like Snow White with a tan. As a teenager, she had plenty of dwarfs who hung around, too, in the form of teenage boys.

Edith had a record player in her room and we played Ted Weems's "Near You" over and over. She taught me to shag dance. Everyone in South Carolina needed to know how to shag when they were old enough to dance at the pavilions at Myrtle Beach, Ocean Drive, and Pawleys Island, or go to formal dances at the Poinsett Hotel in Greenville. And so I perfected the art through Edith until I reached the appropriate age.

Edith didn't do anything that wasn't cute. Whenever I did something cute, Mother would say, "I wish I was as cute as some people think they are." This was how she let me know I was not cute. Edith said funny things like, "If I don't hurry and shave my legs, I'm going to have to plait them."

Mother told me not to shave my legs, or I would have to do it every few days, but Edith told me, "If you go ahead and shave your legs, it will be too late for her to fuss at you." Edith knew to ask forgiveness rather than permission.

When Edith got into high school, Polly insisted that she take me on her dates. I'm sure Edith didn't want me to tag along, but she didn't complain. At the end of the evening, after her boyfriend Ted had taken us to a movie and for a milkshake at the drive-in, he parked in front of the house. I waited for him to open the door for us, but no one moved. Edith sort of shuffled in her seat, which might have been a hint for me to go inside, but the hint was too subtle, so I just sat there. It occurred to me that they might want to kiss goodnight and I was in the way, so I gazed across the street and counted the red bricks on Buford Street Methodist Church. I hoped Edith and Ted would pretend I wasn't there. After what seemed an interminable length of time, Ted got out of his side of the car and opened my side for me to go in the house.

The Scotts were members at Buford Street Methodist where we went to Sunday school and church. Polly went early to play the piano for one of the Sunday school classes; Edith and I found our way to her classroom.

Their church had a revival one summer. We had to go to church services

Grandparents Polly & "Pop" (Carl) Scott.

every night that week. On the last night the preacher finished his sermon and told the congregation, "Now turn in your hymnal to page 240." The organ began to play "Just As I Am," and the music filled the room.

On about the forth stanza, I realized Edith had popped out of her pew and walked toward the front of the church. So I reacted by sort of running to follow her to the altar where we gave our lives to Jesus Christ. Methodists are big on going to the altar.

After I was grown, Edith told me that I was sent to Gaffney so Mother and Daddy could try to work out some marital problems. At the time, I simply knew that things were peaceful and secure at Pop and Polly's house.

25. A Stretch Toward Maturity

I started junior high school in the red brick building at the foot of McBee Avenue where my parents had gone to high school. The teachers wanted undivided attention in class, but I gazed through the tall metal-clad windows and designed tree limbs inside each pane, or instead of doing math problems, I sat mesmerized when I watched Teddy Davis apply perfect shading to pencil drawings he made.

The popular girls in my class wore Jonathon Logan cotton dresses in Easter egg hues, except for an only child named Janet whose mother was a nurse. Janet's mother had taken her to the shoe store and told the salesman that her daughter was swayback, knock-kneed, and pigeon-toed, so they put her into boys' wingtips to give her something sturdy. She wore plaid skirts with different colored tops.

I looked around my classroom at the other girls and wondered who had started their period and whether I ever would "start." When Janet had the curse, or "pip" as Mother called it, Janet's mother made her wear heavy socks with her wing-tipped shoes, and she wore sweaters even in warm weather on "those days." She couldn't wash her hair during her period either. You could tell it was "her time of the month" by the way she was dressed and how shiny her hair was or wasn't.

We had moved into a brand-new house at 802 Bennett Street in the fall of 1948. Daddy bought a desk where he typed business letters and resumes. He forever searched the want ads for a job that might make him happy. A metal file held copies of his job applications and served as a nightstand next to his bed.

Mother used the desk for her correspondence to friends and relatives when Daddy wasn't at work there. Postcards, letters, and greeting cards kept her from being forgotten or ignored. She had a built-in audience since everyone reads their mail. She sent them chunks of her stick-on address labels so they didn't have to write out her address. She also asked friends for chunks of their labels for her use. This was before word processors, and before Avery came out with Template #5267; she was ahead of her time again.

Her fleeting thoughts were jotted down and punctuated with lots of "HA"s in place of an emoji. When she finished with the last of a stack of postcards, she jumped into the car to rush them to the downtown post office. On a card to her cousin Mildred in Hendersonville, she neglected to fill in whatever message had flown in and out of her mind. Mildred received a blank card and wrote back to ask, "What did you say?"

———

When I turned twelve Daddy told me, "I was driving by your age. Would you like to learn to drive?" We went out early Sunday mornings when traffic was at a minimum. I just knew I could do this, especially after I watched how easy it was for Edith when Mother let her drive around Cleveland Park.

It was not enough to sit behind the wheel, know where the pedals were, and how to change gears; I endured long lectures on cylinders, pistons, spark plugs, oil gauges, brake shoes, drive shafts, and how an engine worked. I won points when I laid on my back and helped him change the muffler on our maroon Ford. When I turned fourteen, I was more than prepared to get my driver's license on my birthday.

We made biannual shopping trips to Atlanta each spring and fall. While we shopped with Mother at Rich's and Davison's, Daddy took the car to a garage to have muffler experts put dual exhausts on his new navy-blue Mercury sedan. The duals gave me a savvy reputation with some of the boys I knew, and once I got my license, I never turned down a challenge to "scratch off" or drag race at traffic lights. That was as close to cool as I came.

My cousins got their licenses by age fourteen, too. But Jane didn't really like to drive. Aunt Mary B. had never learned to drive and depended on Annelle to drive her to the grocery store, beauty shop, and to their monthly Daughters of the American Revolution meetings. On the way to a meeting, Aunt Mary settled into the shotgun seat of their little white Plymouth. Annelle pulled away from the curb and flinched when Aunt Mary shrieked, "Stop."

Annelle slammed on the brakes. Aunt Mary's slippery silk dress lined with an equally slick slip nearly dumped her into the floor because seatbelts had not come into use. "What, Mother?"

Aunt Mary pointed straight in front of her and shouted, "Can't you see that?"

Annelle looked at the windshield. "You mean the bird dookie? I saw it, but I figured the next rain would get it." Annelle shifted into first.

"Stop the car! We can't go to a DAR meeting with bird dookie on the windshield!" Aunt Mary B. shrieked.

Annelle's people-pleasing persona made her pull to the curb, go into the house for a damp paper towel, and wipe the excrement away. She had to scrub harder at the dried edges. Back in the house she threw the towel away and washed her hands, now well mindful that no lady would go to DAR with bird dookie on her windshield.

26. The Kitchen Table

Mother, Daddy, Dicky, and I went over to the Powells' for supper on Aunt Mary's birthday, September 5, 1950. Daddy warned us, "Don't mention it being Aunt Mary B.'s birthday."

"Why not?" we asked.

"She's not too happy about getting older," he said.

Mother chimed in. "Some women don't like to celebrate when they get into their forties." She herself was nothing like "some women." She relished her birthdays.

I had heard Mother say, "Mary B.'s main role in the family is to be the self-appointed worrier, and she does a real good job at it."

Oh, Lord, I thought, if Aunt Mary's in a bad mood, then Daddy's liable to get angry too.

Daddy argued a lot with his older sister and often came away from her house mad about something. When Daddy was in a bad mood, everyone had to be quiet so as not to antagonize him.

I knew we'd find Uncle Harry in the kitchen. He made a pot of spaghetti whenever we came over. He called Daddy to fix them a drink. I walked into the den and saw Aunt Mary in her rocking chair in front of the television, her left hand wrapped around the fat of her right upper arm. A filter-tipped Viceroy draped between two fingers. Her right hand rattled the ice that cooled her cocktail; this was the pose she struck every time we went to their house.

She handed Mother a new pack of snapshots. "You want to see the photos Jane's boyfriend took of her at the beach?"

Aunt Mary doted on Jane, who seemed way older than I felt. Annelle and I nicknamed Jane "The Jewel" because she was so precious in Aunt Mary's eyes. With a sister who looked like Elizabeth Taylor, Annelle competed by making people laugh. I didn't have a sister to compete with, just a mother, and that was a race I couldn't win.

Mother didn't hide the fact that she thought Jane had a prissy streak. Mother liked Annelle better and didn't deny that Annelle was her favorite of the three of us. I took advantage of this and asked, "Can Jane and Annelle come spend the night with us tonight?" I whispered to Mother, "It might give Aunt Mary time to get over her birthday blues."

When we got back to our house, Annelle and Jane in tow, I asked if we could pop some corn. We hadn't bought an electric popper, so Mother used a lidded pot that saturated the kernels of corn in a blob of Wesson oil. She rotated the pot over the hot burner.

"I wonder what would happen if the lid wasn't on the saucepan," Mother mused. I knew that Mother didn't wonder about things very long before she found out for herself. First, we heard a puny pop of a kernel or two, but when the corn reached its peak, Mother lifted the lid.

Puffs of corn hit the ceiling, bounced all over the kitchen table, onto the top of the fridge, landed on the floor, and into the pots of African violets and begonias she rooted in the window sill. We squealed and tried to catch kernels in our open mouths.

"Get the broom and dust pan, and y'all get this stuff cleaned up, Betty," Mother chuckled as she helped herself to a bowl of popped corn and left the kitchen to plop in front of our new television set.

About this time, food coloring came on the market. No food went untouched by Mother's ingenious uses of the new-fangled hues. She never learned that too much of a good thing was pretty much too much.

My intake of color-coded food destroyed my appetite. If Dicky and I grew tired of cornflakes, we were introduced to cornflakes with blue milk. We were served red coconut sprinkled over green Jell-O, even when Christmas was months away. She turned our hard-boiled eggs Dr. Seuss green with a drop or two in the cooling water. Dicky's Lionel electric train didn't escape either. With a drop of red into the smokestack, the puffs of smoke turned pink.

Colorful food was more of a treat to Jane and Annelle, who experienced the rainbow menus only at our house. Jane's favorite dish of Mother's was an imitation of a fried egg on toast. Mother bought rectangular pound cakes at the Dixie Home grocery store. A toasted slice on a dessert plate was crowned with half of a canned peach, flat side down, to simulate the yoke, which was surrounded with whipped cream that she squirted from a can.

Mother was no Betty Crocker. She opened many a can of Van Camp pork and beans or LeSeur English peas and served them with fried Vienna sausages and sliced tomatoes from the curb market or plants she grew in a bed by the driveway. She did have a green thumb and grew tomatoes that challenged *Ripley's Believe It or Not.*

The sunlight through the kitchen windows nourished huge African violets. The plants began with someone else's leaf laid on fertile soil in a pot. Most of our shrubbery started as sticks cut from someone else's shrubs that she stuck in the ground. The sticks always flourished.

She bought berries from a farmer who pulled his truck into our driveway and tapped on his horn. She washed and drained the fruit in a colander, put them into the white crock with brown stripes, and covered them with a heavy sprinkling of sugar. I knew just how long to let them sit before I snitched a few berries.

She made a point of being at home on milk delivery days, so she could pass on a joke to Clyde the milkman. She had a wooden disc with a straw-like siphon attached through the middle. After the cream rose to the top of the milk, she opened the bottle cap and pressed the disc into the cream to siphon it into a cup at the crooked end of the straw. We loved a dollop of whipped heavy cream on top of the sugared strawberries or blackberries.

On Saturdays, she helped me make my bed so we could rush to the curb market before the good stuff was picked over. One time she picked up one of the same pillows she had placed on either side of me the night before. She threw it and hit me in the face with a soft thud. I had just placed my hands on my hips and opened my mouth to ask, "Why are we always in such a hurry?"

After fourteen years on this earth, I still had to run behind my mother and wonder how I fit into her unpredictable existence. When I caught my breath, I realized I hadn't gotten an answer to the "why" other than her evil chuckle at my unamused expression from a pillow in the face. We continued to rush wherever we went.

Mother whirled through life like a dervish, but Daddy was never in a hurry. He was deliberate, and he calculated every move, lest he make a mistake, which never happened. Thank goodness Daddy didn't rush, because I wouldn't have had the nerve to ask him why he rushed.

When we arrived at the curb market, we stepped onto the concrete floor and dodged rivulets of water. Puddles formed where a lady watered potted geraniums, zinnias, and marigolds until they peed on the floor. The corrugated tin roof of the huge shelter trapped the green scent of squash, hairy okra, cucumbers, string beans, butter beans, and corn still hidden by its own silk and green husks that cut you like blades if you weren't careful. Mother headed toward the bin of Big Boy tomatoes grown by Stanley, the farmer who hauled produce from his farm out toward Paris Mountain. The tomatoes were enormous and begged to be sliced or diced. Mother and Stanley exchanged ideas.

Stanley told Mother, "I cook them, add leftover sweet corn, baby butter beans, and okra slimy enough to slide down your gullet without being chewed good. You just can't beat good old succotash." When he talked about it, I saw a little drool glisten and run through creases in his skin before it disappeared into the black and gray beard that hid Stanley's chin.

Mother countered, "I put a thick slice of tomato on a wedge of black-skillet cornbread right out of the oven." She left off the part about the huge blob of Duke's mayonnaise she slathered on the cornbread and how she shook so much salt and pepper on the slice that it hid the innards.

We didn't have separate salt and pepper shakers on our table like ordinary people. Mother combined both salt and pepper in a small Ball jar and punched holes in the lid. It saved shaking time. She also invented pre-mixed peanut butter and grape jelly, a product later seen on shelves at the A&P.

I had seen Mother chomp into the layers of her cornbread as though it was dessert. I watched as the pressure of her teeth made the mayonnaise squeeze from between the tomato slice and the coarse yellow bread. It settled in the corners of her Helena Rubenstein cherry red lips. Somehow this ritual didn't entice me, picky eater that I was. I was grown and gone before I learned to appreciate a juicy tomato sandwich.

"You eat like a bird" was the judgment I heard at every meal, except for fried-chicken Sundays, or when Mother and Daddy had their gang of friends bring a steak over on Saturday nights. Dicky and I ate alone at the kitchen table while the grownups downed their beer or bourbon.

One of the gang had given Daddy glass tumblers that were a big hit. Daddy kept them with his liquor. I examined them one time when he wasn't around. The outside of each glass had a pin-up picture of a pretty lady in an elaborate costume. After you drank the contents of the glass, the inside revealed a naked woman.

Maybe on a Sunday when we had fried chicken served with rice and gravy or potato salad and the whole family ate in the kitchen, Mother might use a tablecloth. The colors matched her set of Fiestaware, usually saved for the dining room and spaghetti suppers with the gang or when Pop and Polly came over. I loved to set the table with the festive dishes and mix-match the colors into pleasing arrangements.

At the kitchen table, Mother sat to my right, closest to the stove. Dicky was opposite me, in front of the windows. Daddy sat across from Mother on the other long side. I set the table with the silver-plate flatware kept in the drawer on Mother's side. Mother hopped up often, to get the forgotten butter, to move the uni-shaker from the stove to the table, or to serve second helpings. This irritated Daddy. "Clara, for once I'd like for you to bring everything to the table before you sit down, so you won't have to pop up and down every few minutes." She couldn't do it.

After work and before weeknight dinners, Dad might crouch too often in the opposite corner of the kitchen where he kept the bourbon and the naked women tumblers. On those evenings, I slinked toward the enamel table with dread. Mind your own business and excuse yourself to your room, was Dicky's tack. When he was old enough to drive, he excused himself from the table and drove to the Clock Drive-In for a hamburger and vanilla shake in the Jeepster he had bought with his paper boy savings. He wasn't into Mother's cooking and was ravenous all the time.

When Dicky disappeared, I was left to wonder, would this be the meal when Daddy repeated his threat to squeeze a grapefruit half into Mother's face? I asked Mother one time while I set out the flatware, "Why does Daddy talk about squeezing a grapefruit in your face lots of times?"

"Years ago he saw James Cagney do that in the movie *Public Enemy*."

"Why would he want to do that?"

"I guess he thinks it would be a clever way to put me in my place," she said.

He excused his temper and blamed Mother by saying that she provoked him. I lived in constant dread. Will this be one of those nights when Mother "got his goat"? Will he want to debate some issue with me? Will I be able to avoid the fray when he baits me for an argument?

I suppose I should have felt grateful when he said, "Our debates will train you to someday be one of the first lady lawyers."

Did he love me so much that he thought his attacks would strengthen me? Would I have to remain at the table until he finished his diatribe? Did he know that this harsh attention tied my stomach into knots?

As Daddy's rants grew harsher, even Mother became reticent at dinner, so out of her bubbly comfort level.

Another winter came. Snow covered the ground. We had out-grown the sled inherited from Mother, so she got a screwdriver and dismantled the painted legs from the kitchen table. We trudged toward Hillcrest Drive, plopped our bodies in tandem on the underside of the enamel-topped table. Mother ran behind like a bobsled Olympian before she jumped on the back—no rudder to guide this contraption. The white shroud of snow announced, "A new beginning and another day to wonder where the kitchen table will take us next."

27. Ballrooms to Beach Dunes

Greenville Senior High School was built in 1936, the year I was born. It stood on a green hill off Augusta Road. I started there at age fifteen in 1951. My cousins Jane and Annelle went there, too.

Jane grew into the Elizabeth Taylor look-alike beauty just as Aunt Mary had predicted. She was very popular at school. She made sure Annelle and I were included in all the right activities. Through Jane, and Aunt Mary's social connections, I had been invited to join the Elfa Sorority in junior high and I followed Jane as a member of the Philaphronian Club in high school. I was dependent on Jane and Aunt Mary to know how to involve myself in all the right activities. Mother considered these clubs or pseudo-sororities to be snooty.

Algie Brown & Betty, age 17, at the Philaphronian Valentine's Dance, 1954.

We met in the home of a member every Sunday afternoon to plan social events and benevolent civic activities. We avoided the snobbish label through volunteer work in the community. We were asked by the Community Chest to take surveys in the slums, two by two. We knocked on doors of shanties near the high school and asked personal questions like how many people lived there and how many rooms and bathrooms they had.

We organized square dances, hayrides to the mountains, and house parties at Myrtle Beach, Ocean Drive, or Pawleys Island. We played hostess to elaborate formal dances in the Poinsett Hotel ballroom. The hostess sorority members and their dates processed through an arched trellis decorated with ivy and flowers for a grand march. We danced under the crystal ball and brought in big-name bands. My favorites were Ray Anthony, Charlie Spivak, and Stan Kenton. My favorite slow dance was to "Tenderly."

I didn't have a steady boyfriend during high school; come to think of it, I had never had any kind of boyfriend at that point in my teens. It wasn't easy to invite boys to dances and parties or find one who could accommodate my 5' 8" in flats. I watched the 6' 4" Brothers boy who starred on the basketball team, but he just looked right over my head when we passed in the halls. There was one neighborhood boy that made my heart leap, but he worked at one of the mills after school and couldn't go to the dances and hayrides. His family moved back to Tennessee and that was over.

A guy named Jo-Jo crashed every dance anyone ever hosted. Toward the end of the dance, he and several of his cronies dropped by. A buzz of "here comes Jo-Jo" spread through the ballroom when they appeared. The other guys were larger than the slight-framed Jo-Jo, but you could see that Jo-Jo was the leader. They ambled around the perimeter of the dance floor and stopped at Jo-Jo's signal. We watched him remove his overcoat, fold it across the extended arm of the largest bodyguard, and without a word, take the hand of one of the most popular girls. The head cheerleader was a good choice. He led her to the center of the dance floor where they shag-danced, encircled by the rest of us. Even the band members perked up and watched. He has since gone down in history as one of the best old-time shag dancers and was inducted into the Beach Shaggers Nations Hall of Fame in 1985. I can impress ardent shaggers when I tell them I went to high school with Jo-Jo.

The local radio station started to play rhythm and blues music at 3:30, when classes were over. The Lindy Hop and R&B led into what we called beach music, the music we shag-danced to. Legend tells of a night spot for blacks in Columbia where whites who watched from the balcony of that dance hall adapted what they saw into the shag dance.

Mother discouraged my listening to that kind of music, but I managed to listen when she wasn't around and on the jukeboxes at the beach in the summers.

Trips to the beach were pretty safe in those days. Local people allowed us to sleep on their porches if we came down the day before our designated check-in day. We liked to be early so we could move in to our rented house and not waste a precious moment at the beach.

Most of the boys who came from Greenville slept on people's porches, in their cars, on the beach, or wherever they could find a spot. But the label "beach bum" was reserved for the local guys and dancers like Jo-Jo who hung out all summer and danced at Spivey's rather than at the Pavilion. They bleached their hair and brushed it into "ducktails" in the back. The nickname "Whitey" was pretty common. They also made the rounds of the girls' house parties, and we danced with them into the wee hours. The next day, large blisters popped out on the balls of my bare feet.

Just before we left for the beach the summer after my junior year at Greenville High, Dad kept me seated at the kitchen table after supper. "I know you don't think that smoking cigarettes is bad for you since I smoke, and I know some of your friends have started smoking. But I want to make a deal with you." I squirmed and wondered what was next.

"If you will wait until you turn twenty-one, I will give you a nice reward."

That sounded easy enough at the time, so I agreed to fulfill my end of this pact. "I can do that," I said to him.

Once my friends and I got to the beach, several of them experimented with cigarettes and the peer pressure overcame reason. It wasn't really serious smoking since none of us tried to inhale at that point. We simply lit them and puffed at them a little until they burned down. The very first day that I tried it, I lit sixty-six cigarettes. Later that evening one of the girls told a guy that hung out with us, "Betty smoked sixty-six cigarettes on the first day she smoked."

The guy stared my way and said, "God, I'd hate to be around when she starts drinking."

Later that week, Dad came down on business and took me to a nice dinner at the Ocean Forest Hotel in North Myrtle Beach. My conscience prompted my confession, and I never received the nice reward. I often wondered what it might have been.

Even though I was on a college preparatory track, Mother arranged with the school counselor for me to get out of school early for a job at Myers-Arnold Department Store as assistant to the sportswear buyer. I was to save the money I made for college and buy clothes with my employee's discount to help with expenses. My junior and senior years, I left school early, caught the bus downtown, and worked at the store every day except Sundays, when they were closed. The job was not so bad except when I wanted to do other things.

28. The Threats

My very particular father often stood me, and sometimes Dicky, before his maroon throne for inspection before we left for church on Sundays. Mother, on the other hand, couldn't have cared less if our socks were rolled down crooked, a slip showed, whether or not people could see through my dress without a slip, or if my blouse had been pressed. Mother had decided that the new self-service launderette could replace our washerwoman Daisy and save some money, but neither she nor I wanted to iron our cotton clothes. She had no plans to teach me how to look presentable, so I was on my own to pass muster with Daddy. Yet no one enjoyed dressing up for the camera more than Mother. She played the role of the jack-in-the-box who popped out at inappropriate times and places. I tried hard to hold down the lid of that box.

Clara, age 45, in 1958.

I was the target when Daddy imposed his unbendable standards. "Anyone can make a C. That's why they call them average, and you are better and brighter than the average person. There's no excuse for falling short of your potential," he preached. Even a B drew a lecture. Mother didn't care about our grades in school, other than to keep Daddy happy. As I matured, I realized Daddy was too precise and particular for his own good, and his rigidity affected my sense of well-being.

Daddy's gang of Runt, Tokey, Jimbo, Hugh, and their wives became busier with their own families and came by less often. But Daddy didn't seem to need his cronies now. He drank each evening without them. Sometimes he limited the sessions to a few beers, but other times, when he had what he called the "mulligrubs" or the doldrums, he resorted to the hard stuff kept under the counter next to the fridge.

A strange car was parked in our driveway on a Sunday afternoon when I came home. I went inside and saw our preacher, Dr. Smith, seated on the sofa in the living room. He looked different without his long black robe and the King James Bible in his hand. He sat on the jungle-print slip covers in a navy blue suit, his hands folded at his knees. Daddy sat in his usual place and Mother looked stiff, balanced on the edge of one of the ladder-back chairs by the fireplace. Other than a handshake after church, I had never spoken with Dr. Smith, so I nodded to him and tried to make it to my room without seeming impolite. Then I realized he had said his goodbyes. I watched him and Mother ease toward the front door.

As the door clicked shut again, I heard Daddy say, "What the hell did you do that for, Clara?"

"I just thought you might need some advice from him, since you are so unhappy in your job."

Mother's explanation disguised the fact that Dad's unhappiness led toward more excessive drinking. His boss at Judson Mills had passed him over, several times, when promotions should have come Dad's way.

After Dr. Smith's visit, Daddy refused to go back to Sunday school and church and retired as secretary to the board of stewards. He sulked over the audacity of the minister who had butted in on our personal lives. I heard him tell Mother, "Dr. Smith needs to mind his own business." Mother's efforts had backfired, and Daddy continued to complain about the people he worked with at the mill, especially the boss he resented.

In spite of my ignorance of physics, I do know that two magnetic entities have the ability to attract or repel each other. I read in a magazine that, indeed, opposites do attract; however, two people can be so different that they have few opportunities to meet in the middle where a strong union might develop. I began to see that the frenzy present in Mother's life and my father's perfectionism got in the way of their meeting at the equator of their marriage.

<hr>

When my friend Gwen and I were seniors at Greenville High, in the fall of 1953, we stayed downtown to watch the Thanksgiving parade. Spectacular floats rolled by and bands marched down Main Street to open the Christmas shopping season. The segregated Greenville and Parker High Schools couldn't compete with the marching band from the black Sterling High School. The Sterling band marched toward the end of the parade, not because of segregation but because they revved up the crowd for Santa, who rode on the last float. We could hear the music from as far away as the Ottaray Hotel. Their drums set the beat of the crowd's gigantic heartbeat. The spectators stirred as the sound moved toward us. We heard the applause billow down Main Street as the Sterling High drum major and their majorettes came into view.

Their show made the white schools' bands look like a corps of inflexible tin soldiers. The Sterling band didn't just march, they jived down the street with exaggerated dips and strolls to the beat. What better way to introduce Santa than this?

Gwen and I wiggled into the crowd at the foot of Washington Street where it intersected Main. Gwen drew attention as the "pretty one" when we were together, but this time we didn't seek looks from the scruffy man who seemed to follow us. When we moved to be closer to the front of the crowd, he moved too, until he was directly behind us. The man moved closer and wedged his body against us. After feeling his body gyrate against me, I turned to glare at him; his grin showed yellow teeth. His eyes were green under bushy eyebrows, and a billed cap tried to hide curly reddish hair. Pimples and a day-old beard covered his ruddy face. He wore a dirty tan windbreaker over a plaid shirt and smelled like a drunk. We were repulsed and frightened as his movements seemed more aggressive. Gwen and I sent messages to each other with our eyes before she pushed through the crowd like a flying wedge. I grabbed her belt with both hands and followed her. We drew looks from the spectators we knocked out of our way, but we escaped the obnoxious creep who had violated the space of two teenage girls. Seeing Santa and the Sterling High School Band seemed trivial next to an escape.

"We'll have to walk home. The buses won't run until the parade is over," I told Gwen. "Let's get off Main and go around all these people."

We ran until we reached Park Avenue and walked five more blocks at a brisk pace. I said goodbye to Gwen at Galvin Avenue and continued another long block up Bennett Street.

The trudge home hadn't lightened the trauma. I stood in the dining room. I sobbed, wiped my swollen red eyes, and told Mother what had happened. I heard Dad's Mercury turn onto the gravel driveway and glimpsed the car when it passed the dining room window. Mother met him in the kitchen and gave him a preview of what I had been through. He burst through the swinging door from the kitchen and demanded "What did you do to egg on such behavior from that man?"

I racked my brain to understand his question and asked, "What … what do you mean? We went to the Thanksgiving parade."

He muttered, "You bleached your hair like Frances at my office who comes to work with different dye jobs every time I turn around."

Did he call Frances and me tramps? Does a change of hair color make me a tramp? I had put peroxide on my hair at Ocean Drive Beach last summer.

"Daddy, I never enticed … He was a disgusting drunk man," I said, my eyes wide from his accusation.

Then Daddy back-handed my right cheek. My head slammed into the door jamb between the kitchen and dining room. The corner edge creased my left ear and I heard a loud ring. The edge of the door hurt more than the actual slap but not as much as his words. My father had called me a slut.

Like a chameleon, Mother blended in with the jungle-print slip covers, invisible. Daddy walked toward the kitchen corner where he kept the liquor. About that time, Dicky came in the back door. His expression didn't change, but he sensed trouble; he went straight to his room.

I knew the drinks would make Daddy angrier, so I mumbled in his direction, "May I be excused?" I followed the path Dick took and went to my room. I closed the door without a sound. I left Mother to settle matters, but the discourse through the thin walls told me she was unable to calm the storm that I had brought home from the Thanksgiving parade. Fear surged through my stomach, and I longed for silence from the muffled voices. I pretended this was happening to someone else, not me. It didn't work.

I couldn't focus on geometry and tears blurred the words in my book.

Later, I heard Mother whisper outside my door, "Do you want something to eat?"

"No, thank you." I kept a box of Toll House cookies hidden in a drawer.

I sensed when to turn off my light after the muffled words heard through the walls subsided. I knew that meant Daddy was preparing to go to bed. I heard a tap on my bedroom door. Daddy tiptoed into my darkened room for a moment. He never spoke, and I did my best imitation of a hungry, sleeping teenager. I hoped that the ruckus had ended, and the pillows around me could absorb any further battle.

~

Tensions continued to intensify with each groan of discontent during my teen years. Even though he looked comfortable, hunkered down into the feather cushions of his easy chair, a closer look into his eyes and at his clenched jaw revealed the passion, and Dad's moodiness escalated. When he finally let out his feelings, it was like fire spewed from a dragon's tongue. His words pulsated like a relentless pound of a drum. Finally, he threw down words like a gauntlet to test our ability to cope.

"I think the best thing I can do is get a gun, put it in my mouth, and fire it."

I couldn't believe this was the same father who played "Chopsticks" with me on the piano and taught me to dance by letting me stand barefoot atop his feet. If I couldn't watch sad or violent movies without being haunted for weeks, how could I bear to hear his words? This was no movie. How could he be so tormented and still be the Dad I knew, the man so strong and all-knowing, the man who never made a mistake?

I don't think I heard those ominous words from his mouth until we lived on Bennett Street. It was hard to tell what Dick heard and saw. I don't believe he allowed himself to absorb the threats because he slipped into his room and closed the door. Mother, too, became quiet, a silence strange for her, as Daddy's moods worsened.

Daddy's words of self-hatred were repeated as part of a ritual. How were we supposed to deal with this? If Mother didn't know what to do, I certainly didn't know. It hadn't worked when she called Dr. Smith from Buncombe Street Methodist. It just increased Daddy's broodiness and self-loathing fury.

Part 3

...And the end of all our exploring
will be to arrive where we started,
and know the place for the first time.

T.S. Eliot

29. Out of the House

We heard Mother's warning as we matured, "You have got to take care of your stuff, because we don't have the money to replace things."

Daddy told us we could have anything we needed. "You can go to whichever college you chose, but you have to do the research and decide where you want to go," he said. He didn't comprehend that at age seventeen I didn't have the maturity to be in charge of that decision. I chose Stephens College in Columbia, Missouri, because Jane told me, "Movie stars send their daughters there and they offer horseback riding."

I changed my mind when Mother told me, "It is so expensive that movie stars are the only people who can afford to send their children there."

Mother's solution was for me to go to Queens College in Charlotte, North Carolina. She said, "They offer a two-year Secretarial Administration associate's degree. That ought to be enough to get a job—no need to get a BA. If Queens doesn't suit you, there's nothing wrong with staying home and going to Furman. That would save us a lot of money."

She was right. I could have joined millions of Baptists in Greenville and attended Furman University right under my nose. So I went to Queens College, a hundred miles from my burgundy-colored bedroom on Bennett Street. I began my freshman year in the fall of 1954, in a new environment, but the old one still preyed on my mind.

Before I left home, Mother found it necessary to teach me to play the game of bridge and to drink coffee, so I would feel comfortable at the compulsory "After Dinner Coffee" soirees in Queens College's Burwell Hall on Friday evenings. Mother even sat me down at the kitchen table and split a beer with me. "This is to teach you what a buzz feels like before you are away from home," she said, but I had read in the catalog that Queens shipped ladies home if they partook of alcoholic beverages on or off campus. I drank the half beer anyway.

Mother wrote letters and told me, "Be sure you get your money's worth. It's not easy for Daddy on his salary," and she enclosed five dollars a month for extras. She had taken a job at the pharmacy near our house to help out with finances.

I hated to let her know "I ran out of money and need Kleenex for a runny nose" or "I'm out of toothpaste."

I accumulated a wardrobe with the money I earned at Myers-Arnold Department Store. I used my discount on a red wool jer-

Betty, age 18, in front of the Bennett Street house.

sey dress with matching jacket and a flat beret that perched on top of my head. It had a Robin Hood feather that pointed diagonally toward anyone or anything that followed me. This outfit could make a male cardinal jealous.

Even though Queens ladies were not allowed to drink alcoholic beverages, I bought a token cocktail dress in bronze taffeta with a black soutache braid that trimmed the empire waist and the edge of an inverted pleat at the front. I took the blue and brown wool tweed trench coat I had worn through high school. It could have kept a Russian toasty on a Siberian morning. I used the coat in the spring to conceal my red Campbell-clan plaid Bermuda shorts when I crossed front campus where shorts were forbidden.

Lib, a Greenville girl and a rising sophomore at Queens, was assigned to be my big sister. It was her job to help me make the hurdle from home to college life. During this age of young women who looked for an M.R.S. degree, Lib advised me, "Take every blind date that comes your way."

I knew the M.R. types, specifically the men from Davidson College, just twenty thumbing miles north of Charlotte, would not be interested in a gawky girl like me, the opposite of Lib. I doubted Lib ever worried about her social life. The Greenville High *Nautilus* yearbook had pictured her in the "Beauties" section every year, and she was a cheerleader.

I had heard the stories about a mile-long line of beaus at Mother's doorstep when she was young. They vied for her attention or offered a date to a dance. In contrast to Mother and Lib, I spent hours at my dresser and gazed at my scrawny self in the mirror. I practiced imaginary conversations to use when I mustered the courage to invite an unattached boy to a Sadie Hawkins Day party. On actual dates, I threw out clever lines to deaf ears and heard Mother's voice in my head, "I wish I was as cute as some people think they are."

I grew weary of blind dates by December, but Rose from down the hall came to my room and begged me to go out with her sorority sister's brother, Charles. The sister was a big wheel on campus, president of the senior class, and she roomed with the student body president—more than enough to scare this lowly freshman. "It's for a Sigma Phi Epsilon party at the Policemen's Club."

"If you check with everyone else on the hall and can't find anyone, I'll think about it," I said. I should have known she would take this as a "yes."

I wore my hair rolled up in socks all day. I slipped the bronze taffeta over three crinoline slips. When I reached for my tweed trench coat, my suitemate Kit grabbed the bulky coat, tossed it aside, wrapped me in her mink jacket, and insisted that I wear it. The rustle of taffeta over my slips and the clomp of my black suede pumps echoed across the courtyard toward Burwell Hall, where I met my date, Charles Brown. He and his Sig Ep brother Ken met me and Ken's date Mickey in the south parlor of Burwell. As was his routine on party weekends, Charles had borrowed the two-toned Chrysler from his Uncle Buck, who lived in the Brown family homeplace near Davidson.

Charles was talkative and came up with clever remarks, comfortable in the company of his Sig Ep brother Ken. We danced the night away, which I loved. Looking back, it occurs to me that I'm not sure Charles has ever been that lively, clever, conversant, or danced quite that well since. But he was in good form that Saturday night.

Queens girls had to sign in at Burwell Hall by midnight on Saturdays. Upper-class Davidson boys knew these rules. They returned to campus early, then waited for the curfew in the nearby parking lot of Myers Park Baptist Church. Charles knew this trick and mumbled something about curfew as he whipped into an empty space. Under the watchful eye of the Baptist steeple, Mickey and Ken were already going strong in the back seat. We rolled down our windows a little so they wouldn't fog up. Mother's axiom popped into my head. I had heard it so many times, "Never kiss a boy on the first date. You will seem too easy." It worked for her, and it wasn't difficult for me, since no one tried to kiss me on first dates.

Charles followed Ken's lead however, and jumped in with a passionate smooch onto the lips of the same head in which Mother's admonition bounced around. He never gave me a chance to hold his interest with the "too easy" strategy.

The pressure of Charles's passionate kiss had mashed my face against the edge of the partially rolled down window. Worrying about wrinkles in my bronze taffeta seemed minor next to the excruciating pain on my cheek bone. I did derive pleasure in the thought that Charles might be attracted to his taffeta and fur-clad date, but I wondered how I could let him know about the agonizing pain on the side of my face. I barely knew him well enough to just come out and say, "You are mashing my face into the edge of the window." So, I suffered and waited for a pause and a shift in my position.

I put my hand to my cheek when I walked through Burwell and back to Morrison Dorm. No one noticed until I reached the room.

My roommate Betty Ann looked at me funny. "What's that red mark on your cheek?"

~

I accepted Charles's heart-shaped Sigma Phi Epsilon pin by the following spring. I wore it just above the Maidenform peak of my left bosom, to signify that we were engaged to be engaged. My freshman year at Queens College was where I found my future husband Charles and my escape from the confines of a small bungalow in Greenville, South Carolina, where Lucky Strikes and Schlitz permeated my father's easy chair throne. A loyal subject, I had for seventeen years walked a narrow path between Dad's explosive temper and Mother's frenetic behavior. I felt relieved that home was behind me, but I worried about the situation I had left.

30. The Escape

Charles continued to thumb and catch rides from Davidson to Charlotte on weekends. To spend time with him seemed natural. Once I tried to break up to make sure there was no one else out there for either of us, but he wouldn't hear of it. I guess the relationship felt comfortable to him too.

I had landed a job as a private secretary for a Davidson grad, not much older than Charles, at Blythe Brothers Construction Company in Charlotte. I wore an aqua chambray Jonathan Logan summer suit with a peplum and portrait collar to the interview. My short white gloves fastened with pearl buttons at the wrist. My white straw hat had a brim like the wingspread of a seagull.

Charles and I planned to marry as soon as he graduated, on June 16, 1957, Father's Day. I replaced my father with someone kind and gentle. I worked in Charlotte until Charles fulfilled his obligation to Uncle Sam at Fort Jackson, and I commuted to Columbia on weekends. I was twenty years old and he was twenty-two.

Eight months later, we moved to Charles's home in Ivanhoe, North Carolina, northwest of Wilmington. His plan was to work in the Brown family wholesale lumber business. Ivanhoe was not the most exciting place to live, but I likened us to Ruth and Boaz and adopted Ruth's "whither thou goest" outlook.

It took me all morning to prepare a big meal for my new husband who came home from the mill for lunch each day. The rest of the afternoon made me stir-crazy, so I sat on the front porch steps with my eyes closed and tried to recognize the sound of his car engine. I thought having children might cure my loneliness and efforts proved fruitful—it didn't take but one unprotected try to get me pregnant.

I endured a long labor and thought of how Mother coached us to stifle expressions of pain. "It is tacky to holler out when treated by a doctor or dentist." We named our firstborn Elizabeth and called her Lisa. This eldest daughter of an eldest daughter, me, of an eldest daughter, Clara, followed tradition by being born "looking at you." Charles Brown, Jr., was born one year and eight months later. We nicknamed him Chuck.

I paid my maid, Ruby, fifty cents an hour to help me with the housework and the children. She had thirteen children herself, so my two were like a vacation for her.

I loved my two children more than I had imagined possible. As a mother still in her twenties, demands on my ability to remain calm overwhelmed me, particularly when fueled by PMS. I understood the need to exercise self-restraint, and I fought the frustrated urge to slap—an urge my father handed down to me. After an incident similar to what I had endured, I decided to break the cycle of uncontrolled anger. Perhaps my parents had done the best they knew how. I had to learn to do better.

～

I had left my brother Dick behind to fend for himself. Dicky, as a young boy, was Mother's delight. He had loved her joy rides from the time she plopped him into the basket of her Schwinn bicycle. He was her hood ornament, a perfectly-crafted boy with a toothy grin, thick curly hair, and chiseled features. As he grew into manhood, he was Clark Kent down to the perfect physique. In her eyes, Mother had given birth to Superman.

Dick grew to be more like our father, and he savored that identity. He and Daddy were like Piper Cubs whose propellers were wound a bit too tightly. Dick kept his Jeepster as shiny as Daddy had kept any of his own cars. The smile on his boyhood face changed to a passive grin by the time he was a young man. I asked him years later how he felt about the time Dad slapped my face. His answer, "You must have deserved it."

When he graduated from high school, he announced, "I plan to join the air force and become a pilot. I can go to college later."

Mother and Daddy liked the idea of four more years of tuition money delayed. After Dick enlisted, however, the air force denied his wish to become a pilot. The physical revealed a heart murmur, so they trained him as a jet mechanic instead. Dick sent home a portion of his pay each month and asked Mother and Daddy to deposit the funds in an account for his tuition following this four-year commitment.

After the air force, he enrolled at Clemson University to major in mechanical engineering. He was captain of the swim team and he earned money as a model for a menswear store.

Once Dick left for Clemson, and I settled into married life in Ivanhoe, Daddy felt free to quit his job at Judson Mill, where columns of figures had bored him every workday since 1944. Cooped up for so long with his head stuck in accounting books, he vowed to escape the stuffy building.

He had the idea of selling the house in Greenville and moving to Renno. Daddy withdrew his savings and borrowed additional funds to buy out his siblings, who had also inherited land from Grandmother and Granddaddy Bell. Daddy took a job as a traveling salesman, and he sold sheet metal strictly on commission. Months passed with zero sales and zero salary.

Mother and Daddy chose a site for a four-room house on a knoll that faced the Whitmire Highway. Rather than travel the fifty miles back to Greenville each day, they camped out in a tent while they built the house with the help of a sub-contractor. Mother thought of camping as a grand adventure, but Dad saw it as a way to save money.

They moved into the new house on the hill in March 1962. Mother named the place "Ding Dong Hill." Daddy had planned his dream house down to the last nail. The cottage had rough-sawn flitch-pine siding, hauled in a rented trailer from a saw mill in the mountains. A pathway of concrete stepping stones kept people from tracking red clay into the porch that was closed in with awning windows. They put a picnic table there to eat meals in pretty weather. At the far end of the new porch, they placed the glider sofa that had graced our porches for as long as I could remember. The one extravagance was Daddy's idea taken from a magazine. He used wide maple flooring held together with pegs throughout the house.

When not on the road, Dad spent the spring and summer clearing the top of the hill of unwanted brush and Mother rooted some forsythia, weigela, and viburnum. She staked them to protect the plants from the John Deere lawn mower they had purchased.

Dick went to the new house over Labor Day weekend, 1962. He needed to withdraw tuition money for his next semester at Clemson. Mother fixed a little something for their dinner on the Saturday evening before Dick planned to head back to school on Monday. When she went to the kitchen to do the dishes, Daddy looked across the table at Dick and asked, "Do you think you could scrounge up some more funds for your tuition this semester?"

Confused, Dick told him, "Well—that's why I'm here. There should be plenty left in the account you opened for me at Piedmont S&L."

"My new job doesn't pay much," Daddy said. "Mom and I had to dip into that account since we used our savings to help buy this land and build the house. I'm afraid your account is empty now." Dad matter-of-factly delivered the news that he had depleted his son's tuition savings. Mother futzed in the kitchen. She put away leftovers, washed the dishes, and became invisible.

Dick's persona didn't allow him to question our father, his idol. He took this news without blinking. However, Mother and Daddy may as well have sucker punched him. While Mother seemingly tossed off the injustice, it must have been unbearable for Daddy to confess his wrongdoing. Daddy had to have been desperate to take his son's money. He finally made a mistake that belied the perfectionism we had known.

Dick retreated to the porch glider. The crickets had begun to chirp at sunset and fireflies decorated the darkness for as far as he could see. By 9:00 p.m., the television blared and Mother served ice cream with chocolate syrup drizzled over it, their evening ritual before bedtime. She took some to Dick on the porch, but he set it aside. Vanilla and chocolate puddled in the bowl.

Daddy took his and Mother's empty bowls to the kitchen during a commercial break. He noticed that Mother had rinsed out the can of syrup but dripped a sticky path across the kitchen floor from the sink to the pantry where they deposited empty cans in a box. The cans were supposed to be rinsed thoroughly and placed in this box until Daddy hauled them to a gulley in the woods behind the house. Daddy hated water bugs and blamed Mother for providing a picnic for the bugs when she failed to wipe up thoroughly.

"For God's sake, Clara, can't you do one thing without making a mess all over the floor?"

Trapped on the porch in the dark, Dick listened as Daddy's fury escalated.

31. Olin Leaves

The Sunday before Labor Day of 1962, at about two o'clock that afternoon, a distant cousin of Dad's called me in Ivanhoe to tell me my father had died from a gunshot wound in the woods behind the house. A Dali-like scene melted before my mind's eye. Years of worry accumulated, and I imagined that I had seen the incident before it happened.

When I hung up, I wondered why Mother had not been the one to call me. I guessed that she had her head in the sand somewhere. She denied the truth and protected herself from unpleasantness.

I relayed the information to Charles, as though this sort of trauma happened daily. I remained calm and composed for the sake of my children. I felt anesthetized. Numb and out of my body, I imagined the events played out like a movie.

Charles called his parents and asked them to take care of our children. When my in-laws arrived, my voice revealed my father as though someone else spoke the family secrets. I heard myself explain, "My father was an alcoholic." I had never used those words, nor had I heard anyone in the family say them, but that is what I told my in-laws. While I packed for the trip, I reeled off instructions about the children's bedtime rituals, potty habits, and food preferences.

I wore my blue and brown plaid shirtwaist for the five-hour drive to Renno. We left before dark, then watched the night gradually deepen into a dense black. I usually slept on long trips, but my eyes never left the road, and my position in the passenger seat didn't shift. Conversation was futile and competed with uncertainties—*Did this really happen?—Why does my chest feel tight, and what causes that muscle cramp in my left side?—What will we find out when we arrive at the house?*

Charles and I drove up the rutted driveway about nine o'clock that evening and found every light in the little house burning like a beacon at the top of Ding Dong Hill, unusual since Mother turned off lights whether someone needed light or not. Clusters of men leaned against cars crowded into the yard. The red dots from the mourners' cigarette tips broke the darkness with each drag. Word spread that we had arrived. Daddy's cousin, Willie Mae, held the screened door for us. The house overflowed with neighbors, friends from Broad Street Methodist, and distant cousins I didn't really know.

I didn't see Mother, and a stranger from the crowd had been designated to explain to Charles and me that, although Daddy liked to sleep in on Sunday mornings, the cawing of crows woke him. He had often threatened to shoot them. When Mother awoke, Daddy was not there. She went to Dick's room and saw that the shotgun was not there. She assumed Daddy had taken the gun and gone into the woods to shoot at the crows. She knew he got a headache if he didn't eat soon after he rose, so when he didn't come, she woke my brother Dick. "How 'bout going out back to find your dad. I don't know why he doesn't come in and eat breakfast."

Cousin Willie Mae joined the conversation with the stranger, and told us, "Dick walked toward the back acreage but saw no sign of Olin. By noon, Clara called your Uncle Chick since he knew the woods so well."

We were told that Mother explained to Chick, "Olin must have gone out back to shoot the crows, but Dick can't find him. Could you go back there and find him? I'd appreciate it."

Willie Mae told us that, at around twelve-thirty, Dick and Uncle Chick walked into the woods together. They found Daddy at a gap in a fence with a shotgun blast to his right temple. Each spoken word formed visuals in my head. I was glad I hadn't witnessed the scene, although I pictured Daddy sprawled on the floor of a quiet forest, thick with trees, next to an open field of broom straw. He lay near a fence, the shotgun thrown out of his hands. At age fifty-one, he fulfilled the threats he had made over the years with a shotgun to the temple rather than a gun in his mouth. Mother was forty-eight.

The visitors soon left as though a magic wand had waved them away. I guess they had planned to stay until Charles and I arrived. I didn't want them to leave, and I dreaded going over the incident with Mother, Dick, and Charles. I didn't have to because Mother's best friend, Bet, from Greenville, stayed and slept with Mother in my parents' bedroom. They were in bed with the door closed by the time the last person left.

All was quiet. Dick made a bed on the studio couch that pulled out of the wall in the living room. Charles and I settled into the second bedroom. I told Charles, "You sleep next to the window." The windows and front door were open to cool the house. I felt uneasy with only a flimsy window screen to separate us from the out of doors and the scene of the tragedy in the woods behind the house. Charles was tired from the drive and went straight to sleep.

I lay there in the iron bed Grandmother Bell had given my parents. With my eyes open, I tried to make sense of what I had been told, and I heard my father's threat in my head: "I should put a gun in my mouth and fire it." I felt worse when I closed my eyes, because the ghostly images of my father deep in the woods haunted me. We had gone there to cut Christmas trees or to shoot tin cans balanced on fence posts. I felt the angst of my grandmother when someone shot a songbird in the woods. I knew I wouldn't go back into those woods for the rest of my life.

I could smell the night air through the windows of the house. I could sense the promise of fall as it pushed summer away. Only the crickets interrupted the night until I saw a figure framed by the open doorway of our bedroom. Lit by a single nightlight in the hallway, Dick's stance pleaded for me to help him. I had convinced myself since childhood that I was a better mother to Dick than our real mother. My maternal drive flooded to the forefront, and I approached Dick to console him. "What's the matter?"

"I don't want to sleep in there."

"Why not, you'll be fine."

"Daddy is back," he shuddered and looked past me.

"No, that can't be. It's your imagination, Dick. Please don't worry."

He didn't move. "I saw Daddy come through the door and into the house."

Helpless, I wished Charles would wake up. "Tell you what. I have some sleeping pills left over from when I was pregnant with Chuck." The doctor had given them to me when I couldn't sleep in the August heat of my ninth month of pregnancy—before we had air-conditioned our house.

I rummaged for the pills through my Samsonite train case and went into the bathroom to fill a paper cup with water. After some additional persuasion, I ushered Dick back to bed and assured him that everything would be all right in the morning. I settled again into the bed next to Charles and tried unsuccessfully to remove the mental picture of a ghost that walked through the front door. I had hardly settled down before Dick appeared again. "He's here, I saw him."

"Where?"

"He is in the house. I saw him."

A chilly presence tried to convince me that this might be, yet I knew better. I now fought to maintain my own sanity and control my fear.

"Do you have another one of those pills?" he asked.

I refilled the cup of water and placed another pill in his out-stretched hand. I watched him swallow the pill. I nestled him onto the studio couch again and placed an extra pillow between his body and the front door. I positioned myself so that I could back out of the room to avoid a glance toward the front door.

Twenty minutes or so later, I was startled to see the silhouette of Dick's body in the door again, his face as white as the moon it reflected through the window. This time, rigid arms clenched his own shoulders, as though he hugged himself in a vain prayer for solace. His body shook from the catatonic stance.

I woke Charles. He turned on a dim bedside lamp. Dick's eyes looked wild, like an animal in a trap. His silence pleaded for help. Where was the fearless younger brother I had known? His usual determined spirit could not combat this horrible trick his mind played on him.

"What should we do, Charles? I don't know what to do for him. I gave him two of my sleeping pills, but something strange has come over him." I talked to Charles about Dick as though he wasn't there—and he wasn't.

"We need to get him to a doctor," Charles said.

I looked in the phone book and found an emergency clinic in Clinton and called to let them know we were on the way. I tiptoed into Mother's room and whispered to Bet, "We are taking Dick into town. He isn't feeling well."

We held his elbows on either side and guided him into the car. Charles drove toward Clinton faster than Charles ever drives.

I explained what had happened to the doctor and told him I had provided two sleeping pills. I showed him the pill vial. He gave Dick an injection of an additional sedative. We took him back to Renno and put him to bed. He slept until morning and never mentioned the previous night or his fear again.

When Mother got up, she didn't talk about what had happened, nor did she express how she felt. She didn't ask about our late-night trip into Clinton. She didn't cry that day, and I'm not sure she ever cried. Mother was calm, as though nothing extraordinary had happened the day before. We tucked this shadowy topic into a box and sealed it, not to be brought into daylight again.

Uncle Chick came out that afternoon to tell Charles there was to be an inquest. I didn't know exactly what that meant, until Chick explained that the insurance company wanted to rule out suicide. If the coroner's jury ruled the death an accident, they would pay Mother double indemnity.

On Thursday afternoon, Charles, Chick, and I went to the inquest. Dick went with us, but he was so quiet we hardly remembered his presence. We climbed two flights of creaky stairs to the musty top floor of a building in downtown Clinton. Small groups of men looked our way when we followed Chick into the room. A hush fell, the kind of hush that lets you know you have been the subject of gossip before your arrival. Most of the faces were unfamiliar to me, but I had the distinct feeling that the strangers knew me.

The sun, through tall paned windows, created elongated shadows on the bare wood floor. We took our cue from the others and sat in the folding chairs around the walls of the otherwise empty room. I guessed the strangers had come to see how the panel would deal with the crisis that Daddy had inserted into the Bell family history. Another group of men entered, scraped metal chairs from under a table, then sat. The metallic noise and the murmur of the strangers hushed, and the moderator called the meeting to order.

After several people, including Uncle Chick, testified, the panel of men at the table ruled the death to be accidental. The panel assumed that Daddy had caught the trigger of the gun on barbed wire as he passed through a gap in the fence.

The onlookers stirred in their seats and whispered their reactions to one another. Camaraderie ran deep within this small community. After all, population statistics showed that 99 percent of the residents were natives. That meant that only a very few people moved in or out of the area.

We stood when the men at the table left the room, then we walked toward the stairs. The shadows on the bare floor reached from wall to wall now, and the scene felt surreal. I had left the inquest with the impression that the men made their decision based on what would best provide for Mother—accidental death—and now double indemnity would be awarded.

With each step down the creaky stairs, I heard my father's voice. "I should put a gun into my mouth and fire it." I heard the voice all the way back to Renno, and I watched as wooded scenes, similar to the one behind Mother and Daddy's house, passed by my window.

Charles found Clara in the kitchen and explained to her that the inquest had gone in her favor. She turned toward him but looked past his face and out the front window toward the grass-covered knoll. She responded with an understated "hmmm" sound. I translated that as "something for nothing." She knew as well as I that it was no accident, but we never took that topic out of the sealed box and into the daylight.

I knew, too, that Daddy was astute enough to make it look like an accident and provide the insurance for Mother. After all, this plan had been on his mind at least since I was a teen. I was twenty-six now. The men on the inquest panel knew that hunting accidents were common when a man attempted to maneuver through a fence gap. Dad's practical mind knew that too.

We had a small service at Gray's Funeral Home, followed by a burial at Rosemont Cemetery on the Whitmire Highway. The casket remained closed. I was told that the funeral workers were unable to make his face presentable after the shotgun blast to the right side of his face. Another visual for me to fight. We sang his favorite hymns, "Lily of the Valley" and "Old Rugged Cross." I wished I had practiced the piano longer, so I could have played them for him.

We stayed long enough to help Mother with some final settlements of the estate. Estate? Can that word properly denote a four-room house named "Ding Dong Hill," down the Whitmire Highway from Clinton, South Carolina, at Renno?

On the drive home, Charles relayed a conversation he had with a police officer at the inquest. The officer had pulled Charles aside to say that he knew Daddy's death was not an accident. He explained that there were powder burns on Dad's left hand, presumably how he steadied the gun aimed at his right temple. Nevertheless, the coroner's jury had ruled the incident an accident.

Grandmother Bell would be beyond angry and sad if she had known that her son shot himself in those woods. She saved many a songbird, but no one saved her own son, Olin Bates Bell.

32. After Daddy

Mother was unstoppable after Daddy died, as though she stepped on the gas pedal and off she went. She kept his death tucked away without a tear. But when she spoke of him, he was the finest person to have ever been a part of her life. I tried to take things in stride like she did, but I experienced irregular menstrual cycles, had migraine headaches, and went into a deep funk.

Clara riding her John Deere on her seventieth birthday in 1983.

An outstanding loan for construction of the house on Ding Dong Hill hovered. The Farmers Home Administration assigned a slight man named Rufus to deal with Mother. Rufus was either divorced or a widower, and he took an interest in Mother that surpassed the FHA debt. He found numerous excuses to stop by and check on things at Ding Dong Hill. He took Mother out to eat several times and brought his daughter to meet her.

Since Daddy's death, she had hauled rocks in the trailer of her John Deere tractor to fill the ruts in her driveway. Rufus, smitten by Mother, offered to have her red mud driveway paved in asphalt.

Mother bragged to me about her new driveway. In a telephone conversation soon after Rufus finished the paving job, I said, "That was very generous of Rufus. Are you getting serious?"

"Naw, I don't give a hoot about him. In fact, he huffed off into the sunset when I told him I didn't want to go out anymore." Rufus realized he had been used when Mother gave him the heave-ho. She didn't grasp why Rufus was miffed—men like Rufus, after all, were put on earth to meet her needs.

Later, Mother took up with a red-faced man named Roy. When she brought him to our house for a visit, I found Roy difficult to talk to. He acted edgy around our family and didn't look me in the eye when I tried to converse. The children seemed to get on his nerves.

Mother's relationship with Roy concerned me, and I wanted to know more about him. I called an old friend who lived in Roy's town. I asked if he knew the guy. My friend told me, "I think he might have a problem with alcohol from what I've noticed at the country club."

Before I could broach this subject with Mother, she had figured it out herself and broken off the relationship. She said, "I don't need that again."

Renouncement of male companionship came when Mother declared, "I don't want a man in my life. Besides, I could never find one equal to the one I had." She ended her courtships and instead mowed the acreage with her John Deere. She ran all over town on errands and popped in on friends.

Mother adopted a gray cat for company since Daddy wasn't around to complain of headaches from cat fur. She named the cat "Nosey" because he put his nose into whatever rug she hooked or doily she crocheted. Poor Nosey wasn't able to be very nosey though, because Mother had him declawed and kept him in the house so he couldn't run away.

She wrote a letter to me that said, "I'm sending you a picture of my new cat sitting on the high stool in the kitchen." The photograph was of the kitchen stool with a smidgen of gray cat's tail sticking straight up from the bottom edge of the photograph. On the back, she explained, "The cat wouldn't cooperate. Every time I posed him on the stool, he jumped off before I could get a good picture."

Nosey must not have been sufficient company. We guessed she was a bit frightened to stay alone in her hilltop house when she bought a German shepherd she named Sam. Poor Sam was forced to stay within a circle of wire fence that Mother rigged up just outside the entrance to her house. If Sam had

Clara & Nosey hooking a rug.

tried, he could have jumped that fence, but Mother so intimidated him that he left the pen only when leashed. She sent me a photograph of Sam in his pen. He wore an avocado knit golf shirt of Dad's. On the back she noted, "It was cold so I put an old sweater on my dog. He kept it on for three days."

Mother realized she could not manage financially on the meager life insurance policy Daddy had provided. She found a job as a matron at Whitten Village, a home for disabled and special needs children. She shared stories with us about how she outwitted the troublemakers under her supervision or how she beat little Sara Jane or Mary Lou at Monopoly and Chinese checkers. She taught them to play Rook and showed off her skills with the colorful puzzle, Rubik's Cube, when it became a popular craze. She didn't have far to go to reach their level and to wear down the tough veneer of the "residents," as she referred to them.

On the days she worked, Mother was given her meals at "the village," as she called it. After services at Broad Street Methodist, she ate at the Presbyterian College cafeteria. She took plastic bags and containers so she could fill her pocketbook with leftovers for her Sunday supper. "It's a real bargain," she bragged.

Soon she had saved enough to buy a Chevrolet Nova. The Nova was Hi-Yo, Silver, and Mother was the Lone Ranger. She equipped the automobile with a citizens band radio and told us it made her feel secure when she drove alone to visit us in North Carolina. She also had the CB radio equipped with a public address system.

"Why?" I asked.

"What if I run off the road into a gully and am trapped in the car? I can call for help on the P.A." Years later, she claimed the idea for GM's OnStar system.

The CB radio also enabled Mother to fulfill her lifelong need to connect with people, like every trucker between here and there. She thought they would be her friends who looked out for her. Never mind that the truckers were long gone before her fifty-five-mile-an-hour pace got her to wherever she went. "It takes less gas to drive at the exact posted speed limit," Clara explained. "I don't have much money, so I try to save on gas."

Among the truckers on Interstate 385 to I-26 to I-20 to I-95 to I-76, she was probably known as the crazy lady in the white Nova with the handle "Ding Dong." Once, she drove back from our house and came upon an unfamiliar body of water. A roadside sign welcomed her to the state of Georgia. She had been on Interstate 20 until the Columbia bypass was a dim memory. She grabbed her microphone and conveyed her confusion to the next trucker. He told her, "Ding Dong, you must have missed your Exit to I-26 at Columbia. Just head toward Greenwood, past Strom Thurmond Lake, and cut across toward Laurens. That ought to get you there. Copy?" He closed with the standard screech of static.

"Thanks, over and out."

Another attentive trucker called on her CB and asked, "Are you getting tired or sleepy, Ding Dong?"

"No, I'm wide awake," she answered.

"You are going from one lane to the other. Looks like you might need a break," the trucker urged.

"Oh, I do that on purpose. It saves time and gas to take the inside of every curve."

The trucker scratched his head and pulled off at the next stop. He had decided that he needed the break. "Over and out, Ding Dong."

Another gas-saving practice was to take her foot off the accelerator when she saw a traffic light turn red. "No need to waste the gas between here and the light when you have to stop anyway."

She kept a shoe box stuffed and bound by a fat rubber band with jokes typed or jotted down in shorthand onto scraps of paper. The box lived in the trunk of her Nova until she pulled it out at stops to share with travelers who enjoyed a joke—or not. Some were corny, some off-color, some funny, and some flat. It didn't matter. It was all in the telling.

Navigating distances triggered Mother's need to record insignificant information. She knew in her mind that Ding Dong Hill was 7.4 miles from the exit for Clinton off Highway I-385. She counted off the hills and coasted all the way to her mailbox at the foot of her paved driveway to save a little gas. She knew the exact mileage from one point to another all over the South—from her door to Buddy's Hardware Store, to Polly's house in Gaffney, and from her door to Broad Street Methodist Church in Clinton. She was way ahead of MapQuest and the Global Positioning System.

When the children fidgeted on trips, she told them, "Trips to a new place seem to take longer to get there because you don't know how much of the road is still ahead. A trip back home seems shorter since you already know how much road is behind you."

"Hmmm?"

Several stop signs around her stomping grounds drew Mother's comment. "You sure better come to a complete stop at Main and Grove in Clinton or Limestone and Rutledge in Gaffney." This was a sign that Mother had been ticketed at those places at some point in her years of driving.

When Charles or I were with her, we preferred to drive, for our own safety and sanity. I compared the Nova to a sewing machine on wheels; the motor seemed about as powerful as a Singer. Charles drove Mother and me to Spartanburg to pop in on Edith. It didn't matter if Edith was at home or wanted guests; the kick for Mother was simply the process of going somewhere—anywhere. Mother insisted we take a short cut across back roads and through small mill villages toward Spartanburg, a larger mill village. She drove from the back seat and instructed Charles about which way to go, when to take his foot off the gas, and when to brake or accelerate. Charles assured her that he had things under control, but he finally grew weary. He pulled a dollar bill from his pocket. He slapped the money onto the edge of the front seat and said, "Clara if you hush between here and Edith's house, that dollar bill is yours." Mother loved a dollar bill, especially out of someone else's pocket, but she didn't get that one. Couldn't do it.

The Nova brought Mother to visit us in Wilmington three or four times a year and we visited her in Renno between her visits. Charles often commented as we set off for home, "Three days is pretty much your limit for being around her, isn't it?"

33. Migraines and Muscle Spasms

Some ten months after Daddy's death, in the summer of 1963, we took Mother and our children to Wrightsville Beach for an afternoon. When it was time to leave, Charles led the way with Lisa in tow, and I followed Mother across the dunes with Chuck riding my left hip. Her chartreuse boy-leg swimsuit reminded me of the two-piece Jantzen I wore during high school days at Lake Mont where I hung out with friends. I noticed an odd track Mother left through the hot sand. Her left foot dragged each time she took a step and there was a faint tremor in her left hand. Before she left, I mentioned the drag and suggested she go to Greenville for a checkup.

She saw Dr. Daniel, who sent her to Dr. Monroe, a neurologist. He diagnosed Parkinson's disease at fifty years old. I wrote Dick a letter to tell him about the diagnosis, but I don't remember a reply. The disease didn't slow her one iota. I thought the affliction had probably resulted from her bottled up trauma after Dad's death. She minimized the diagnosis and told us, "It's only on the left side."

Dick had continued at Clemson with some financial aid and a co-op with Chevrolet. I didn't know if Mother ever sent him money, but Aunt Mary helped him with tuition payments. When Charles and I realized his financial difficulties, we sent checks a few times.

Except for Aunt Mary and Annelle, Dick kept a distance from the remaining family. Mother didn't miss an opportunity to type a letter and scold him for not coming to see her, as though that would bring him running.

When Dick lacked one semester before graduation, he took a job as a tools analyst for Delta Airlines in Hapeville, Georgia, near

Atlanta. He didn't come to family reunions or visit anymore. I tried to keep the lines of communication open but saw him only at an occasional wedding or funeral. No one knew the reason for his estrangement, although I assumed he blamed Mother for Daddy's death when she provoked the argument they had the night before Daddy died.

He sent Mother a picture of him and his wife several years after they were married, but this marriage didn't last.

We visited him when we took the children to Six Flags over Georgia. Anna was just a baby, so I stayed with her at his apartment and nursed my migraine, probably induced by the stress of being there.

Charles and I took our family on a trip to California the summer after Lisa's high school graduation. We wrote Dick that we wanted to stop by to see him when we passed through Atlanta. We altered our path and went to nearby Hapeville, Georgia, where he lived, convenient to his work at Delta. We found him working on one of the Corvettes he collected and restored. A friendly young woman named Olga was with him.

We knew he ran races, so Charles invited him to run in a race sponsored by his Rotary Club. He came to Wilmington and brought two friends and Olga with him. If Mother's name came up in conversation, a wall of ice went up.

I was still unaware that my parents had depleted Dick's savings account he had set aside for his education. I just knew I didn't want to lose my younger brother through estrangement. Even these few encounters with him gave me migraine headaches and muscle spasms in my back.

———

Charles and I were strapped by our debt to the bank after we bought a retail lumber business in Wilmington, North Carolina, with his brother-in-law. His brother helped finance the deal. We moved to Wilmington on Christmas Eve, 1965, with Lisa, Chuck, and six-month-old Anna. I loved to be close to the beach, where we dangled our feet in saltwater and made slippers of foam for our toes.

34. "Chunny Cruckers"

Descendants of the Scott family referred to themselves as "Chunny Cruckers," derived from a private language created by my grandfather Pop and his siblings. They invented the language to communicate with each other behind their stepmother's back. To further throw off listeners, they used the opposite terminology to convey the intended meaning. For instance, the literal translation for "Chunny Cruckers" was "country cracker," but it meant the opposite—sophisticated people.

Mother invited the Chunny Cruckers to Ding Dong Hill for annual reunions of Scott descendants in the 1970s. The highlight for the children was when she hauled them in the utility trailer of her John Deere mower over terraces in her yard. A John Deere salesman had given her a billed cap, free with her purchase. When she plopped it on her head, the children knew they were in for a thrill.

A bumpy ride for the youngest Chunny Cruckers.

By now, Charles and I had four children. Our youngest, Douglas, was born in 1969. Our children called Clara "Geemommy," Lisa's pronunciation for Grandmommy as a toddler.

My children plus Edith's Tommy and Jana; Aileen's grandchildren;

and Jim's children took turns going on "bumpy rides" over the terraces. She kept the children entertained for as long as they could stand it since Mother herself was indefatigable.

The adults sat around to sip iced tea and lemonade, or to sneak a beer when Aileen didn't watch. She didn't approve. They told stories about the iron gate that fell on Clara as a child and the dirt and jelly sandwich she spread for their cook. "She hasn't changed a bit," they agreed.

Aileen loved to brag to the family of their accomplishments, and she also relived the feuds between her and Clara. Aileen told the next generation, "Daddy had no money left to send me to college because Clara used all the money to go to Draughon's Business College." She implied that the money would have been better spent on her rather than on the ne'er-do-well Clara. Grudge.

Aileen's recollections resurfaced with every reunion. "Clara was always self-centered and incorrigible," she'd say. "I caught her going through my trousseau just before Dave and I married." Those who knew Clara never disputed Aileen. They chuckled at her antics as much as Aileen fumed. Granted, Aileen had endured a bigger dose of Clara than all those who chuckled.

Aileen and Dave had fulfilled their dream to become successful business people. They manufactured a line of blouses with Aileen's signature as the registered trademark. Mother loved to stop by their plant in Columbia on her way to or from our house in Wilmington. Aileen complained to Mother, "You only stop by here to get blouses." Her objections weren't enough to stop Mother from stopping by the plant for a new supply of free blouses.

Mother's niece Jana, Edith's daughter, once came home from a visit with a friend and said, "You know, Mom, Lynn has parents and I have parents. She has grandparents and I have grandparents. But Lynn doesn't have an Aunt Clara."

It was well-known to the children that Mother slept with a flashlight, used a baby pillow to improve her posture, and snuggled two regular pillows on both sides of the children so they wouldn't feel alone in the bed. They knew she promoted regularity with a mellow apple or a bowl of Raisin Bran at bedtime. The children knew, too, the thrill of the enamel kitchen table top as an un-guidable missile down the snowy terraces of Ding Dong Hill. They all knew about life's dangers—things that could kill you, like an aspirin with a "co-cola," a drink of milk with fish, or a mash behind someone's ear lobe. They knew not to use other people's combs (lice), and not to play with Spanish moss (lice). "Only tacky people and pigeons have lice." Mother didn't like for us to sit next to windows where pigeons might roost in the eaves, because we might get lice.

She watched a commercial on her TV and told the children, "That idea for pumped toothpaste was mine. I wrote Colgate-Palmolive a letter with the suggestion. They got it wrong, though. I dropped them a postcard to let them know, 'That's not what I meant. I wanted it to be more like liquid soap,'" which she also claimed to have invented after she collected shards of used bars of hand soap into a Ball jar that sat on the lavatory with enough water in the jar to liquefy the soap.

I'm sure there were icicles in hell when one of Mother's favorite columnists, Heloise, published her suggestion soon after Right Guard aerosol deodorant came on the market. Mother wrote Heloise, "It's a good idea to put a large bath towel around your neck and shoulders so the deodorant won't spray you in the face when aimed at your underarm." Mother laminated the article in plastic and tucked it into her bulging billfold along with other items of interest. She carried those plasticized suggestions in her billfold next to Daddy's obituary for as long as plastic lives.

She wrote her name and social security number with a bold Sharpie pen on all new appliances or items of value. "If they are stolen and recovered, I can prove to the police that they belong to me." Identity theft was of no concern at that time. Her name was written on the television set, clothing labels, magazines, and even Kleenex pocket tissues—she wrote "Clara S. Bell" across the package and was never without a Kleenex.

Cousin Jana was a frequent visitor. She remembered other of Mother's sayings: "Not I, said the pretty little girl," and "I wish I were as cute as some people think they are," and "Only flush when you really *need* to." "Aunt Clara's house was the only place where we were encouraged to go to the bathroom outside, to save flushing water," Jana said. "Once she let me drive the lawnmower. I ran right over a six-foot-tall pecan tree she had planted the year before. I didn't fess up and she didn't mention it.

"When we visited Aunt Clara in the summer we did cool things like fishing. Then we cleaned and cooked the fish and ate them for supper. Once she was out of cornmeal, so she fried the fish without it. She told us, 'When you live in the country, you can save gas and make do with what you have.'

"When she dropped by our house in Spartanburg, she announced that it was 37.7 miles from her door to ours. Then she hollered out, 'I need to use your bathroom.' Off she'd go to the powder room, then leave in the same hurry. 'Bye, got to go.'

"Our mouths gaped, without a chance to speak," Jana said.

Penny's husband, Tom, piped in, "She did the same thing at our house. We were 54.5 miles from her door."

Now that I am the same age Mother was at that time, I understand her urgent focus on bathrooms. I have also located every bathroom across the Carolinas. My gynecologist has a name for it—prolapsed bladder.

The children all remembered how Mother greeted any man with a beard. We could see the words form on her lips before we heard Clara say, "What did you do with that man?"

The butt of the joke asked, "What man?"

"That man who stole your razor."

One more connection cultivated, a friend made.

And Jana reminded us, "We knew to hold on if a squirrel was in the street when Aunt Clara drove her Nova. She'd swoop across two lanes to run down a 'bushy-tailed rat.'"

35. Super Bowl VII

"**I** won a contest from a Nescafé ad in the *Reader's Digest*," Mother announced over the phone one Sunday evening. She entered sweepstakes and contests with the hope of easing all her monetary woes while gaining another way to connect with people. She used Daddy's old metal file cabinet with records of what, when, and where she entered each competition.

"And just what did you win?" I asked.

"Two tickets to the Super Bowl. It's a football game they have every year. They've already done six so this one is called Super Bowl VII. I don't give a hoot about it. Do you and Charles want to go in my place?"

"My gosh." I put my hand over the phone and got Charles's attention, "Mother has won a trip to Los Angeles for the Super Bowl." That got his attention.

Chuck wasn't in the family room at the time, but Charles and I knew our thirteen-year-old son would be the most enthusiastic about the opportunity. He'd been a Redskins fan from the time he played Pop Warner football. The Redskins quarterback, Sonny Jurgensen, was a Wilmington native, so Chuck followed the team passionately. He wore a red wool jacket with white leather sleeves and the Indian insignia embroidered on the front.

"Let us call you back, Mother. We need to talk this over." Just before I placed the phone on the hook, I added, "Don't offer it to anyone else until you hear back from us."

Charles said, "Chuck should be the one to go. It wouldn't seem right to leave him behind. I'll take him with me with the second ticket."

"But she's my mother. I'll take Chuck. I don't care about the game but would love a trip to Los Angeles. I might be able to catch the Johnny Carson show."

"I wonder if Nescafé would allow us to pay Chuck's way, and all three of us go."

When we called Mother back, she said, "Good idea. I'll call the Nescafé people in New York City on Monday and ask if we can do it that way."

Monday evening, she called back, "They told me you could take Chuck along at their expense." Lord knows, we were so excited. Mother drove to Wilmington and stayed with the other children while we flew out on an icy January day that broke records. My fake fur winter coat kept me warm.

On the Piedmont flight, the attendants served cocktails from cute miniature liquor bottles. I knew I could find a good use for them now that I was into decoupage, tole painting, and other crafts. I asked the flight attendant to save some empties for me, so every time she walked by, she dropped bottles in my lap. When the plane landed, my lap was full. I looked around for something to hold them and stuffed them into the vomit bag that I grabbed from the seat pocket.

I had arranged for tickets to *The Tonight Show* with Johnny Carson, which meant we had to catch a cab straight to the NBC studio from the airport. There we sat in the audience, a vomit bag full of mini bottles in my lap, and more in the pockets of my fake fur coat. Little beads of perspiration broke out on my forehead, dressed for below-zero temperatures in this seventy-degree oasis. Maybe because it was Los Angeles, no one stared at us. Johnny Carson was on vacation, so Liberace filled in for him and Bob Hope was one of the guests.

We were happy to get to our hotel room. Nescafé welcomed us with a big arrangement of flowers and a basket of fruit. They ordered a fold-out bed for Chuck. They arranged cocktails and dinner with famous football players including Merlin Olsen, Deacon Jones, and Bill Mathis, who had played for Clemson before going pro.

I wore a full-length floral polyester skirt I had made. I had trimmed it in blue lace to match my blue puckered polyester Aileen

Pennington blouse. I had my hair teased into a Gibson-Girl-do, bouffed up with curls piled onto the top of my head. I hoped the look would last the length of the trip, so I wrapped it in toilet paper held by a pair of nylon panties each night.

In every way, we were treated like royalty by Nescafé, and Mother had found another connection and a way to keep busy with Dad not around. She continued to enter contests.

36. Mastectomies and Funerals

Mother was prone to having small nodules or lumps in her breast that turned out to be benign. In November 1973, she turned sixty, and she wrote me that she had found another lump in her breast. She saw a surgeon in Greenville and went into the hospital the next week to have it removed.

I didn't plan to go for the surgery. I thought it was just another false alarm. On the day of the surgery, Annelle called me at about 10:30 a.m. "The doctor thought Aunt Clara's lump was malignant, so he removed her left breast."

"I'll get there as soon as I can," I said.

When I hung up the phone, I put on my dutiful eldest-child mask and began to pack bags for Doug and me. The other children could fend for themselves under Charles and Lisa's supervision. I picked up Doug at nursery school on the way out of town, and we headed for Greenville. We stayed for a week after Mother got out of the hospital. Annelle assured me she would continue to look out for her until she was better.

Years after Grandmother Bell lost her breasts, Dad's sisters, Aunt Mary and Aunt Martha, had mastectomies. Eventually, all the female cousins on the Bell side, except Annelle, and my one cousin on the Scott side walked the path. This included me when I turned sixty in 1996, the same age Mother was when she had her surgery. The Bell trait was to accept what we must do without fanfare. Mother, by contrast, wore her mastectomy like a badge of honor and revealed her scar to anyone interested—or not. This irritated the life out of

Aunt Mary. "I am not interested in your scar, Clara," Aunt Mary said more than once.

Mother called me in March 1981 to say that Dad's younger sister had died. I promised Mother I would come to Clinton and take her to Aunt Martha's funeral. I drove down the following Saturday in time to pick up Mother and get to the church before things got underway.

After I located a parking spot, I realized the trip had left me stiff when I lifted my body out of the car, but Mother bounced out like the first circus clown from a packed Volkswagen. We walked toward the entrance of the red brick Methodist church. I struggled to keep up with Mother, to make sure she didn't trip or fall when she bounded up the concrete steps.

We walked through the vestibule with carpet the color of Holy Communion grape juice. An usher with a big smile offered me a worship leaflet. His head was bald in the front and the back, I recalled one of Mother's jokes. "Men who grow bald in the front are thinkers and those who grow bald in the back are lovers. Those who are bald in the front and the back think they are lovers."

Another usher directed us toward the registry and I signed for both of us while Mother flirted with the bald usher. The church was about three-quarters full.

Martha's friends had sent sprays and wreaths in a breast cancer color scheme. Pink carnations and white mums were much softer hues than the jewel tones in the stained-glass windows. The scent of carnations that filled the cavernous room was sweeter than I cared for at that moment. Flowers banked the altar where Aunt Martha lay in her coffin.

I started down the aisle, scanned the crowd, and looked for a pew. I stepped back to let Mother into the row and realized she had broken away. She was halfway down the center aisle toward Aunt Martha's open casket.

My wayward mother whipped out her Instamatic camera and flashed it toward Aunt Martha, laid out on tufts of pink satin. Mother had time for three good shots of Aunt Martha's peaceful, pallid countenance before I could get within tackling distance. The big grin across Mother's face irritated me when I ushered her back to a seat. As we walked up the center aisle, a glance at the congregants told me they found the sideshow for the price of a couple dozen pink carnations to be a true bargain.

37. Change to Come

The policy at Whitten Village forced Mother to retire from her job when she turned sixty-five. She left the girls at the village in December 1978. Upon retirement, Mother latched onto a widow lady named Paula. She was eighteen years younger than Mother, ran a hardware store she owned downtown, and owned some land that she farmed. Paula had no immediate family and loved to have a friend like Mother who enjoyed a trip to Myrtle Beach or the mountains whenever they felt the urge.

Paula provided a room in her house for Mother when it was too late to drive her back to Ding Dong Hill, or when they planned to leave in the wee hours on a trip. Paula, aware of the age difference, even called Clara "Mother." Mother fulfilled Paula's need to nurture, and to assuage her own loneliness. Mother soaked up Paula's attention like a Bounty paper towel soaks up a mess.

When they came to visit us in Wilmington, I felt that Paula had the resources to pick up the tab when they ventured out. Something free had always delighted Mother, and this good fortune was no different.

Eventually, Paula, began to call me with concerns about Mother, who didn't take her meds as instructed. I knew Mother had once told Dr. Monroe, "I only take my pills when I feel like I need them."

Dr. Monroe asked her, "From which medical school did you graduate, Clara?"

Mother's friends and acquaintances began to complain to Paula that Mother had become a nuisance with telephone calls all day long. They softened their complaints and added, "Bless her heart." Yet the phone calls continued. When friends told Mother they couldn't talk, she hung up but called back minutes later, "Can you talk now?"

Mother had written in her journal,

> *Eula Hunter was elected to take my place after fourteen years as secretary of the Wesley Sunday School Class.*

With her Draughon's Business College background, Mother had loved to volunteer as secretary. This might have indicated that Mother's friends had grown weary of the pushy company they had endured in the past, or her pushiness had increased to unbearable.

Paula told me that Mother had received some stalker-like notes in her mailbox, so Mother allowed her German shepherd Sam to sleep inside the house rather than in the pen outside. The only dog our family had had when I was growing up was Skippy, the blonde mutt we had in Brevard. Skippy was not allowed in the house; it was Daddy's rule. Mother continued to live by many of Daddy's dictates. The German shepherd in the house was a big surprise.

Paula told me that Mother had become less steady on her feet, too. Mother confessed to Paula that she had put Sam on his leash to take him outside about midnight, and she got tangled up in the leash. She fell and hit her head on Rufus's asphalt driveway and woke up some unknown length of time later with the dog cuddled by her side.

Charles and I had also noticed Mother seemed more combative when we visited Renno, and she was stricter with Sam and Nosey than she needed to be. She insisted they obey her every whim. Paula invited her on fewer jaunts. Mother didn't bathe regularly, wore the same old ragged clothes that had been Daddy's work clothes or castoffs her friends had given her to make hooked rugs. Her thick, brown curls had turned to thinner waves, with a minimum of gray for her age. Her steely blue eyes were still there, but she peered through a cloudy veil.

Her connection-seeking endeavors had paid off for her most of her life, but the charm and the fun had ceased to be charming or funny. My children had thrived on Mother's energy, but as they grew older, her constant attention-seeking was a funhouse with no exit for them.

Daddy had insisted that Mother throw out leftover food. With him gone, I discovered that she saved even the smallest morsel. Her fridge had become a landfill of leftovers. I saw containers, foil-wrapped morsels, and other unidentifiable contents stuffed into the far reaches of this airless box. I asked Mother, "Why is this Duke's mayonnaise jar in the back of your fridge? And why is there money inside it?"

"I decided it was safer to close my bank account and keep my money in the jar. If I have a fire, it should be safe in there," she explained.

By 1985, I had dropped numerous hints to Mother that she wouldn't be able to live alone at Ding Dong Hill forever. I called Dr. Monroe and reported all the bizarre incidents. He backed up our plan to move her to Wilmington.

~

Mother wrote in her journal on October 3, 1985,

Betty and Charles came down to see how I was doing. Then the next day we went to see Dr. Monroe in Greenville. He said I shouldn't live by myself out in the country, so I put my name on several waiting lists in the area.

With the help of Dr. Monroe, Charles and I finally convinced her to move to Wilmington. Paula had gotten married and her spare time was consumed by the new husband.

Charles and I drove down to Renno and began to pack Mother's things and clean out her house. We started a pile for a garage sale to benefit the Renno Volunteer Fire Department. We placed the furniture and clothing that went to her new home in a U-Haul trailer. We set aside another stack with a few keepsakes for me and our children. These included Grandmother Bell's chocolate pot and gravy ladle in the "Grapes of Wrath" pattern. Charles planned to haul the largest heap to the trash dump in the woods behind the house.

Mother disorganized our attempts and pulled items out of the piles. She grabbed a rusty metal grater she had used to make pimento cheese from the firemen's stack. "Here, you could use this."

"I have a Cuisinart, Mother. That's how I make my pimento cheese."

She had us on a merry-go-round, and we were dizzy.

I put my hands on my hips and watched her rummage through the trash to rescue a two-inch tall bronze statue of Robert E. Lee, a gift from her savings and loan in nearby Clinton. I made three attempts to discard a collection of rotten rubber bands that encircled a batch of pencil nubs and broken emery boards. She continued to rummage through the trash pile. She declared, "These things are perfectly good," and tucked whatever she'd found back into a box intended for Wilmington.

I jumped off the merry-go-round and gave in to her wiles. We looked like the Beverly Hillbillies going down Highway I-26 toward Wilmington.

We had called Dick to tell him about Mother's move to Wilmington. My father had promised Granddaddy Bell's roll-top desk to Dick. It waited in a corner for him. He came to Renno for the desk and that may have been the last time Mother saw her son; she continued to scold him in letters that nagged him to come see her. It made me sad to see her yearn for him this way.

Mother had sold a large parcel of the Bell land that included Grandmother and Granddaddy Bell's home, built around a log cabin, to a paper company. They cleared the land of the house, all the barns, and outer buildings, and planted pine trees. Mother sold twenty acres of cow pasture just west of and down the hill from her house to Uncle Chick's brother. She was left with about twenty-six acres that surrounded the house, and later we sold those. The land in Renno had been in the family since the Bells emigrated from Scotland and came south from Virginia in 1760.

I felt sad to sell the remaining Bell land, but I was more than glad to leave the haunted forest in back of the house where Daddy had died at the gap in the fence.

38. Catherine Kennedy Home

Mother perked up over the move to a new place. She arranged her furniture and met new people. I think she knew this move to a retirement home was inevitable. She was headstrong, but all of her life, she plowed through adversity and made a party out of things she couldn't control.

We felt anxious about how Mother might fit into this genteel setting, as though we had moved a two-year-old into Windsor Castle to hobnob with Queen Elizabeth.

Several residents welcomed Mother when they poked their tightly-permed bluish heads into the open door of her room on moving day. Mother wore miniature cowbell earrings after she had her ears pierced. She ignored her admonition to me as a teen, "Not a good idea, Betty. Only gypsies and prostitutes pierce their ears." She also wore a miniature brass cowbell on a chain around her neck. She shook the bell in the new ladies' faces and announced in her best Miss Congeniality voice, "Hey, I'm Clara Bell. I moved here from Clinton, South Carolina." I cringed and watched to see how they took her gusty greeting. The near-deaf ones couldn't pick up the clues that labeled Mother as trouble; they smiled and moved on. Others stepped back when Mother came toward them with such enthusiasm. A few retired school-teacher types dispensed patronizing looks and recognized a two-year-old in their midst.

I adapted my custom-made raw silk drapes, the Williamsburg blue ones with twelve-dollars-a-yard fringe, to fit the one window in her small room. Wilmington's venerated interior decorator

Robert Nash Cooper had designed them for my dining room, but I was ready to redecorate.

I took Mother to K-Mart and bought a chintz comforter with pink cabbage roses and a coordinated dust ruffle for her twin bed. We found space for her La-Z-Boy recliner, her iron floor lamp with the carved seahorse design, and a lampshade she had salvaged by wrapping rows of string around the worn-out frame.

"And hey, I can put one of my crocheted doilies on top of the file cabinet and display my bell collection there." She didn't truly need Daddy's old metal file cabinet, but that's where she kept carbon copies of her correspondence typed on the Underwood typewriter she inherited from Dad. I found this example:

December 11, 1981

To the Editor:

 I don't see how the people, who run the gasoline, utilities, grocery stores, etc., can go up on their prices, on account of inflation, when people who live on a fixed income have to make-do with what they have. Why shouldn't those businesses have to make-do on what they receive?

Clara S. Bell

She and the Underwood spewed a stream of journal-like letters about her life to friends and relatives. She continued to write letters to the editor of the *Greenville New-Piedmont*, to politicians, and businessmen. Some contained thanks or praise, and others complaints that they were greedy or unfair. She had better ways to do things and offered unsolicited advice to all. She blessed Heloise with letters and kept records of all the sweepstakes and contests that she continued to enter. She dropped postcards to the minister of her former church in Clinton to let him know that, "You won't have a financial worry in the world after I win Publishers Clearing House Sweepstakes."

Mother relished the routines imposed on the residents at CK, and glorified the meals in letters to her kinfolk, "We have breakfast every day at 7:30 a.m., dinner at noon, and supper at 6:00 p.m." She loved the repetition of meatloaf Monday, fried chicken Tuesday, pork chop Wednesday, spaghetti Thursday, fish on Friday, and light pick up meals over weekends; linen napkins for laps and paper napkins for faces and fingers; and meds dispensed three times a day and at bedtime. A white board reminded everyone, "Today is Friday, April 25, 1986. The weather is sunny and warm." The azaleas were in full bloom and so was Mother.

Administrator Abbott made the rules so that Catherine Kennedy Home ran smoothly. The rules were not hard for residents to follow, but Mother assumed they were for everyone except her. As she became more comfortable in her new surroundings, her belief about rules made to be broken surfaced in her speech and actions. She joshed around with Mr. Abbott and the nurses; she barged in on other residents. "Just trying to help," Clara reasoned. Mr. Abbott seemed amused by Mother at first, but his welcome soon waned. Her charm became a Whitman's Sampler eaten in one sitting.

Residents were restricted from the kitchen, but Mother insisted, "I can go into the kitchen whenever I want because I have made friends with the people who work in there. I like to go see them, and maybe they'll find some way I can help out."

The ladies in the kitchen abided her intrusions and took bets as to how long it would take Mr. Abbott to discover her in their midst. Some of the kitchen workers encouraged her; her presence broke the monotony of their routines. Mother must have informed them about her unique birthday, 11/12/13. One of the cooks baked a birthday cake for Mother. The inscription thrilled her:

11/12/13
Jesus loves you
& so do I!

The board hosted a Silver Tea for CK's residents before Christmas. They polished the sterling punch bowl and trays and served petit fours, open-face cucumber sandwiches with a sprinkle of paprika, bite-size ham biscuits, and homemade cheese straws. They invited the families, the mayor and his council, and county dignitaries, all of whom attended without fail, especially in election years. The ladies on the board didn't hold back when it came to making the residents feel special. Every year Mother called me. "The girls on the board have their Silver Tea for us next Friday. They really put on the dog."

When Christmas rolled around Mother put on the dog too and switched her cow bell jewelry to large jingle bell earrings and a larger bell on a red cord around her neck.

Mother kept a medicine cabinet in her half-bath, chocked full of over-the-counter meds forbidden by the home's policy. She fell into her old need for the self-medication she had enjoyed when she lived the life of the Renno hermit.

She pestered the nurses to dispense her meds early. "It won't hurt a thing," she nagged. She appeared at the nurses' station at least thirty minutes before the scheduled time. On one occasion, Mother was caught inside the unattended station. She scrounged for her own meds. The nurses wore black thunderclouds over their heads after that one.

One summer evening, the nurses allowed a gentle breeze to come through an open back door. A harmless homeless man noticed the open door and strolled down the hallway. He startled the nurses, and a nurse called the police, who escorted the man out to Fourth Street. The residents had watched *Wheel of Fortune* in their rooms and missed the whole thing.

On a slow day at the *Wilmington Morning Star,* the incident made Tuesday morning's Police Blotter. Mother clipped the article out of the newspaper, took it downtown to PIP Printing Shop, and had it laminated. When new residents filled vacancies after others moved closer to their children or passed on to be with Jesus, Mother used the article to introduce herself to new ladies.

After reading Clara's clipping, a new resident ran to her room, called her family, and revealed that they had placed her in a crime-ridden retirement home. The upset family called Mr. Abbott, the ever-present cushion between Mother and the rest of the world. With a stern look that caused his thin mustache to twitch, Mr. Abbott paid a visit to Mother in her room. "Clara, I want to see the news article you show to the new ladies who move into Catherine Kennedy Home."

"I took it to PIP Printing and had it laminated just like my letter published by Heloise and Olin's obituary," she said.

"I'm going to take this with me, Clara," he said.

With one hand on her hip, a finger wagged just about level with Mr. Abbott's twitching mustache. "I didn't say you could have it."

"You're upsetting the new people," he said.

"Hmmph! I paid for that lamination myself."

When she knew Mr. Abbott had left the building to go to his private dwelling behind the home, Clara came up with a plan. She slipped into the room near the nurses' station where the snacks, ice, and drink machines stayed. She had spotted the key to the Coca-Cola machine on a high nail across the room. After she put her fifty-cents into the slot, a Coke clunked down the track. She made a noise in the ice to disguise her purpose, stole the key from its nail, and trotted back to her room.

She didn't wait for the Coke man to arrive and look for the key the next morning. She marched into Mr. Abbott's office with a defiant look and announced, "If you ever want to see the Coke machine key again, you need to return my laminated welcome." After a day of high-powered dickering and summit meetings, Mr. Abbott convinced Mother that the news article was not a good idea. Also, the nurses and the agitated ladies with Coca-Cola addictions pressured Mother to return the captive key so the machine could be refilled.

To give Mother an inch meant she took a mile. She might run the joint pretty soon. When Mother saw a person with a letter or card to mail, she bounded up to the resident like an eager Newfoundland pup. She snatched the mail from the lady's hands and ran to drop it in the outgoing letter slot. Some of the residents complained to Mr. Abbott about Mother's unsolicited service. Bless his heart. I should have baked him cookies every day of his put-upon life.

The ladies congregated in the front parlor before meals. "You might want to sit over here, dear. That's Clara's place," they warned newcomers and guests. Mother didn't hesitate to physically move someone from her seat in the parlor. From there, Mother could see when a kitchen worker was about to ring the bell for a meal. "Sadie's about to call us to dinner," she announced to all in earshot. She popped up from her spot and bounded down the corridor to be the first in the dining hall. That was another of her self-appointed jobs, to announce that the dinner bell was about to announce a meal.

Her journal revealed other ways she stuck her nose into others' business.

> *February 4, 1989 – There is a lady (Mrs. Maready) who sits at a table in the dining room near me. When she leaves the dining room, she takes a stack of paper napkins anywhere from ½" to 1" every morning. One night I put a note in her mail box and asked her, "What do you do with those napkins you take out of the dining room every morning?" Someone told me she throws them in the trash in the utility room. I looked there later and saw a bunch of napkins in the trash can. So I put another note in her mail box and said, "Don't you know it is a sin to steal and also to waste napkins?" For a day or two she stopped taking them, and then she started taking them again. She would roll them up in her hand or put them in her pocket, inside her sleeve, or under a scarf she wore around her neck. So I put another note in her box and said, "God sees you, no matter where you hide those napkins." So now she doesn't take any. The reason I put the notes in her mail box was because she wears shoes that are too big and she flops her heels, and I told her one day to put pads in them and they would fit better, and she said, "Aw shut up."*

> *February 17, 1989 — I put another note in Mrs. Maready's mail box and I said, "You're getting better and I am very proud of you."*

Many of Mother's antics continued under the guise of "helping" others. The hot water heater went on the blink in the south wing on a cold winter evening, so half the ladies were unable to take showers or even a bird bath at their private lavatories. The breakdown happened on a weekend when plumbers tend to go fishing.

Mother to the rescue! She remembered that she had seen some big buckets left in the kitchen. One of the volunteers had left them there after she delivered cut flowers for the tables. After she pilfered several buckets, Mother spread a towel over the floor next to her bathroom and placed one bucket at a time onto the towel. She filled her cookie tin with hot water, dumped it in the bucket, careful not to get it so full that she couldn't lift it. As soon as she finished the second bucket, she picked up one on each side, proceeded out her door, down the corridor, and past the office Mr. Abbott had vacated for the evening. She went through the front parlor, through the Florida room, and down the corridor past the dining room. She took the elevator to the top floor, intending to work her way down, furnishing hot water to the residents who lived in the waterless south wing. Mother went about her business in such a determined yet stealthy way that no one noticed her fast gait and sly smile.

On her way back from her second trip, Mr. Abbott happened by his office and noticed the Hansel-and-Gretel trail of sloshed water. His twitching mustache planted in her pathway, Mr. Abbott stopped the good deed in its wet tracks.

And so, Mother launched her own fabled life at CK. She settled into her determined routines, but at the same time, she managed to unsettle the routines of the other residents, the staff, and bless his heart, Mr. Abbott. They could've named the place "Clara's Retirement Home for Ladies." She would have liked that.

39. Aunt Mary B. Leaves

Aunt Mary was diagnosed with cancer in the fall of 1989 and had a matter of months to live. I promised Mother I would take her to Greenville to visit her only remaining sister-in-law. "I'd like to leave early, so be ready about six-thirty in the morning."

"We can go earlier than that if you want to. We might catch a tail wind and get there real early," Mother said

"Six-thirty," I said.

The next day, I pulled into the back parking lot of CK where several of the early risers rocked on the back porch and waited for the breakfast bell this crisp fall morning. I parked and went inside for Mother. I nodded to the ladies as I walked past them. One lady oozed, "Oh, what a pretty dress."

I wore a new Hawaiian print on a teal background with a plum and yellow floral motif. I mustered some graciousness and thanked the lady for the compliment before I made my way through the screen door toward Mother's room, surprised that she had not waited on the porch. Just as the screen door closed behind me, I heard a lady's audible whisper, "Sure don't have trouble seeing her coming in that dress." I gulped and questioned my choice of attire for the trip.

I settled Mother into her seat and placed her train case, Fig Newtons, and Bran Flakes behind the back seat of my station wagon. Even with a few swigs of Benadryl, Mother struggled to sit where the seatbelt tried to keep her, but we got to Greenville in time to get in a visit with Aunt Mary B. at Annelle's house, where we were to spend the night.

The next morning, still dark outside, Mother flicked the over-head light on and off and nudged me out of my dream. "C'mon, if we get an early start, we might catch a tail wind," she insisted. "We can save some time if we pick up a sausage biscuit at McDonald's on the way home." A groan started deep in my belly, came up, and out of my mouth.

We left Greenville on I-385 and maneuvered through the morning rush traffic at Mauldin, now a bedroom community for Greenville. The traffic congestion amazed me in this once-tranquil communi-ty where our egg man had lived. The egg man, his chicken coops, and all the adjacent farms had been eaten alive by Holiday Inn, Red Lobster, and Burger King, with fancy suburban homes just off the highway all the way to Simpsonville.

Just past Fountain Inn, I had reached my usual five miles over the sixty-mile-an-hour speed limit when my seventy-eight-year-old Mother unbuckled her seatbelt and climbed from her shotgun seat over the two rows behind us. She rummaged around in the back before I could blink.

"What the...? Where the heck are you going, Mother?"

"Just want to get one of my mellow apples and see if I remem-bered my Fig Newtons."

How had she gotten back there so fast?

"Get back in your seat and buckle that seatbelt," I told her, as I pushed "resume" on cruise control to return to sixty-five-miles-an-hour.

Later, Mother reached for my steering wheel, blew the horn with her left hand, and waved to the trucker we passed. She gave him a toot-toot signal with the childish hope he would blow back at us. "Mo-ther, puh-lease! I will have a wreck if you don't calm down and sit still." I thought I had driven a carpool of unruly kindergarteners to South Carolina.

I told Mother up front that I didn't plan to make pop-in calls on her friends in Clinton on the way back to Wilmington. We compro-mised, took the long way around, and swung by Ding Dong Hill instead.

She felt it was her duty to check on her old place whenever she came within ten miles. She wrote postcards to her friends in Clinton and asked them to ride by and let her know if the strangers who bought her house had mowed the front acreage. As we coasted down the last seven-tenths of a mile, the grassy knoll was gone. Instead, a healthy crop of broom straw waved at Mother as we passed by. "Those people need to get a John Deere mower," she grumbled. "I don't know what in the world is wrong with the Renno Volunteer Fire Department! I have written them six postcards to tell them to have those people mow that yard. As soon as the first smoker drives by and tosses a cigarette in that direction, the fire will swoop up that hill and burn the house to the ground."

"The house no longer belongs to you, Mother. You don't have to worry about it."

"I will drop them another postcard when I get back to CK. I may even get Donald, your lawyer friend, to send something official-looking."

In the middle of her rant, she rolled down the window and threw her Fig Newton wrapper toward the ditch.

"Mother, will you please stop littering? There's a sign, right there—a $200 fine for littering. Do you have that kind of money? I want you to roll up that window, wipe that mellow apple off your face, and sit still for the rest of the trip back to Wilmington. I don't want to hear another word out of you until we get home."

My pleas ran off her like syrup poured over a plastic pancake, but she settled down for a while. She possibly strategized at how she could pass off that $200 fine to the driver of the car.

We turned down Bell Road at Tip Top Store and passed the cleared site of Grandmother and Granddaddy Bell's home. Just after we had passed this faded memory, we saw the remains of cousin Johnny Bell's general store where the road leads to our ancestor Hayne Bell's house. Hayne Bell was one of the few Bells who owned slaves and Daddy told me his great uncle had slept with one of his slaves. I wondered about secret kin in and around Renno. There could be distant cousins other than the Copelands.

I turned left after the railroad crossing, past where Grandmother Bell was reared on the other side of the tracks. My orders to Mother worked until we approached the ramp to take us back onto I-26 toward Columbia.

"You'd better…"

"Shhhh!" I cut her off.

"I was just going to …"

"Not a word, Mother!"

Unstoppable, she blurted it out. "This is the last place to get gas before Columbia and your red light has been on 'empty' since Mauldin."

Without a word, I turned into the station at the top of the ramp and hmmphed while I pumped gas into the wagon. I wiped the crow off my lips and got back into the car, Visa receipt in hand, and I drove to Wilmington without a word.

40. All Around Town

When we first discussed Mother's move to Wilmington, she still drove the Chevrolet Nova that she loved. But the Chevrolet people changed the look of the Nova, much to Mother's disdain. She wrote General Motors a postcard with her complaint and traded to the Celebrity model to show them she meant business. This was the car she brought to Wilmington.

Her concern to save a few pennies on gas disappeared when she wanted to go somewhere and she put many miles on the Celebrity. Mother drove carloads of ladies to my home from CK and announced, "I want to show them your house!" Was there pride in there somewhere, even after she told me the new wallpaper I chose for my dressing room was tacky?

She had contacts all over town—Lucy King James, the volunteer receptionist at St. Andrews-Covenant Presbyterian Church; Edna, who worked in hardware at the K-Mart on College Road; all the employees at Albert Rhodes Jewelers on Grace Street; Al at the Oleander Exxon station; and Donald, our attorney friend on Fifth Avenue.

Mother took the same pride Daddy had taken in his cars, but she ignored his rule against eating in the car. She couldn't pass a McDonald's. "It's about supper time; we may as well pick up a hamburger." After scrutinizing the wall-size menu, she couldn't understood why McDonald's didn't pick up on her repeated tips, such as "Nothing is better than a slice of hard-boiled egg atop a hamburger patty," or "Pimento cheese gives a gourmet touch to a hamburger."

When our children went to McDonald's with her, they pretended to be with other hungry families.

～

She met new people at Independence Mall. After each adventure, Mother dropped by my house to ask me, "Do you know so and so? She knows you." After I acknowledged that I did or I didn't, Mother explained to me, "I made friends with her when she drove me around the parking lot to help me find my car at the mall."

She connected with her "friends" around town while other ladies at the home took afternoon naps and she was left with no one to chat with. Mother left the dining room at Catherine Kennedy after her serving of cherry Jell-O with a dollop of Cool Whip on top, Wednesday's dessert. She knew that Lucy King James volunteered at the church on Wednesdays, and she waited outside the Fifteenth Street entrance to watch for Lucy to return from lunch. Mother's plan was to go into the air-conditioned office and visit with Miss Lucy for a while.

She passed time with the Chevrolet owner's manual from the glove compartment and highlighted things to remember. The monotony was broken when the charming young preacher, new to St. Andrews-Covenant, whipped into a space just in front of the Celebrity. He didn't notice Mother. *Ah ha, here's someone I can talk to*, she thought, as she watched the handsome figure unfold himself from the navy-blue Ford the congregation had presented to him.

She grabbed the PA mike attached to her CB and blasted her question toward the fast-paced preacher, "And just where do you think you're going?" The minister flinched, winced, and looked heavenward, as though God had chased him down.

"Odd for a preacher to act so guilty," she told me later.

Mother didn't care about Sunday school with us, not that I encouraged her attendance. CK was about twelve blocks from St. Andrews-Covenant, so Charles and I took turns and picked her up between Sunday school and the 11:00 a.m. worship service. Lisa and Chuck had gone off to college. Charles, Anna, and I sang in the choir, so we sat Mother in a pew with Douglas and crossed our fingers.

One Sunday, I picked her up at the back entrance to CK. I noticed loud smacking on chewing gum—something Daddy didn't allow us to do. I mentioned the gum and she got rid of it. After the service, Miss Bertha McIntyre approached me in the narthex. She had been seated in the pew behind Mother. She told me, "I think there is something in your mother's hair. Right there," she pointed.

I spun Mother around and saw that she had stuck her chewing gum behind her ear to save it until church was over. She had seen that in a comic book. Mother channeled the voice of Heloise, "Don't worry—it will come out with ice." On Monday, we visited the beauty shop to smooth over the lost chunk where I cut the gum out of her hair.

Mother loved to stop by Charles's building-supply store. One day she pulled into a parking space and just sat there. It was pouring down rain, so one of Charles's employees went to the door with an umbrella. Mother whipped out the PA mike and announced to him, "It's OK, I'll just wait until it stops."

The man flinched at the noisy speaker. He had pretty much gotten the message when he heard, "Over and out!"

After one too many stop sign violations and a stern denial of a renewed driver's license from the North Carolina Department of Motor Vehicles, Mother decided to give her Celebrity to Douglas, who didn't have a car. After that, she invested in a pedometer to measure how far she walked. She started out to K-mart one day but settled for Rose's instead.

Which was worse, I wondered, a threat on the highway, or the responsibility of taking her places? "No, Mother, I'm not planning to take you by the K-Mart to visit Edna in hardware or to pop in on Miss Lucy at the church. Donald has more to do in his law practice than to chat with you about leaving me and Dick out of your will."

She had learned at Broad Street Church that drinking alcoholic beverages was a sin, and she fussed about beer in the overflow fridge in my studio; it was enough to get me disinherited. Dick was out of her will since he ignored her existence. She qualified the threat with, "Except for a $2,500 CD that I have saved for him. That's all he gets."

Mother no longer tootled around Wilmington in her car; she roamed the halls of CK. She kept a set of keys, one to her room, her file cabinet, her train case, and her lock box at First Citizens Bank that held the $2,500 certificate of deposit for Dick. The keys were strung onto a large safety pin attached to her waistband. I think it was an old blanket pin for a crib. Ever since her years at Broad Street Methodist in Clinton, Mother preached how God looked after her and answered her prayers. When she returned to her room she bowed her head and prayed, "Lord, if it be thy will, please help me find the key to my room." When she opened her eyes after each prayer, the keys appeared, pinned to her waistband. Miracles never cease.

I had converted a storage room downstairs into a place for me to paint. Even though I told Mother that I liked to work in my studio during the morning hours, she made a point to call me early and interrupt my work time. I bought my first answering machine to screen her calls and encouraged her to wait until I took a break at lunchtime. Didn't work. The days went like this:

Betty at the easel, 1980.
Photo by Philip Morgan

8:30 a.m. – Mother called and hung up when she heard the machine.

9:00 a.m. – Repeat—another hang-up.

9:15 a.m. – "I have something for you. Pick up the phone." I guessed the "something for me" was leftovers smuggled from the dining room.

10:00 a.m. – "What are you

doing that's so important? I need to talk to you."

11:05 a.m. – "You stinker, I know you are there. Pick up that phone."

Lunchtime was close, so I answered the phone, "Hello." The scenario didn't vary much from day to day.

She often walked to St. John's Museum of Art at Second and Orange Streets, just a block from CK. Mother had convinced a Mrs. Pearson to accompany her since painting was her hobby. They saw one of my paintings that hung in an exhibition. Later that day, Mother called and said, "Mrs. Pearson saw your painting at the museum. She said it was marvelous and went on and on about it. I didn't see any big deal myself, but she just loved it!"

"Thanks, Mom."

I tried to give her outings whenever I had errands to run. I called ahead, and she waited in one of the rockers on the back porch. As soon as my station wagon pulled into the drive, she hopped up, waved her arms to motion me forward, and pointed her finger as though I didn't know the way to the pickup spot. My resistance to these flamboyant directions cast a mood over our outing before she sat her butt in the car. Later, she walked out to the sidewalk and down the street to watch for me. To try to teach her a lesson and with a little meanness, I drove past a few times and pretended not to see her. But that seemed to hurt, not help. She began to wait in the middle of the street where I wouldn't miss her.

～

Mother continually took food back to her room from the dining room. Her passion to save leftovers overcame all self-discipline. Mother recycled plastic containers before it was the green thing to do. She had put containers to good use before the Tupperware people breathed their first creative breath. A rusty cookie tin served as her storage bin for unused or even partially used packets of sugar, sweetener, and individual jelly containers. She surreptitiously slipped the contraband into her container the way a convict might conceal a table knife from the watchful eye of prison guards.

She tagged along on my trips to Harris Teeter every Thursday. Mother saw me pick up a container of Ruth's pimento cheese spread, even though she had taught me to make much better pimento cheese than Ruth's, but I was in a hurry.

Back in the car, she announced, "I want that pimento cheese container when you finish with it."

"Well, you are not getting it." I answered.

"Why not? I need that container."

"You might die of ptomaine, too." I fought the visual of chicken breasts crammed into a tin on her metal file cabinet.

"You are going to give me that container because I am your mother, and I am telling you to."

She was ready to fight over a plastic container. "There's a North Carolina law that makes the help in the kitchen throw away any food that has been served and that's plain wasteful," she said.

━━━

Sometimes I wondered if I should get Mother out more. If I didn't go by and take her places, she told the nurses, "Betty is picking me up. I'm going to walk out back and meet her." If I wasn't truly coming that day, Mother just walked the 5.3 miles to our house. On his way home one afternoon, Charles saw Mother on busy Dawson Street halfway between CK and our home. She tried to cross in the middle of the block in front of the Dairy Queen. He pulled over and quickly got her to a crosswalk and into his pickup without incident.

If she came to our house and I was not at home, she went to one of my neighbors to hang out until she saw my car back in the driveway. One hot August afternoon I came home and found her seated on the steps at my kitchen door with a cone of chocolate Dairy Queen ice cream that melted down her wrinkled arm and dripped off her elbow. I unlocked the door and ushered her into the house as she explained, "I brought you some soft serve, but it didn't travel too well." She started toward the taffeta-covered seats on the Queen Anne dining room chairs, chosen by Robert Nash Cooper of Robert Nash Cooper Interiors himself.

"Not there!" I shouted.

~

A man rang our doorbell on a Sunday afternoon and asked, "Do you know a Clara Bell?"

"Yes," I paused. "She's my mother."

"Well, she's lying in the grass with her feet propped up on the brick pillars at the entrance to South Oleander. I stopped to see if she was all right. She told me she got tired and thought she would just take a break before she walked the rest of the way to your house."

With gratitude, I brushed off the man, got in my car, and rushed down there to find her in the exact position described by the stranger. "Did that man tell you I was here? I told him where you live," she said as she got into my car.

~

After graduation, Lisa took a job in Orlando, Florida, and married John. For Christmas, 1990, our family planned a trip to be with them in Florida. Guilt made us invite Mother. Charles had the perfect solution. He rented a fourteen-seat van from Triangle Car Rental. "We can take turns driving. Between you, Anna, Chuck, Doug, and me, we can drive all night and have plenty of room to stretch out for naps when one of the others takes the wheel," Charles told me. "We should arrive at Lisa and John's in time for breakfast."

"Great idea," I said.

We stuffed the van with our suitcases and gifts and swung by Catherine Kennedy to pick up Mother at about 9:00 p.m. She brought her cow-hide Samsonite weekender, her bulky blue train case, her shoebox full of jokes, and plastic grocery bags with her Bran Flakes, mellow apples, and Fig Newtons. She also brought a large cardboard box filled with unwrapped things she had accumulated during the year—prizes out of the Bran Flakes boxes, calendars from George Chadwick Insurance, scratch pads and ballpoint pens from businesses around town, and so-called "free gifts" from Robert Schuler and Billy Graham. Mother was well prepared to stand before the family on Christmas morning and hand out her assorted gifts.

With a few grumbles and two aspirin, Charles scrunched Mother's stuff between and under the seats of an already full van. To pack and travel seemed to bring out Charles's grumpy side, and Mother's necessities did not help his mood. We heard him mumble something about getting Geemommy into the van and told us to stop filly-fartin' around. We looked at each other and tried to stifle our guffaws at the term we hadn't heard before. Filly-fartin'? Charles didn't use profanity—that was as close as he came.

Excitement was in the air and conversations were lively over the first couple of hours, but about the time we approached Orangeburg, South Carolina, Mother's fun accelerated and the family's fun waned. Charles had driven since we left home and was ready to turn it over to one of the children. He knew I didn't like to drive after dark, in the rain, through road construction, or at all if I could help it.

Chuck took the wheel, and Charles settled down for his nap on the seat in the back of the van. The conversation had settled into a quiet comprehension of the long trip ahead with the idea that everyone should catch some sleep, until Mother chirped, "It came upon a midnight clear…"

"Mother, we need to settle down now and let Charles get some sleep before he has to drive again."

A few seconds passed before we heard, "Si-uh-lunt night. Hoe-uh-lee night…"

"Mother, shhhh."

Her efforts to organize a choir failed, so she stepped up her game. "JING-GUHL BELLS, JING-GUHL BELLS…." She accompanied her lyrics by shaking the brass bell around her neck. Mother had begun swigging Benadryl along the way, but it must have been a non-drowsy version.

"MOTHER! We have to be quiet and let everyone get some sleep. We will drive all night and need to get some rest before we get to Orlando."

"Shoot," grumbled Mother, "I slept all day so we could stay awake and have some fun on the way to Lisa's."

She had her fun, but the rest of us didn't. Most people get carsick or fanny fatigue on long trips, but my irritable bowel syndrome flares up and Charles gets headaches. About the time we crossed into Florida out of Georgia, the IBS rumbled and the headache arrived as predicted. We limped from gas station to rest stop from there to Orlando and ate away the time we had saved.

CK was still at the corner of Third and Orange Streets when we returned. However, I wouldn't have been surprised if they had moved away and left no forwarding address while we were in Florida.

41. The Camel's Back

Mother found that walks downtown entertained her for one reason or another, or for no reason at all. She had lost a stone out of her wedding ring years earlier and it made her paranoid that she might lose another tiny diamond. One of her favorite pastimes was to go by Albert Rhodes Jewelers to have her stones checked and cleaned for free. It was a ritual she indulged in far more often than necessary. Sometimes, she had them check the crystal on her watch. She was in and out of there about once a week. She claimed the staff as intimate friends and pecked on the window like a mocking bird for them to let her in before they had opened for business.

My watch had acted up so I asked Mother to take it into Rhodes for repair. I circled the block and picked her up. The next week, I stopped to see if my watch was ready, but the lady couldn't find it under my name. She pulled out a big log and scanned the names to see if she could figure it out. I read the list upside down and saw the name Clara S. Bell next to a watch repair. I pointed it out to the clerk who said, "Oh no, that couldn't be it. That's some nutty lady who comes in here all the time."

"Bingo! That nutty lady is my mother and that's my watch."

"I am so embarrassed," said the jewelry clerk. "I didn't realize…"

"Don't be. I can be embarrassed enough for both of us."

Sloshed buckets of water and stolen Coke machine keys and many similar episodes prompted Mr. Abbott to invite me to his office to hear his latest complaint. His implied threats to expel Mother scared the pudding out of me. Mother walked a tightrope with very little balance, and I stood on the ground to catch her. By spring of 1991, I daily expected that final leap from grace at CK.

Age and the acidity of the Scotch tape that held photos and news clippings to her walls caused the tape to curl. It grew brittle and left messy glue marks on the walls of her room. No matter—she patched fallen items with another application of tape on top of the old. That was good enough for her. But her attempts to patch her social life and to maintain friendships were in no way sufficient. They became as brittle and messy as the old Scotch tape.

I was desperate to understand why Mother indulged in "socially unacceptable behavior," the label the retirement home people used. I made an appointment with the neurologist, Dr. Queen, to whom I had taken Mother when she first moved to Wilmington. "If there is some hidden reason for her behavior, I want to know what it is," I insisted.

"Has she ever experienced a severe blow to the head?" asked Dr. Queen during an examination of Mother, now in her late seventies.

"There is a story about an iron gate that fell on her when they lived in Charleston. Mother was about five years old then. I don't know for certain if a blow to the head occurred. Mother's mercurial personality has been hard to figure out all her life. She is as busy as a bee hive, and she thinks she's the queen bee." Dr. Queen decided to send Mother to a geriatric psychiatrist to see if he could help unravel the mystery of Mother.

The psychiatrist was up in years himself and it didn't take long for Mother to have him as addled as she had me. Her rat-a-tat-tat chatter and constant movement flustered him, I could tell. She was on a high, flattered that this elderly doctor had asked her to talk about herself. She wound him up like a toy, making it harder for him to maintain his even voice and gentle psychiatrist's manner.

"Here is a prescription for Ativan. This should calm her so she can fit into society more aptly."

"Ahhh, maybe this will do the trick. Thank you, Doctor." His quick solution gave me hope.

A few days after that appointment, I called to see if Mother wanted to accompany me on a trip to Florence, South Carolina, a two-hour drive from Wilmington. I had developed a painful shoulder and my orthopedist decided to send me to Florence where a doctor had done some innovative work with arthroscopy on shoulders.

I pulled into the back driveway at CK. There she sat in a rocker—was this a sign that the Ativan worked? Mother hadn't bounced out to the street to meet me, but before we crossed the bridge out of Wilmington, she began to fidget. She opened up every flap and zipper in the Dooney & Bourke purse handed down from her friend Paula. She rattled cellophane, opened tins of pills, closed the purse, put it away, and then repeated the previous actions. She reapplied her lipstick and fumbled for a Luden's cough drop. This happened about three hundred and forty-two times, to and from Florence. I decided the Ativan was not a suitable tranquilizer, so we didn't see the geriatric psychiatrist again.

In later years, I found a note Mother entered into one of her composition book journals:

> I think when I was 77 years old, plus about 3 or 4 weeks, my nerves started acting up (as I would repeat everything I thought of, but not out loud.) Betty has taken me out in her car on Thursdays, when she doesn't have something else to do. Last Thursday we went to Phar-Mor. I talked bad to Betty when she asked me to go by myself while she waited in the car. I told her, if she and Dick and Charles didn't pay me some attention that I was going to change my will and give the money I have left when I die to church or CK or somewhere else. Betty said, she didn't care. I walked all over the store and bought only one thing that I had on my list. It was all I could find that I wanted. I think when I get used to my new medicine I will do better. Meanwhile, I tell Betty and Charles to wait until they get to be my age, and they will know how it feels.

Mother accused me of moving her to Wilmington without introducing her to people who would be her friends. However, she had exhausted any friend candidates among the sixty-plus ladies who lived in the home. She ran out of people to give her that cherished attention she craved. Now she considered her most loyal friends those who worked in stores around town. Sales clerks smiled and chatted with her.

However, a large quiet woman with a kinky reddish permanent who looked through narrow eye slits was pleasant as could be to Mother. Mrs. Lula Fletcher befriended mother. I thought it strange that Mother was nice to a lady named Fletcher, since I remembered how she frowned when I asked Jackie Fletcher to a Sadie Hawkins hayride in junior high. After she lived next door to the boisterous Fletchers on Rutherford Road, Mother had harbored a prejudice toward people named Fletcher. She called them tacky.

Mother told me that Mrs. Fletcher had taken a fall and broken her arm. I prayed the fall had nothing to do with Mother. It must not have, or I would've had a call from Mr. Abbott. On day one after the fall, Mother hot-footed it two doors down to help Lula dress. Then she returned at bedtime and helped her into her nightgown. It was the third morning of the routine when Mother barged into Mrs. Fletcher's room and slapped the face of the nurse who blocked her way. This prompted the last call from Mr. Abbott who demanded that I remove my mother immediately from Catherine Kennedy Home for Ladies. Now I had no place for her to go.

42. The Search

I brought Mother to our house, but agonized about what I should do, and how long it might take to find another place for her. I knew well my three-day limit for sharing a roof with her. My chest hurt from the stress, as it had when the children were little and I had to take all four of them downtown, to the mall, or to the beach by myself. The spasm in my left side wrapped around my midriff.

Mother had pushed Mr. Abbott to the edge. I resented her putting me through this problem with little hope of finding a solution. *Who?* I asked myself. *Who will want to take Mother with her record?*

I didn't speak to her for the next eight hours. She was even quiet herself. I wondered if she knew it might be appropriate to keep quiet. Then, reality registered—no, she's just playing it safe, "flying low" as Daddy would have put it. I put her suitcase and train case in a corner of the pink bedroom, now vacant since Anna had enrolled at N.C. State University. Pink—perfect! Law enforcement people put criminals in pink rooms to calm them.

Charles came home from work, and after a silent supper, he and I tidied the kitchen. We went to our bedroom and closed the door so that I could convey the whole story to him. I cut loose; all my rage and helplessness spurted out like lava.

"Mr. Abbott says we have to have her room cleaned out by the first thing tomorrow. What will I do?"

"I'll go by in the pickup before work."

He turned on the television for the news. Charles didn't fret or spew frustration the way I did.

Within five minutes, Mother bounded into our bedroom, without a knock but with a big grin and a, "Hey, let's watch the news." She knew very well I was not receptive to her charms, so she put Charles to the test.

"Clara, go watch the television in the family room if you want to watch the news," he told her.

A few minutes passed, and she was back. After several further attempts to invade our bedroom, we locked the door.

The next morning, I opened the yellow pages and looked for retirement homes. I devoted the week, and we visited each one. Mother had the nerve to turn up her nose at some of the nicer places. "Too prissy," she'd say, "Mark that one off your list." And to complicate matters, her reputation had preceded her at every home within New Hanover, Brunswick, and Pender Counties. An extensive grapevine among the nurses, aides, and kitchen workers in the area had spread Mother's story like a Kudzu vine.

A friend from church stepped in to help. She was not allowed to admit Mother where she worked—a place that had been at the top of my list, but, as a nurse, she helped me place Mother on a probationary stay at Harrington Health Care in Burgaw, a thirty-minute drive from Wilmington. The bumfuzzled psychiatrist we had seen had suggested that we put some distance between us to avoid the walk to our house, so maybe the thirty miles between us was a good idea.

"Your mother will be asked to leave if she steps out of line," they told us at Harrington.

Step out of line? The rumors must not have traveled to Burgaw. At best, I hoped the trial basis might give us a couple of months before the new place had a stomach full of Clara S. Bell.

43. Harrington Health Care

It has been said that the name Burgaw is Native American for "mud hole." The new place was no Catherine Kennedy Home— they were more likely to throw a catfish fry on the riverbank than a silver tea in a formal dining room. No more white linen napkins and table cloths. No more private room with a carpeted floor or Robert Cooper drapes. No more well-coiffured volunteers from First Presbyterian Church who arranged buckets of fresh flowers into vases on the surfaces of every heirloom antique in each cushy parlor. The bouquets at the new place were plastic. The wind was not knocked out of Mother's sails. She could live without all the airs, but my sails were slack, locked in without a breeze.

After I settled Mother into her semi-private room, her half-sister, Edith, called to let us know that Mother's stepmother, Polly, had died. Polly had been in and out of the hospital for a while. Her circulation failed and her legs had to be amputated. No one wanted to see Polly suffer. She had provided a soft lap for all of us at one time or another—except for maybe Aileen.

Mother went along for the ride to the funeral, but she showed no outward emotion over Polly's passing. The family met at the funeral home in Gaffney prior to the service. Aileen's daughter Penny and her husband Tom brought Aileen from Columbia. Penny's older brother didn't attend. He had pulled away from Aileen much as Dick had alienated himself from Mother—yet another ironic comparison that Penny and I observed about the sisters.

Aileen feigned a sick headache and car sickness. Rather than go to the church for Polly's funeral, she curled up on a sofa at the funeral home and asked the funeral director for a damp paper towel for her forehead and an afghan for her legs. Several of us witnessed Aileen's perfect rendition of an aunt with a psychosomatic illness. The rest of the family went to Buford Street Methodist for a service that befit this respectable Southern lady.

⁓

Soon after Mother settled in at her new home in Burgaw, we realized that funds for her care had nearly run out. The expenses had depleted what little money she had left from Daddy's insurance and the sale of Ding Dong Hill. Even though her assets dwindled, she continued to tell me, "I'm not leaving a thing to Dick unless he comes to see me." She maintained that the $2,500 CD in her lock box was for Dick and repeated once more, "That is all he gets."

That was pretty much all there was. Her $600 a month from South Carolina employees' benefits plus social security would not cover her monthly bills, but she continued to send a meager tithe to her church in Clinton, as well as regular checks to Robert Schuler and Billy Graham. In return, she received massive quantities of brochures, propaganda, and an occasional coffee mug from the two religious icons themselves. But it gave Mother one more connection, albeit empty and inauthentic. She wrote in her diary:

I listened to a program on television tonight. Billy Graham was the preacher, and it was real good. I think I got saved that night by Billy Graham.

The administrator at Harrington advised me to put Mother's pittance of a checking account into my name and have our attorney friend Donald draw up power-of-attorney papers. I also made an appointment with a CPA and asked his advice. He recommended I go ahead and turn over the CD to Dick and have him sign a statement that confirmed the receipt of the CD that finalized any and all inheritance he would receive at Mother's death. I called Dick and explained the situation, but he refused to sign a statement. "She might win the lottery the day before she dies," was his offhand logic.

I lost the control I had held onto for so many years. "What is it that bothers you, Dick? Why have you cut the family out of your life with no explanation?" The question shot out of my mouth—the question that had bothered me since Dick withdrew after the death of my father. At that time, I had no knowledge that our parents confiscated his educational fund. Even so, how did I fit into his grudge toward our parents?

"I just want to be left alone." It was an icy tone. His obstinate disregard of our marred relationship opened the gate, and my emotions stampeded like a herd of beasts.

"Well, that's just what I plan to do!"

I slammed the receiver down. I knew I'd lost my composure—lost it big time. I cried until Charles came home from work, and for days, whenever I recalled the conversation. I agonized over the loss of my brother even though I had truly lost him the day Daddy died. And I still didn't have an explanation as to why. I fantasized about a pseudo-funeral for my brother to escape the reality of a broken relationship.

In addition to my commitments to Mother, Dick, and Harrington Health Care, Charles and I struggled with the business he had bought with his brother-in-law in 1965. It failed in 1992, due to complicated adverse financial demands. Liquidation seemed to be the answer.

I noticed that when I stretched out on my bed to watch the news after dinner, I experienced severe pains in my mid-section, different from the pains in my back and chest from stress. Dr. Queen referred me to a family physician since our doctor had retired.

When the new doctor walked into the examination room, he asked about my symptoms. I told him, "My stomach hurts; I have tendonitis in my shoulders; I have acid reflux, IBS, PMS, and frequent migraine headaches."

"Is there anything in your personal life that might worry you?"

"Mother could be kicked out of the only nursing home that will have her within three counties, and I'm the one person in the world who takes responsibility for her. My brother has alienated himself from the family, my husband lost his business and doesn't have a job, and I can't find any uninterrupted time to paint." I may as well have melted into a puddle at the doctor's feet. He didn't bat an eye. I guessed that similar sob stories were not uncommon to him. I remembered that Daddy warned me not to complain. He said, "There are always people in the world who are worse off than you."

The doctor wrote down the name of a therapist so that I could begin counseling. "I can't do that. I don't have the money."

"If you don't do it, you will ruin your health and that would be even more expensive." He handed me a slip from his prescription pad with a name and phone number scribbled there.

The therapist listened to me tell my story over a period of time, in one-hour sessions. She rarely interjected comments but took copious notes about my childhood, my brother's withdrawal, my mother's eccentric ways, my father's stern ways, even my relationship with Charles. She had Charles come in for a session. Asking Charles to talk about his feelings was like asking a blind man to describe a painting. He couldn't do it.

The therapist advised me to put my relationship with my brother to rest. "Write him a non-accusatory letter to let him know that you love him and that your door is always open to him, but that you plan to 'leave him alone' as he requested."

I followed her advice and tried to put Dick out of my mind.

44. Old Habits Don't Die

I received the first call that Mother was acting out—something about pushing the residents around the hallways in their wheelchairs. "We can't let her push the patients because we would be held liable if anything happened," the head nurse said. I drove the twenty-eight miles up Interstate 40 then took the Burgaw exit at Highway 53. Her misbehavior necessitated a lecture, so I drove Mother to the central square in downtown Burgaw.

A few outdated stores and abandoned spaces surrounded the courthouse, itself surrounded by trees and green. Since nothing much ever happened in Burgaw, I had no problem finding a parking place. After I pulled into a diagonal space, I ushered Mother toward the ornate wooden bandstand on the grounds. I sat her down on the steps to the stage and launched into a preaching that made Jimmy Swaggart look like an amateur. My childhood training for show biz made me a star who poured out advice to my audience of one.

"It will not do for you to get kicked out of another home," I told her. "No one will have you. You must stay on your best behavior, or we will all be yesterday's grits." I preached and paced back and forth in front of my congregation, a little old lady who behaved like a two-year-old.

While I defined her destiny, Mother sat in the shade of the shelter with a serene gaze into the live oak trees. In my desperation, I soon realized that my voice traveled from one end of a long tunnel where no one listened on the other end. In my summation, I leaned forward, took her by the shoulders, looked her square in the eye, and pleaded, "Don't do this to me, Mother." Why did she have that twinkle in her blue eyes? Did she enjoy my angst? This wasn't a game—or was it?

I stepped back from her and she stood. "Let's go by Dees Drug Store and get a fountain Coke before you take me back," she said. I followed her order and bought her a Coca-Cola. We drove back to Harrington and, after I took her to her room, I went by the office of head nurse Linda to take one last stab at smoothing ruffled feathers.

I dropped whatever occupied me and raced the twenty-eight miles to Burgaw every time the home called to report Mother's bad behavior. I whisked her away from the facility, took her to Dees Drug store, and ordered her a Coke and a pack of Nabs so we could use a booth for our heart-to-heart talks. Over and over, I warned Mother she would be kicked out of this new place if she didn't straighten up.

A couple of days might go by before another call came. "Your mother rushes too fast through the corridors and bumps into other patients. They lose their balance," or, "She helps other patients with their wheelchairs, even though we've told her not to touch them." Each call threatened to be the last, but Harrington continued to let her stay.

The following weeks were up and down. I averaged two to three trips a week to Burgaw. Every time Harrington called, I drove to Burgaw. Mother delighted in setting this up for me. She was the elephant trainer, and I was the big old elephant performing her tricks.

Lela, the activities director, and I put our heads together. We realized we had been manipulated and the little old lady outsmarted us. Mother had learned to act up just enough to get me up there to "visit." So Lela and I devised a plan. I would limit my visits to once a week. If Mother misbehaved during that week, my trip to Burgaw was canceled. I was grateful that the staff at the home worked with me without threats of expulsion. The plan worked pretty well.

After my visits with Mother, I stopped at the Exxon station on the edge of Burgaw and rewarded my diligence with a Baby Ruth and a Diet Coke, then I headed back onto Interstate 40 for Wilmington.

My therapist said, "I want you to find a support system. Take a friend or family member along each time you visit your mother. You need someone to keep you company before, during, and after your visits." I took her advice and invited friends on my weekly jaunts. I tried to spread the joy amongst those who loved me enough to understand. I treated them to a Baby Ruth and Diet Coke on the way back to Wilmington.

My preacher told me, "Even though you yearn for a 'normal' mother, you will not have one since people don't change. She is who she is." He also told me, "Oftentimes one family member stays true to a difficult relative, as a co-dependent; others deal with the problem and remove themselves from the situation as your brother has chosen to do."

I dragged Charles away from the ball game on TV, and we made the weekly visit on the next Sunday afternoon. Guests who came to visit on Sundays were invited to crowd into the living room off the front hall, much like relatives visited prison inmates on weekends, minus the screen mesh or thick glass that separated inmates from their families.

Charles and I ushered Mother into the visiting room and found two seats on a far sofa and a stack chair next to it. We were barely settled onto the burgundy-and-blue-striped upholstery before we noticed a lady resident move into a chair from her wheelchair. She tried to fold the wheelchair into a space-saving position. Mother bobbed up from her stack chair like a jack rabbit. She tugged at the chair until she pulled it away from the lady. I took off, exasperated. Charles scolded Mother for disobeying the rules. He tried to escort her to her room, but Mother broke away and ran toward the parking lot after me. She outpaced Charles, who followed her like a big sweet collie dog. She got to me, and I spun around. "You've been told not to mess with the other patients, but you do whatever you damn well please." I looked squarely into her steely blue eyes. "Don't you?"

Mother pondered the question only too briefly before she replied, "Yep, pretty much."

No "pretty much" about it—she had forever done whatever she damn well pleased. She knew it, I knew it, and Charles knew it.

I lived the frustration Daddy had lived—if I drank bourbon, this would be the night I crouched in the corner of the kitchen, but I don't drink bourbon. I do drink a gin and tonic with a lime twist, and I had just that when Charles and I returned home.

45. Fields of Flowers

The next week a group of my artist friends planned a day trip to paint at a flower farm just outside Wallace, on the other side of Burgaw. Fields of larkspurs, gladiolas, Shasta daisies, and dahlias grew there, and the fields were about to peak. I asked my buddy Gladys to ride with me. I hoped she wouldn't mind a stop by Burgaw to fulfill my weekly visit. Mother considered Gladys one of us since she had grown up in Greenville too. We found Mother as she left the dining room after breakfast. The three of us sat on a deacon's bench along the wall in the wide brightly-lit institutional corridor.

"There is a flower farm up the road where we plan to paint," I told Mother. About that time, I noticed decrepit old Miss Eula Mae Pridgen snailing down the hall toward her room. She rolled the wheels of her chair at a speed of about an inch every fifteen seconds, minus time spent in a rest between wheel turns. Jack Rabbit Clara went into action and raced from the bench toward Miss Pridgen. She grabbed the handles at the back of the wheelchair like the bars on her Schwinn bicycle and trotted toward Miss Pridgen's room. The old lady's eyes widened in surprise.

I went into action, too, and fulfilled my pledge that I would not visit Mother when she disobeyed the rules. I spun on my Reeboked heels and huffed toward the exit. "Come on, Gladys." Gladys looked dizzy and confused but followed me to the car. Mother caught up about the time we jumped into the car. I left her to stew in her own juice.

Once we pulled away from the parking lot, Gladys said, "After you turned to leave, I looked back and watched your mom. When she saw you leave, she hunched over the back of that wheelchair, clenched the handlebars, and launched that old lady down the corridor with one huge shove!" I pictured Miss Pridgen's little arms and legs flailing in the air as though she were on a ride at the county fair.

My happy thoughts of painting in the solace of the flower farm had vanished, but I stayed on plan and muttered under my breath with every splash of watercolor pigment from palette to pristine paper.

The next week, the activities director called me about an incident in the craft room. Mother's rogue acts had turned more diabolical. Mother had asked for someone to pass the scissors to her. The other ladies in the craft room ignored her and continued to work. Mother picked up an X-Acto knife and demanded that the ladies pass her the scissors. The other women froze, but the bravest of them ran to find the activities director. Meanwhile, Mother took the knife to her room, hid it, and refused to give it up to the director or the head nurse.

Clara carried out these episodes with a Southern belle smile on her face. When she was accused of misbehavior, she pretended to play around. The patients were not so sure of her playfulness, but Mother had ways to win them over. She offered to show a movie on the VCR that her niece Annelle had sent.

Lela restricted Mother from the activities room because of the disruption. I knew that it was best to keep Mother busy and occupied. I worried about how this new tactic might work.

She also walked into the rooms of male or female residents who were in various stages of undress. The nurses chased Mother as she darted through the halls. She was so fast it was hard to catch her for a scolding. On one of these times, she dropped and broke her pedometer, but she didn't care. She told me, "I already know that I walk these corridors an average of three miles a day. Pretty good, huh?"

The home had required her to use a local physician, and we had chosen Dr. Rella, who seemed confused by Clara and her Parkinson's diagnosis. He decided to bring in Dr. Franzen, the resident psychiatrist. The doctor didn't tell Dr. Rella anything we didn't already know, but Franzen wanted to rule out bipolar disorder, obsessive-compulsive disorder, and Alzheimer's disease.

Mother's neurologist in Wilmington, Dr. Queen, confided that she, too, wondered about the diagnosis of Parkinson's disease at such an early age. Our daughter Anna had become a special education teacher in Charlotte. She suggested that her Geemommy exhibited traits of adult attention deficit hyperactivity disorder. But if that were the case, Dr. Queen said medication for ADHD would not be compatible with her Parkinson's meds. No diagnosis was ever clear, so I continued to believe that her behavior amplified traits she possessed her whole life.

When I went to Burgaw to check on Mother, I often found her moved to a new room with a new roommate. Mother wrote in her diary, *I don't know whose fault it is but they are always finding new roommates for me.*

Even the patience of Charles waned with time. We had brought Mother to our house one Saturday for a visit. We had worked in the yard. Charles stood near the garage when Mother said to him, "I want to borrow some tools from Olin's toolbox that I gave you. I need a Phillips screwdriver and a monkey wrench to fix some things at Harrington."

When he refused, Mother slapped him on the face. Over the years, Charles, bless his heart, had been far more patient with Mother than I had ever been. But when Mother slapped him, Charles's patience toward his mother-in-law hit a new low.

46. Matters Deteriorate

Mother continued to save packets of sugar, sweetener, plus plastic containers of jelly from the dining room. My therapist advised me, "Just take the items, dispose of them, and look at your mother, not as the person who exasperates you, but as a little old lady who now needs your love and support."

I said, "Fine. But the little old lady has been this way all her life. What's new?"

However, I noticed that Mother had slowed down, and I saw her in a different light. I watched her from the parking lot in front of Harrington as she toddled down the walk and back into the facility. The old Clara was still there, but she now needed help that I could not deny. I started to walk her into the building and back to her room. My therapist seemed to be right.

One day my rain-or-snow postman rang my front doorbell. He shifted from one foot to the other, a look of dismay crossed over his shiny-hot brow. He reached toward me and presented a flimsy Lance cracker box tied up with string. A fine white substance that resembled sugar or sweetener sifted into the weave of my doormat. Sticky purple jelly oozed from the corners of the cracker box. I took the package and the postman reached for his sweat-soaked handkerchief. "So sorry. I'll get you a damp paper towel. Just wait right here."

I had missed my weekly trip to Burgaw to pick up her "something-for-yous," so she had collected them into this flimsy box and taken the smuggled goods to the post office for a trip to Wilmington. A few days later I received a postcard from Mother. She asked, "How 'bout bringing me some small sturdy boxes?"

A postman stopped by Harrington and explained that the post office machinery was too rough for her Lance cartons filled with the jelly, sugar, and sweetener packets she had mailed to relatives across the Carolinas. "They have ruined other people's mail and we need for you to please stop."

Other problems with the postal service arose when Mother's lovely cursive began to deteriorate in about 1992. By 1994, I could barely read it. Her forward-slanted handwriting looked shaky and angular. She often re-wrote over the top of words she had already written, her own style of hieroglyphics. Return address stickers from her friends got the addresses right, but the handwritten messages were impossible to read. I replaced Mother's old Underwood typewriter with a Smith-Corona electric. She couldn't get the hang of the electric part and fussed when she rested her fingers on the home keys, which produced *dddddddd* or *kkkkkkkkkkkkkk*. A letter to her favorite niece Annelle read:

> *Dear Annelle, and all,*
>
> *Betty brought this electric agtypewriter to me to use to use when I wanteer ddtp wrote them a letter so they could read itlll..I'm not used to it yet so please exccuee all*
>
> *The mistakes I make in it. I don"t know any bews as all we do around here is eaat aand sleepraoond here and andread letters and newspapers and blooks, and aamagazines like the ones yoou send me. I enjou getting them and any mail that I get.*
>
> *I go to the dining room and read a book.... I have read 9/1/9 books aso far....... As it is easier to read them in in there. Tjere are///tablew' in there and you can read better when you have ////some.where to prop your book.. there is nothing in our room but a bed and chest/// of drawwes and a TV in my room. I have a room mate and an/// and I can't tallk after dinner ao we get along OK. So don't all me on the phone... as I won8t t be able to talkl to uoi. I would rsther get some mail anyway.*
>
> *I guessthis is all I know to tell you. For this time....I hope you can read this...*

Today is Lisa's birthday and I have a card to snq send her bubut tshe is moving up norrh somewhere and I don8t have her new addrews so wioll have to wait and gdt it later. I guess it is better llaate than never.

I don't know any news to tellll you so will close for this time.

Love

aunt// Clara

When the price of postage stamps increased, I furnished one-cent stamps for additional postage on Mother's envelopes and postcards. I must have given her more than she needed, because I received a postcard covered with the leftover one-cent stamps, with just enough room for the address label in the center.

Her obsession with the postal service was mild next to several episodes when Mother choked on her food and the orderlies rushed her across the street to Pender Memorial Hospital.

After additional incidents, Dr. Rella recommended a series of cookie swallow tests administered by speech therapists at the hospital in Wilmington. Mother loved the attention from the technicians, but she failed the tests miserably. I could see the cookie go into her lungs while I watched her profile on the X-ray.

I dreaded the cookie swallow tests that she always failed, but Mother loved the free cookie. The home was advised to serve a soft diet to her, but I'm not sure she adhered to this, which might explain all the times the nurse's administered the Heimlich maneuver on Mother in the dining room.

After a serious bout of choking, they called for me to come to the hospital. I was escorted into the hospital's intensive care unit. I walked through a maze of cold metal machines to where she lay on a stretcher with a respirator attached to her mouth and nose. She was attended by a flock of nurses. It was the first time I saw her exhibit fear—she had lost control with no way to manipulate out of this situation. Unable to speak, she pleaded to me in the language of her blue eyes, "Get this contraption off me and get me out of here!"

I understood the message as though it had been shouted. I

explained with my own blue eyes, "I am as helpless as you and don't know what to do."

We both remembered Dr. Queen's explanation that with a Parkinson's diagnosis, the time would come when Mother might be put on life support. When Mother first saw Dr. Queen we talked about stomach tubes, respirators, and such. Mother assured her doctor that she wanted no part of life-saving measures to be taken. We set up a living will as the nursing home had advised. The will provided final decisions for Charles and me. In a few days, Mother recovered and went back to Harrington, as she had done on many other occasions when she choked and developed pneumonia.

Edith sent money for me to have someone give Mother a manicure and pedicure. She knew Clara would love to be pampered.

47. Sisters Part

A few weeks later, Harrington sent Mother to Pender Memorial with her most dreadful case of pneumonia yet. Dr. Rella's examination also found an unexplained mass on her kidney, but he thought she was too sick for him to send her from Burgaw to Wilmington for further tests. When she slipped into a coma, the nurses let me believe that she might rally and go back to Harrington, as she had done so many times before.

Over the next few days, I broke my rule about visits to Mother only once a week and was back and forth so I could I stay in close touch with the nurses. She remained in an unconscious state. Dr. Rella had gone out of town and his stand-in was a doctor whose thick accent was difficult for me to understand. However, I heard every word when he told me he planned to put a stomach tube into Mother. I glared at the doctor across the bed and informed him, "She has made it clear to me and her doctor in Wilmington that she doesn't want a stomach tube."

He fixed a defiant stare toward me. "You will starve her to death!"

"No! I will not allow a tube." I had raised my voice at the doctor, and I stormed out of the room.

I bumped into a nurse at the door and repeated my orders. "Do not let that man put a stomach tube into my mother." I drove home, cried into my Diet Coke, and skipped the Baby Ruth.

I slammed my front door behind me and went for the phone to report to Dr. Queen what the doctor in Burgaw had said to me over Mother's bed. I sobbed, "I've heard all the stories about how people in comas can understand conversations around them even though they are unconscious, so I was livid that he argued with me in her presence. She lay there so still, but I knew she could hear him, and I knew her wishes."

Dr. Queen told me, "You did the right thing." Then she added, "Nature has ways to deal with the needs of a patient, and your mother will not feel pangs of hunger, but will endure the lack of nourishment in a peaceful way. She will not suffer."

After I called the family to let them know about Mother's hospitalization and how sick she was, Aileen called me back. "I am coming to check on your Mother. I'll get Penny's husband Tom to drive me there. I've always worried about Clara and her spiritual life," Aileen said. "I feel called to go to her and make sure she has been saved."

To make sure she has been saved? After I hung up, I digested Aileen's irritating comment. Why would she accuse Mother of not being saved? Surely, God creates impulsive, attention-seeking, fun-loving people like Mother—on rare occasions, at least. The money Clara sent to Billy Graham and Robert Schuler alone should have amply fulfilled her Methodist good works that would save her. Too bad these facetious comebacks weren't available earlier.

From the day Mother moved into Harrington, five years earlier, she longed for Aileen to visit, so she could show off her new accommodations. But Aileen didn't find the time until her sister Clara was comatose.

The next day Aileen and Tom arrived on my doorstep just before lunch. They wanted to go for a seafood platter before we headed to Burgaw. Aileen's craving for shrimp and flounder moved her visit with Mother into second place. It was just like any other day in the life of Missionary Aileen. She didn't ask for an update on Mother, but she chatted non-stop about her latest accomplishments—her election to an international office of Altrusa and her oversight of the renovation of the downtown library in Columbia. What a busy woman.

When we reached the hospital, I didn't go into Mother's room with Aileen. Some ritualistic laying on of hands might have sent me over the edge. I flipped through a magazine while Tom and I waited for Aileen to come out of Mother's room. She didn't comment about the visit—but what could be of interest about a visit with a comatose eighty-three-year-old? Their chance to be fond sisters was over. Aileen tried to commiserate with me about dealing with Mother over the years, but I would not take her bait to expound on grudges I might harbor. Tom chauffeured Aileen back to Columbia.

48. Clara Leaves

The Sunday afternoon after Aileen had visited, Chuck and his daughters came to Burgaw from Raleigh to see how things were going. Lisa and her family had relocated to Wilmington a few months earlier that year. She rode with Charles and me from Wilmington to Burgaw. We had lots of questions for the nurses, but each nurse who popped in and out of Mother's room told us that she would have the head nurse come by and answer our questions.

We waited for the head nurse to come and ease our concerns. We took turns and checked for her at the nurses' station and in the corridors. She never came. Mother's hands felt cold and swollen. Should that be a concern, I wondered?

Chuck said, "It's late and I need to get the girls back to Raleigh." They had stayed most of the day and evening. Charles had tried to entertain his two girls in the lobby, but they had been there long enough to get bored and hungry.

Chuck, Lisa, and I held hands around Mother's hospital bed. We took her icy swollen hands in ours, and we prayed for her. I closed our prayer and explained to Mother that we planned to go for supper at Holly Shelter before sending Chuck and his family back to Raleigh. "You are in God's hands now. We will come back tomorrow." We squeezed her swollen hands and turned on a lamp. We noticed how odd it seemed to see Mother so quiet and still before we slipped from the tranquil room. No one had ever known Clara to lie so still and quiet—never, in all her years between 11/12/13 and 2/25/96, had anyone seen her so peaceful.

After supper, Charles, Lisa, and I went home, and Chuck and

family left for Raleigh. The telephone rang just as we hung our coats in the closet. The head nurse who had never come by the room asked to speak with me, and I was excited to have a chance to ask all our questions. "What about Mother's cold, swollen hands? What should we do to…?"

She stopped me mid-sentence. "I am calling to let you know that Mrs. Bell died."

"I don't understand. We were just there about an hour ago. We had a prayer and said our goodbyes for the evening."

"She passed away a short time ago, probably not long after you left the hospital." The nurse added, "She was ready, and you gave her permission to leave."

I sank into the bedroom chair; it was soft like arms to hold me. A dimmed light in our bedroom made it feel warm and serene. I sensed the peace that Mother must feel now.

But then I stiffened and thought of things to do. The nurse told me that they would notify Andrews Mortuary for us. I thought of people to call—Lisa, Chuck, Anna, and Doug. I didn't want to deal with Dick—I asked Annelle to call him, Jane, our cousin Anne, and anyone else in Greenville. Edith could call the Scotts, including Aileen. Aileen would let the Weavers in Atlanta know. Oh, and Paula could call people in Clinton and Renno. My eldest-child efficiency rallied into motion. I'd think about missing Mother tomorrow. It was out of my hands now—in God's hands, indeed.

"If there are no roller skates in heaven, Clara will see that there are from now on," Edith told me over the phone.

I knew she was right. "She'll have a big blue Schwinn too."

～

The office at Harrington Health called the next morning by 8:30—the day after Mother had surrendered and died. The administrator's assistant asked us to come remove her belongings. Charles and I took his pickup to Burgaw and loaded the Naugahyde vinyl La-Z-Boy, the floral comforter, her two-drawer metal file cabinet, a box full of forbidden over-the-counter meds, and a closet full of polyester clothes with an infinite shelf-life. Several of the nurses and aides came by the room while we packed. "We sure will miss Miss Clara. She really kept things lively and interesting around here."

"You're very sweet. I hope she wasn't too much trouble."

I saw two aides exchange looks before they answered, "No, ma'am, she was just fine. We liked her a lot."

I was sure their days would lack the drama and capricious behavior Mother offered. They did seem to dread the old routine. I thought about the unpredictability of my own days over the last ten years since Clara moved into CK, then Harrington. It was hard for me to imagine how things would now change.

That evening, we went about our routine—ate supper, cleaned up, and watched the news. We had piled Mother's belongings into a corner of our kitchen under the stained-glass window. It looked like a makeshift shrine.

49. The Service

Mother's surviving kin gathered at Edith's house in Spartanburg, where Charles and I spent the night before the graveside service in Clinton. Our conversation filled Edith's family room and the chatter soon turned into Geemommy tales. We laughed hysterically as family members tried to top each other.

"I was mortified the time she lifted her skirt in front of my boyfriend Dave when she backed up to an open fire." Aileen repeated that story again.

Edith's daughter Jana retold how Clara invented pump toothpaste and made Colgate-Palmolive rich. "She always kept me in my place and told me, 'I just wish I was as cute as some people think they are.'"

Cousin Mildred added, "Or, 'I wish I was as smart as some people think they are.'" It was late into the night before folks drifted back to their motels. We had celebrated her life with our own homespun eulogy.

After Mother moved to Wilmington, the Methodist church had assigned a new preacher to the church that she attended in Clinton. The new minister knew Mother best by her reputation and her tiny tithe.

Doug's wife, Mandy, had graduated from a seminary in Richmond, Virginia. The Cooperative Baptist Fellowship Church where she worked part-time had ordained her and hired her full time. Charles and I decided to ask her to co-pastor the funeral with the Methodist clergyman, since he didn't know Mother well. Mandy had passed muster as an in-law, and she had experienced Mother's eccentric ways. She could add a personal touch to the service.

We had arranged a graveside service in Clinton and paid for funeral arrangements back when Mother had $4,000 in her checking account. We planned to bury her next to Daddy in the remaining plot he bought when they first moved to Renno. I ordered a spray of flowers in Rubik's Cube hues for the top of the casket.

I wondered if Dick would show up. I scanned the people gathered for the service and spotted Dick and his friend Olga on the far side of the parked cars. Olga had once told me, "Dick doesn't talk about his family or give any reasons why he keeps such a distance." At least Mother could no longer write letters and pester him to visit her.

Although I knew I was imperfect, I vowed to work toward a happy relationship with my own children. I never wanted to feel the hurt Mother felt from the broken relationship with the son who had been the apple of her eye. Of course, I couldn't altogether blame Dick for this estrangement. Life with Mother proved difficult. Daddy was unable to do it, and I supported her out of a sense of duty.

I was already seated on one of the rickety folding chairs under the Gray's Funeral Home tent. Our chairs balanced on a rug of artificial green turf that caught the heels of my pumps. Mandy whispered to me that she had invited Dick to sit by me on the front row.

"But—"

She was gone before I could react. Mandy ushered Dick and Olga to the tent and seated him next to me. I looked up, but he didn't acknowledge my presence, so I said nothing. My body stiffened, and I sensed invisible magnetic forces of like poles that repel one another.

The Methodist minister opened with scripture and a prayer before he turned the service over to Mandy. Mandy had gathered plenty of stories for her eulogy in Edith's den the night before. She had absorbed everything we remembered about Mother and, without a written note, re-told those stories. She included the one about the preacher who looked heavenward when he heard Mother's authoritative greeting over the PA mike on her CB, "Just where do you think you're going?" The local preacher smirked at that one.

I don't remember whether or not Dick laughed with the rest of us, but my stiffness gave way, and I relaxed upon hearing the tales again. We laughed until we cried at Mandy's anecdotes about Clara. Mandy made the service so significant that I wanted to tie a ribbon around it.

Part 4

*"The habit of judging and condemning others
is usually a great deal more serious blemish
than are the things we so glibly point out
as flaws or faults."*

ANONYMOUS

50. What Is Left

The night we returned to Wilmington from the service in Clinton, Charles said, "I'm whupped. I'm going to bed."

"Good night." I gave him a peck on the lips and felt thankful for a driver and for his being there with me.

The pile of Mother's stuff in the corner of the kitchen tugged at me. Charles had taken her La-Z-Boy straight to the Salvation Army. I had put Mother's clothing in the laundry room to be washed before I offered her well-worn polyester outfits to my neighbor who kept a clothes closet for the needy at St. John's Episcopal. I removed the mink collar from her green wool coat and gave it a home on the dresser in the granddaughters' bedroom, where they played dress up in old bridesmaids' and prom dresses.

I pulled a chair up to the table next to the stained-glass window. The clunky metal cabinet was the most obtrusive object left after the La-Z-Boy and the clothing. The file cabinet held typed pages of Mother's autobiography that covered the years 1913 through 1948. After that, she wrote in black and white mottled composition books through 1957, the year I was married. As though it wasn't enough for Mother to record her own life, she set out to record mine as well. Several of these books use first person as though written by me, but she wrote it in her own impeccable cursive handwriting—probably a continuation of my wordy baby books that contained every gift and inoculation, plus every adorable thing I ever said or did.

Multiple moves are probably responsible for missing years between 1957 until 1979. I found a five-subject theme book Mother had used as a log of every oil change on the Chevy Nova, and letters from Billy Graham that offered a free calendar. *"He paid the postage and I paid the $1.80 for shipping."* She saved letters that contained Easter Seals or return address labels. She listed, to the penny, the amount she paid for meals and gas and the times she offered to pay for meals or gas when she was with other people. She wrote with free pens and pencils from stores or businesses around town. The journals also recorded all the connections she had made with service people who fixed things for her.

> *I got ready to cut the grass with my John Deere and went to the utility shed to put some gasoline in the mower. I noticed a rod underneath had come loose. I went down to the road just as Edmund Taylor (postman) drove up to the mailbox. I asked him to help me fix the mower, but he couldn't, so just after he left, I flagged down a man in the next car. He was a Mr. Brewer Putnam. He told me that there was a broken rod on my mower, and I figured I'd have to take it off and take it to town to be welded, but he said that he works on mowers, and he welds, so he came out the next morning, welded it, put a new air filter in, and a new belt on the front. He charged me $20 for all that.*

When Charles heard about it, he said, "She was the luckiest woman who ever lived. If Clara put herself out there by the side of the road with a broken mower, some mower repairman would surely come along to help her. And Mr. Putnam did."

A September 1981 entry told about a visit to Greenville on the Sunday before an appointment with Dr. Monroe.

> *I dropped by to say hello to Daisy and check on things with her. I spent the night with Ruth Creech, went to Buncombe Street Church on Sunday morning, and to the Robert F. Morris Sunday School Class where I saw lots of people I knew. They seemed tickled to death to see me.*

I found a yellow legal pad with lists written on both sides of the paper, beginning December 1991. The last barely legible entry was

July 19, 1995. The other pages were blank and stopped about seven months before she died.

I found a list of Parkinson's symptoms she had jotted on the back of a page torn out of a calendar and stuck into a book. The draft of an un-mailed letter to Mr. Abbott at CK scolded him for not refunding her last month's fee at CK. *"I hope you will enjoy spending my money. If you don't send me a refund I will know now why you drive a Cadillac and have such nice clothes."*

Annelle had mailed a ten-dollar check for Mother's last birthday. Stingy as she was, Mother had me endorse the check over to the Methodist church in Clinton and put it in the mail.

Carbon copies of all her correspondence were carefully matched to the letters she had received. The onionskin sheets were still crisp but showed evidence of silver fish who enjoyed that environment. Some of the files were left over from Daddy's estate settlement. I read everything in every file and finally came to a bundle of letters from Dick during the time he served in the air force. Some of the letters dated back to when he was stationed first in Texas and later in Orlando. His letters to Mother and Daddy were newsy, and he sounded happy and well-adjusted to his work. In most of his letters he enclosed a check, and asked Mother and Daddy to deposit these portions of his pay into an account so he could continue his education after his four years of active duty.

The tone and length of Dick's letters to Mother changed after Dad's death. Sometimes, he wrote only one or two sentences. Carbon copies of her letters questioned him. "Are you coming home for spring break?"

She received curt answers back. "I will be home on April 20 to check my mail but will not stay."

Both their letters lacked any acknowledgment of Daddy's death. Neither of them wrote one word about the crisis itself. The suicide built a wall of silence between them. And, since 1962, I was trapped behind Mother's side of the wall without a clue as to why.

I read through those files until 3:00 a.m. before I spread her costume junk jewelry across the table where I sat. I placed the worn-out treasures in a ceramic bowl that I had made in pottery class. A plastic imitation cameo had unglued itself from its oval mount; a fan of worn gold metal feather plumes had lost its sheen as a costume lapel pin. I spotted a couple of Daddy's tie pins and numerous single earrings divorced from their partners and saved for no reason. The junk jewelry cried out for attention just as Mother had done all her life, but no one was left to care.

I pulled a wastebasket closer and disposed of the bottles of Benadryl, calamine lotion, clear nail polish that stopped runs in her hose, aspirin, Vick's VapoRub, and a multitude of other expired drugs, considered illegal at Harrington Health Care.

I picked up her hairbrush that felt as warm as her scalp when I had brushed her hair, the same hair that her mother Emily sculpted into spiraled curls while Clara sat at her mother's knees. The hair wove through the bristles of her brush like a braided crown. I felt a morbid sagacity that Mother's hair was a living part of her that remained here with me—almost gray, coarse, still wavy, the scent unmistakable.

I walked through the back door onto the deck. The February night was chill and crisp and the high moon made me aware of the late hour. The light from the kitchen filtered through the stained glass and reflected the colors onto my hand. I touched the loose strands of Mother's hair, grasped a handful, and pulled it from the bristles. My arm extended past the deck rail, and I opened my fingers. The night breeze lifted the last of my mother's hair and carried it away in a farewell to what was left.

51. Elucidation

More than a decade after Mother died, cousin Annelle and her husband joined our family over Thanksgiving 2009. Lulled by the huge meal of too much turkey and dressing, everyone settled in the living room where my now grown children asked Annelle about their Uncle Dick.

Annelle had shared earlier that after twenty-five years together, Dick and Olga had married. As surely as a Southern belle makes a green bean casserole when someone dies, I sent an obligatory wedding gift and chose a piece of pottery I had admired.

Annelle told us they had retired and moved from Atlanta to a lake house in Georgia. Annelle has been the only family member that Dick had not ostracized. Dick and Olga dropped by Annelle's house from time to time. All of us wanted to know what more she could tell us about them.

One of my children asked Annelle, "Do you have any idea about why Uncle Dick withdrew from Geemommy and the rest of us?"

"He's never discussed it with us," Annelle said, "and I've never brought it up." She continued, "I always thought he blamed Aunt Clara for Uncle Olin's death because of the argument they had on the night before he died. But most of all, I'm sure Dick was disillusioned and disappointed in his parents, who had spent the educational fund he had accumulated while in the air force."

"What?" I asked. I sat up straight. I lifted my leg that had been slung over the arm of a wing-back chair. I went from a slump to full attention, both feet on the floor. "What did you say?"

Annelle explained, "He sent money home every month for Aunt Clara and Uncle Olin to stash away into a savings account to pay his college tuition when he got out of the air force, but your parents were in debt and spent all of Dick's savings just to get by."

"They spent the money he saved for tuition?" Stunned, I demanded details from Annelle, "Why?"

She added, "I was never told directly, but I overheard conversations between Mother and Daddy to that effect. It was why my folks sent money to Dick from time to time. And they thought it was why your dad died. I assumed everyone knew."

"I knew he sent money home but had no idea Mom and Dad spent it. We sent money too, and we thought he just hadn't accumulated enough to get through Clemson."

My mind raced, and I tried to figure out the consequences of what Mom and Dad must have done. Also, Dad's betrayal of Dick would have given Dad reason to face up to his own imperfection.

Even after Annelle went back to their motel, I couldn't get it off my mind. "Charles, did you know that Mother and Daddy used up those funds Dick sent home from the air force?"

"I think I remember something about a savings account, but I certainly didn't know they had used the money to pay their own debts." He stared into space. "After your Dad's funeral, I did ride with Dick down to Whitmire to check on an account at the bank there, but the account had been closed. I was just along for the ride and didn't know why or what he looked for."

The certificate of deposit in the amount of $2,500 slammed back into my memory. Mother had reminded me over and over, "All I will leave Dick is the CD in the lock box at First Citizens Bank unless he comes to see me."

"Do you suppose that CD in the lock box was her attempt to pay Dick back what they had owed to him?"

Charles said, "I guess we'll never know for sure."

Ding Dong Hill.

Epilogue

On our way home from my fifty-fifth class reunion at Greenville High School, Charles took a left turn onto the Whitmire Highway near Clinton. I thought he needed gas, but he said, "Let's go see how Ding Dong Hill is holding up." This was in 2009, thirteen years after Mother had died.

We spotted the mailbox where tiny letters named the spot "Ding Dong Hill." But, a larger sign had renamed the site "Cedar Hill." A rusty "For Sale" sign with an attached "Price Reduced" sign nestled in the tall cedars that grew where Mother once mowed. Charles turned onto Rufus's asphalt driveway and drove toward the top of the hill.

The house was pretty much intact, with the exception of broken glass in the storm door that leaned against the mountain-pine siding. The locked front door had a dead bolt. I stuck my camera-phone through a hole in the broken glass and snapped a few pictures.

We walked around the house and found that a bathroom had been added to the master bedroom. There was an open door, so we went inside. "Daddy would not like the sloppy job they did on that crude bathroom that has been added or these scratches and gouged out places in his maple floor."

The tour was short but not so sweet. "We'd better go," Charles said. He looked down the hill toward the highway and said, "Clara was right. A fire from a cigarette thrown from a car would sweep through these cedars and up the hill to the house."

I spotted an old John Deere thermometer attached to a tree with big rusty nails near where the dog pen had been. I tugged against the nails, and I told Charles, "Nobody's going to want this old thermometer," and I pulled it off, "but me," and we left for home.

Afterword

Friends who know about my book have asked, "How is your re-lationship with your brother now?" During the years it took me to write and publish this book, this is what has happened: Since Mother's funeral and in recent years, Dick has revealed a strong in-terest in family history and genealogy, and that interest has brought the two of us back into regular contact. I might say that the research he has shared with me has added to my own understanding of the history we share.

Acknowledgments

I am a painter. When I first began to write, I recognized that poetry, prose, and painting bear great similarities. I am grateful to the people who taught me to see these connections—my writing teachers and notable experts—Kathleen Halme, Michael White, Emily Louise Smith, Darnell Arnoult, Judy Goldman, Clyde Edgerton, Cynthia Lewis, Dana Wildsmith, Maureen Ryan Griffin, Vickie Hunt, and Mel Borjean. I am indebted to my editors, Peggy Payne; Nora Gaskin Esthimer, who taught me things I would not have known without her; and to Dr. Linda Hobson who understood Mother even better than I. Kelly Prelipp Lojk provided expert copyediting and book design.

The Pomegranate Books writing group—Brad Field, John M. Grudzien, Susan Hance, Patricia Walters Lowery, Jeanne Mullins, and David A. Stallman—laughed and cried with me through each chapter. My lunch bunch, Louise, Alida, Glana, Becky, and Emily overflow with their own similar stories. Also, I am grateful for my Figure Eight Island writing group, Drew Etler, Jo Ann Hoffman, Lawrence Davis, Dave Reynolds, and Jan Haack, real writers who know their stuff; for my beta readers, daughter Lisa, granddaughter Hannah, Agnes Stevens, Kim Cannon, Jim and Patty Kauffman, Lou Ann Liverman, Chris Patterson, Alice Osborn, Kay Ballard, and hubby Charles; and for the patience of my art students who set aside principles of design to listen to the stories.

Toward the completion of my story, God dropped Betsy Wade into my lap in the living room of Sea View Inn on Pawleys Island, South Carolina, where I teach an annual artists' workshop. Betsy had been an editor for the *New York Times*. She and her husband, Jim Boylan, both retired professors at Columbia University, listened to my story and gifted me with advice and a discourse that topped anything I could have solicited on my own.

Made in the USA
Columbia, SC
07 July 2019